STYLES FOR FLOURISHING

STYLES FOR FLOURISHING

HISTORIES OF SURVIVAL
IN THE RACIAL NICHE

GABRIEL ALEJANDRO
TORRES COLÓN

Columbia University Press   *New York*

Columbia University Press
Publishers Since 1893
New York   Chichester, West Sussex
cup.columbia.edu

Library of Congress Cataloging-in-Publication Data
Names: Torres Colón, Gabriel A., author.
Title: Styles for flourishing : histories of survival in the racial
niche / Gabriel Alejandro Torres Colón.
Description: New York : Columbia University Press, [2024] |
Includes index.
Identifiers: LCCN 2024013470 | ISBN 9780231215299 (hardback) |
ISBN 9780231215305 (trade paperback) |
ISBN 9780231560726 (ebook)
Subjects: LCSH: Race—History. | Race discrimination—History. |
Racism—History.
Classification: LCC HT1507 .T67 2024 |
DDC 305.8—dc23/eng/20240506
LC record available at https://lccn.loc.gov/2024013470

Cover design: Milenda Nan Ok Lee
Cover photo: Paul Stob. Mask artisan: Orlando Tomasini. A
masked dancer from the bomba group *Majestad Negra* expresses
pride and representation of African ancestry and Puerto Ricanness.

*To Lura and Savi, may you craft styles and flourish,
for you and your peoples.*

CONTENTS

ACKNOWLEDGMENTS

This book includes anthropological work I have conducted since 2004 in Ceuta (Spain), the United States, and Puerto Rico. In each fieldsite, many people helped me with ethnographic research, and a few could be listed as co-authors if I followed the standards of authorship for scientific journals that list all key personnel involved in supporting research and writing. Without them, fieldwork would have been much more difficult, and theoretical arguments throughout this book would not have been possible.

In Ceuta, Mohamed Mustafa Ahmed and the late Pepe Gutiérrez were instrumental in making connections and instigating new directions for research. Mohamed conducted some interviews with me because he cares deeply about his community's past and future, and Pepe welcomed me into his office in the Local Assembly and home to share his love for Ceuta and history. Farid Selam has also been a great friend and strong supporter of my work. Farid's political insights, based on decades of experience as a political advisor, have been very important for thinking anthropologically about governance.

In the US, Larry Young and Eva Jones-Young gave me a robust education in the "sweet science." Coaching is an art form, and they are master who patiently took me as an apprentice to show me the good and bad of the sport. The many awards and halls of fame inductions they have amassed over the last few years are more than well deserved. Many young boxers also entrusted me with their training, and it was a privilege to be in their corners as they strived for glory.

In Puerto Rico, Maricruz Rivera Clemente has been one of Piñones' fearless community leaders. She has struggled for land rights, ecological conservation, anti-racist education, and empowerment of people from her community and other Afro-Puerto Rican communities. The concept of flourishing in this book is a result of many conversations with Maricruz, and it is meant to honor the people, histories of struggle, and the biological flourishment of reforested mangrove trees in the Piñones Mangrove Forest. The maestro Marcos Peñaloza Pica knows that I have no musical skills, yet he has welcomed me into his world of bomba and allowed me to document his vision and journey to open new global pathways to share bomba. I am equally grateful for his dedicated time helping me understand the community's efforts to save the mangroves. The many hours I have spent with him navigating the serene mangrove channels are truly memorable.

In the academy, Lars Rodseth gave me priceless feedback and encouragement on early drafts. Since I was a graduate student, I have admired Lars' dynamic theorizing, and he inspired my attempts here to think bioculturally and through intellectual history. Most of this book was written in the virtual company of Adrian Huerta at USC, my friend and accountability partner. I am indebted to his daily commitment to jump on video calls to write and to all the sidebars to debrief about family and academic life. My former colleagues in the Anthropology Department at Notre Dame helped me gain confidence in thinking across anthropological subfields, and they always encouraged my community work in Larry and Eva's boxing gym. At Vanderbilt, Alex Jacobs has been my most trusted interdisciplinary sounding board and the classiest of office mates. For years, we have had impeccable timing in simultaneously stepping outside our offices for coffee, often leading to valuable conversations—many directly related to this book.

Paul Stob has supported me intellectually and as the best of friends for the duration of this project. He read a rough draft, gave me feedback, and has endured hours (maybe days and weeks) of hearing me talk about every aspect of this book. Of course, we often talk about these things while brewing beer, which made our discussions more bearable and, perhaps, even more productive (but that is debatable). His home has been a second home to my family (thanks, Sarah!), and that type of love is all over the ethos of how I characterize communities in this book.

Outside the academy, my good friend David Friend has always had my back. Our friendship and love for running trails, craft brews, and staring at stars is our version of a style for flourishment. Now living in Colorado, I visit him often, and significant portions of this book were written in his home.

Mami, Titi, and Papi have been my biggest cheerleaders. Their wisdom on life struggles, politics, and love for family undergird my ethics to anthropological research. My cousin Marcos is always down to chill with me. Watching boxing, fishing, and goofing around have been the perfect leisurely counterpoints to scholarly writing.

In this book, I employ the concept of flourishing to do a lot of theoretical lifting. However, we sometimes need palpable examples to clarify such ideas. My wife, friend, colleague, and co-author, Jada Benn Torres, is my living proof of flourishing. Our journey began in 2001 when we were graduate students at the University of New Mexico. Not only did our partnership lead to ethnographic projects and theoretical visions, but her life is a testament to the idea that resilience, perseverance, loyalty, listening, and love are pillars of flourishing. If this book came a little late in my career, it was unquestionably worth the wait because I first had the opportunity to witness a beautiful exemplar of flourishment by my side. Our children, Lura and Savi, are the most significant fruits for seeding future flourishment. The hope of a better future for them is all the motivation we need as parents to celebrate small victories and keep moving through life with good vibes and to the rhythms of our Caribbean roots.

STYLES FOR FLOURISHING

INTRODUCTION

2014, northern Indiana, United States. On a windy, gray October weekday morning off an old service road parallel to the railroad between the Rustbelt cities of Elkhart and South Bend, I parked right in front of The Dinner's entrance and darted into the restaurant. I was a few minutes late, so my friends were already finishing their orders. Michelle, the waitress, welcomed me as I took off my coat and sat down. I exchanged warm greetings with Eva and Larry, married owners of the St. James Boxing Club, which closed in 2021. We quickly agreed that the morning was cold, but the last few weeks had been warm and not so bad. Our conversation quickly turned to the business of boxing.

I met Larry and Eva in the fall of 2009 when I began visiting St. James. I was interested in exploring how gender, race, and nationalism were manifested in the athletic performance of boxers, trainers, and spectators. Over the years, our relationship evolved into a strong and enduring friendship. In 2009, St. James was a small, old boxing club with twelve boxers coming in for weekly evening practices. Since the early 1970s, the gym had existed in various corners inside South Bend and Elkhart buildings: at the upper level of a church, in an old factory, and in a community center. By 2009, the gym was in the back of Eva and Larry's home.

Larry, a working-class white man in his sixties, trained boxers for over forty years and worked various jobs in education, administration, and manual labor. He saw the best in people, and people saw the best in him. Eva, a Black woman in her forties with her own window cleaning business, was a highly accomplished combat athlete with twenty years of teaching karate and boxing. People who did not know Eva well never guessed she had soft spots because she was publicly outspoken and direct when speaking truth to power, but most of the time, she was one of the most friendliest people I ever met. Her personality matched her tenacious spirit as a combat athlete who conquered multiple national and world titles in karate and three professional world championships in boxing. It was during the quest for boxing glory that Eva asked Larry to train her. They then fell in love and married.

Soon after my first visit, I began training at St. James. After a few sparring sessions, Larry asked me what I would later hear him ask many young boxers, "So, where do you want to go with this?" It was a gentle invitation to box at the competitive level. Larry had more faith in my abilities than I did as a thirty-one-year-old anthropologist who was more interested in gentle runs, grilling meats, and finely crafted Midwestern beers. However, I did like the idea of apprenticing as a trainer, which Larry and Eva also offered. I began helping around the gym, dedicated myself to the art of coaching, and immersed myself in the world of boxing and a partnership with Eva and Larry that has continued to last.

Back at The Diner, that morning's conversation focused on funding sources for the gym. St. James would soon be moving into an ample, donated factory space, which needed all sorts of structural repairs, heating furnaces, and money for operating costs. It was exciting and stressful, as the gym had been steadily growing, with two group classes thrice weekly in the evenings. Each class had between twenty and forty boxers, men and women, boys and girls. They also came from different racial and ethnic backgrounds (Latinx, African Americans, and white). Most of them were from low socioeconomic or working-class backgrounds. Many young men between seventeen and twenty-four were at risk for substance abuse, crime, and violence (historically, those youth had a constant and vital presence in the gym). These youths were often successful as amateurs and professionals. Assuring their well-being and those of all boxers was a critical mission for all coaches.

The broader mission of welcoming and educating youth often led to moments of frustration and venting when we discussed the challenges of securing funding for the gym, including our conversation that morning at The Diner. Like many other times, Larry preached, "Nobody wants to touch boxing! Everybody is happy that we get these kids off the streets and keep them busy, but they are scared of boxing. Instead, they give the money to after school programs that don't do anything for those kids." It was hard to ignore that St. James, compared to other after school programs in the area, was very successful at reaching youth and building community. Boxing, a low-brow combat sport in the US, was at least as good as any other alternative in the surrounding neighborhoods for youth to be part of a caring community, but increased national attention on the effects of head injuries combined with the decreasing importance of boxing in the national sports scene made it difficult for the public to see boxing as more than a blood sport.

As we continued to discuss why young men need to be off the streets and in a boxing gym, the conversation turned to

Michael Brown. On August 9, 2014, Brown, an eighteen-year-old African American man, was shot by Darren Wilson, a white police officer, in Ferguson, Missouri. His death was followed by two episodes of social unrest in Ferguson, as protesters joined and fueled a larger national movement against police brutality and the shooting of unarmed Black men. However, our conversation differed from those in academic and political forums. With many of our boxers in mind, we knew from personal experiences that police officers often unfairly harassed and sometimes shot young Black men, but that was not our conversation's driving ethos. "But you have to leave the police alone," Eva explained as common sense advice, meaning that there are better things for a young Black man to do than individually confronting the police in anger.

We started discussing some details of Brown's cases: Brown's reported robbery before being confronted by Wilson and the possibility that Brown had reached for Wilson's gun. It did not escape me that conversations about those details were politicized at the national level. Why should the details matter when we know police often mistreat Black men? But this was an intimate conversation unconcerned with national discourses, and details about someone like Michael Brown or anyone else getting shot *always* generated conversations about how "it went down." Discussing the details matter because people in the gym and neighborhoods like Brown's know youths like him. I had many similar conversations with boxers who had encounters with law enforcement.

Several months after Brown was killed, I talked to one of our boxers, William, about the case details. William was one of our most experienced boxers in his late twenties. He had innumerable encounters with police and endured almost two years of abuse from guards while in state prison for a nonviolent theft crime. "What?" William said and then stared at me as I told him what I had read about the case. He sat silently, shaking his head for a few seconds as we drove to the gym. He lamented, "Now you know if you steal something and get caught, you get caught! You know how many times them guards messed with me when I was locked up? I'd still be there if I reacted. [Brown is] dumb, he's just dumb." Just as William's sentiments did not focus on systemic injustices because he took them for granted as part of his existence, at The Diner, we similarly expressed sadness for Brown's death but talked more about how it could have been prevented. "That's why we need to keep them in the gym," Eva reasoned. In fact, for Larry and Eva, keeping youth in the gym was a life mission above and beyond any political solution being offered by grassroots organizations and politicians. Rather than holding their breath for comprehensive policies to redress systemic racism, their interest was making the gym a place where youth could find hope and family.[1]

Thinking about someone who truly needed to stay in the gym, I asked, "Hey, how's Joe doing?" "Haven't seen him in a while," Larry answered, looking up at me with a stern look that he often managed to pass off as friendly. Always thoughtful and quiet before speaking, Larry sometimes made statements that came across as truth decrees. "Haven't seen him in a while" felt like, "I told you so!" and "Can you believe this guy?" Eva was more forgiving when it came to Joe. When Joe entered the gym, she accepted him as a labor of love. She did not afford him any privileges. On the contrary, she was calculated in demanding from Joe as much and sometimes more than other boxers during training.

Larry and Eva's union worked well in the boxing gym. A young Black man like Joe, who first entered the gym when he was seventeen, received quick schooling in boxing, discipline, and life. It was difficult to stay at St. James without accepting and demonstrating competence in those lessons. However, Joe and others like him also live in a world without the structure of the boxing gym, and there were competing lessons for survival in the streets. A gang engaging in criminal activities also had its discipline or cultural logic for selling dope or stealing. Furthermore, in the streets, being high from alcohol and weed competed with an endorphin-fueled high after a hard workout. Larry and Eva presented Joe with an alternative life, but this was the second or third time that Joe had taken a hiatus from boxing. Eva chimed in, "It's so sad, Gabe. He just needs to stick with [boxing]." She added hopefully, "But I have a feeling he'll come back."

National debates about police brutality and race in the US rarely include insights like the ones I documented in the boxing gym. William's "he's just dumb" and Eva's "that's why we need to keep them in the gym" are nuanced perspectives concerning everyday life in the streets and public policy on policing, respectively. William knows how over-policing and police brutality can change someone's life, but he and many others have adapted to take an active role in their survival. Even while engaging in illegal activities, survival means considering the consequences of embodying a Black body; if you get caught, do not make things worse for yourself by reacting to a provocation from a police or prison officer, even if you have two trained fists that, theoretically, could best the officer in a fair match. Being smart during a police encounter also involves having positive goals and visions of oneself in the future that are not worth derailing by taking the bait in a provocation.

Similarly, Eva has had little time for the politics of police reform. Since I have known her, she has always supported national political candidates backing the Black Lives Matter movement. However, she believes local community action in the boxing gym is more tangible and immediate in its potential to save lives. For Eva, the answer to saving and uplifting Black, Latinx, and poor white lives is in the boxing gym. She has been willing to accept help from anyone to save those lives, regardless of political leanings (including local police departments). William and Eva have developed strategies for survival in sociocultural worlds that are shaped by racial inequality and possibilities; I refer to these strategies as *styles for flourishing* and theorize these racial worlds of inequality and possibilities as *racial niches*.

RACIAL EXPERIENCE, STYLES FOR FLOURISHING, AND RACIAL INEQUALITY

This book examines and theorizes the relationship between racial experience, styles for flourishing, and the politics of racial inequity in liberal democracies. I argue that to imagine and implement anti-racist politics, it is first vital to appreciate racial experiences as rich, complex, and varying cross-culturally. In everyday life and multiple social contexts, racial experiences can be negatively damaging, neutrally mundane, and positively enriching. For example, racial experiences can include discrimination, unquestioned assumptions about bodily existence, or a political sense of solidarity. Moreover, racial experiences can cause one to reflect on individual or collective identity, or racial experiences can go unnoticed in everyday acts of social differentiation. Sentiments, thoughts, and behaviors—deemed happy, sad, or unexceptional—are all dimensions of experiences that individuals and social groups encounter through racialized lives. Such complexities of racial experience are most holistically appreciated if we approach experience as aesthetic and biocultural.

A philosophical pragmatist approach to experience demands that a full range of sensorial emotions—conscious and unconscious—are deemed part of an experiential whole. Experience should be understood as a "sense of experience."[2] Consistent with anthropological theories of experience, aesthetic experience radically differs from any social scientific approach that equates experience with what a person can articulate or what researchers can observe a person experiencing.[3] Overlapping with the aesthetic approach, the biocultural approach attends to the cultural and biological intertwining of the sense of experience. At the minutest levels, the nervous system elucidates bioculturality since humans can neurologically sense the same external stimuli differently depending on cultural context.[4] However, there is more to a biocultural approach since individuals and social groups condition and are conditioned by ecological and physical environments.[5] Pain, for example, is a sensation that cannot be explained simply as external stimuli and sensorial responses. Instead, it is necessary to consider environment, human development, community history, biology, and culture to fully understand how pain is meaningful to individuals and societies.[6]

If we apply these aesthetic and biocultural approaches to racial experience, we open up our inquiry to the myriad of instances when race is immediately relevant in peoples' lives. Moreover, we can be more exact about what we mean when we study the anthropology of race. The theoretical approach to racial experience in this book breaks with the social constructivist approach, but it is not a clean break since I embrace the position that biological races have no scientific validity and, more importantly, that biological races do not account for cultural differences.[7] However, because of the intellectual history of race scholarship, which I fully address in Chapter 1, scholars

have for decades been working with different and contradictory ontological understandings of race and racism. From the
perspective of intellectual history, understanding race as a social
construct is most theoretically useful when positioned against
pseudo-scientific ideas about the existence of biological races
underlying cultural differences. However, once we accept that
race is not biology, the theoretical purchase of race as a social
construct loses value beyond this important pedagogical purpose. Although it is still necessary to educate at many levels that
race is not biology (as most anthropologists and I teach in our
classes), there are more empirical phenomena to examine in the
lives of racialized communities that the social constructivist
approach cannot address.

Scholars are aware of the theoretical limits of the constructivist approach. Clarence Gravlee's seminal "How Race
Becomes Biology: Embodiment of Social Inequality" demonstrates how racism and racist social structures can negatively
impact the health of racialized people.[8] Gravlee's essay and others, like Leith Mullings and Alaka Wali's work on stress and
resilience among Black women in Harlem, were important in
shifting anthropological understandings of race from a construct to a construct with health consequences for individuals
and communities.[9] However, within this new paradigm, the real
consequences of race mostly implied the direct negative result
of racism or the efforts to resist such negative results. Even the
concept of resilience is understood within the context of patho-
logical stress.

Throughout my years of fieldwork, I have also documented
real consequences of racism in various communities. Yet the
racial experiences of Black and Latinx youth in US boxing
gyms, Afro-Puerto Ricans, and Muslims in Ceuta (Spain)
have been much more vibrant, complex, and ever-present than

the instances of racism resulting from interpersonal prejudicial encounters. Racism does not account for the entirety of racial experiences, as emerging literature on Black placemaking in sociology demonstrates.[10] For example, in this book, I give close, ethnographic attention to boxing techniques that youth embody as a "Mexican style of boxing" (Chapter 3), dance forms that are both traditionally Afro-Puerto Rican and present new anti-racist visions that break from Puerto Rican tradition (Chapter 4), and Leftist political visions that privilege the experiences of Muslims through anti-racist ideologies for governance (Chapter 6). Racism and systemic racism undoubtedly have something to do with all three cases. Still, if we only examine racial experience as racism, we are left with many unanswered questions about how racialization plays a significant role in people's lives between racist incidents. Most importantly, we miss focusing on the many instances in which racial embodiments are a source of strength, creativity, and forward-facing strategies for survival.

There is plenty of scholarship dedicated to aesthetic expression or everyday creativity from within racialized communities, but these works tend to fall outside the realm of research that aims to critically engage the political processes that sustain racial structures of oppression.[11] I have not come across any work that explicitly seeks to formulate new strategies for liberal democratic governance from the aesthetic and biocultural complexities of people's everyday lives. *Styles for Flourishing* presents a theoretical framework that does not accept a priori disciplinary divisions of labor that has, for example, social psychologists researching the positive effects of ethnic and racial identification, biocultural researchers looking for the best biomarkers to measure stress from prejudice, political scientists studying anti-racist social movements, or ethnographers elucidating the embodiment of racial constructs. Instead, this book insists that the complex tensions and seeming contradictions of people's racial experiences (good, neutral, and bad) are valuable sources for thinking about the politics of racial inequality in liberal democracies.

Based on aesthetic and biocultural forms of racial experiences, people fashion styles that might reproduce racial orders. However, these styles are performative arrangements through which people embrace, celebrate, and struggle for their racialized selves and communities; that is, these styles are quotidian strategies for flourishing given the prevalence of racial orders. Styles for flourishing are performative manifestations of racialized ways of being in the world that are associated with social conditions of inequality but creatively reconfigure racial existence into expressions of resistance, social assertiveness, desires for recognition, and alternative political orders. Through the performance of styles, embodied racial experiences are more than the oppressive weight of racism. Embodied racial experiences are regenerated into everyday efforts to survive social marginalization, which in time become histories of survival. Ultimately, I argue that these histories of survival must be compared with existing political ideologies and governance practices aiming to ameliorate racial inequity in liberal democracies, for the latter are not always in alignment with the former.

* * *

Months after the morning at The Diner, Joe returned to the gym wearing the physical and psychological scars of a violent shooting incident on the streets. He was slower and easier to hit, and his chances of having a decent professional career quickly faded. Instead of hearing about Joe on national news, you are reading about him here because his life trajectory as a young

Black man has led him to experiences that do not register with the sociocultural mechanisms that recognize his experiences as politically relevant (at least not in ways that matter to Joe, or Eva and Larry). Eva and Larry, among others, did not realistically expect most racial politics in the US to matter in the improvement of Joe's life immediately. This lack of relevancy is partly due to the disconnect between our attempts to help Joe in the gym and racial politics at the national level. Even Joe, along with two other Black boxers in the gym, could articulate how Michael Brown's death was and was not relevant to their lives; sure, a Black man must watch out for police, but, as William put it, "you can't let them get you like that!"

That statement reflects styles for flourishing developed in the gym that reconfigure the Black body as a source of athletic strength and controlled violence. In most anti-racist scholarship, the very idea of Black masculinity associated with hyper-athleticism or violence would be a subject for pointed criticism and deconstruction.[12] In this book, I do not evade such pointed criticisms and deconstructions. However, I also remember instances that significantly complicated these analyses.

For instance, early in November 2013, William invited me to his birthday party with family and friends. Late into the evening, William asked me to go with him and a couple of friends to an after-hours bar outside Chicago. I drove, and we got there before anyone else. As we entered the bar, two off-duty police moonlighting as bouncers, both white and muscular, gave William a hard time about his clothes being inappropriate and made him take off his skull cap. William kept his cool. After they let him in, we leaned over to me, cracked a smile, and said, "Now, imagine if I jumped at [hit] those fools." I smiled back, knowing that few humans on earth can withstand the speed and power of a nationally ranked heavyweight boxer. I told him, "Even if it wasn't your birthday, I'd be buying you drinks tonight, champ. Way to keep your cool."

The style of Blackness that William acquired in the gym might be problematic in some scholarly analyses, but it is the style that allowed him a chance to make money through sport and gave him the discipline to not fight two off-duty cops. He knew very well that a quick victory over the bouncers would surely lead to a no-win situation. Moreover, there was a tangible sense of satisfaction knowing that violence would not ruin an evening out with friends. Williams would often say to me over the years, "I want what you have," referring to me living in a good neighborhood and going to sports bars where he did not have to worry about being provoked. Disciplined violence in the gym, embodied through a racialized style of "how to carry yourself as a Black man" can dissuade men like William from becoming the next Michael Brown and feed visions of a brighter future. *Styles for Flourishing* queries the everyday ways of being and styles that people at the margins of society adapt to as they reimagine the possibilities for flourishing, and, by the end of the book, I take those everyday possibilities for flourishing and reflect upon their potential to teach us about effective anti-racist politics and survival in liberal democracies.

INTO THE RACIAL NICHE

The aesthetic and biocultural complexities of racial experience and styles for flourishing are theorized as occurring within racial niches. A racial niche is an adaptation of the social scientific concept of the human niche that allows us to approach people's experiences as nestled at multiple, intersecting levels: psychological, communal, and societal. The niche concept has been utilized in the sociological study of organizations to account for their function within broader social environments.[13] In this book, however, I adopt Agustín Fuentes's integrative anthropological conceptualization of the human niche:

> These human niches are the context for the lived experience of earlier humans and their communities, where they shared . . . social and ecological histories, as well as where they created and participated in shared knowledge, social and structural security, and development across the lifespan.[14]

This theoretical framework draws from ethnographic and biocultural research and has the same theoretical foundations as my biocultural and aesthetic approach to racial experience.[15] Moreover, the theoretical concept of the racial niche substitutes "racial" for "human" because, as I argue throughout this book (especially in Chapters 1 and 2), a concept of humanity need not conceptually and theoretically supersede the racial lens through which people experience their social existence. Put differently, awareness of the human self is often achieved in relation to already existing embodied social identities. Therefore, there are varieties of human niches that should be first approached and characterized from the already existing embodied social differences of our interlocutors (which in this book is racial in nature) and later compared to other human niches to test the soundness of humanity to account for a variety of social experiences.

My insistence on the racial niche over the human niche also has intellectual, historical foundations. The "psychic unity of mankind," a fundamental concept in early anthropology that established the adequateness of having one science for the study of all humans (and the rejection of racially-based psychic difference), is only partially true.[16] Humans are one species that cannot be biologically divided into races, so that part of the psychic unity paradigm is unquestionable. However, from a psychoanalytic perspective, humans first know their bodily selves in relation to social bodies that social scientists conceptualize as gender, race, ethnicity, and class. Therefore, our knowledge of something like humanity comes after our embodied social understanding of selves and others. In societies whose structures are marked by race, I argue it is more theoretically accurate and productive to conceptualize the niche as corresponding with the social categories most broadly at the core of social stratification, which are racial in all three ethnographic sites I examine in this book. Other social categories, such as gender, nationality, or class, can then be explained as complexities within the racial niche.

The racial niche is also a theoretical mechanism for cross-cultural comparison of race-like experiential phenomena.[18] I say race-like because I want to question the intellectual and popular distinction of embodied cultural forms, such as gender, nationality, and ethnicity. As such, the racial niche is strategically presented as a broad theory of the embodiment of difference to bring the racial niche in direct conversation with theories of gender, nationalism, religion, and migration.[19] Furthermore, the racial niche allows us to engage in a cross-cultural comparison of histories of communal survival without defining people through their oppression and acknowledging their efforts to resist inequality and flourish in broader social worlds.

A more pragmatic justification for the racial niche is the necessity to contextualize the complex aesthetic and biocultural approach to racial experience, which was discussed in the previous section. For example, suppose we want to account for the experiential complexities of community activists who have struggled for decades to achieve racial equality and political recognition. In this case, we must account for the stress of marginalized living conditions, the intellectual contemplation and emotional drainage of social protests, and the momentary satisfaction of won political battles within contexts of systematic oppression that often do not promise long-term changes. The racial niche concept allows us to theoretically locate these racial experiences at various organismal and organizational levels and in relation to multiple social and cultural realms of human existence.

Moreover, if we imagine that the experiences of an individual involved with such struggles are complex and can be understood as various components of a racial niche, then we can also continue to think across generations. For example, biological and psychological stress markers might be through the roof for community activists, but stress in one lifetime can hide the less stressful world left behind for their children and grandchildren. If approached from a racial niche perspective, then racial experience is not just biocultural in the sense that a social form like racism can affect the body; instead, racial experience is biocultural because it occurs within the context of a community's history of racialized existence. Therefore, the racial niche is the context for historical and everyday oppression, but it is also the context for histories of resistance and everyday instances of self-worth and dignity.

In addition to the boxing gym as part of the complex racial niche that is the US, this book engages my work with Afro-Puerto Rican communities in Puerto Rico and Muslims in the Spanish enclave of Ceuta in North Africa. In Afro-Puerto Rican communities, I document how Black Puerto Ricans conceptualize their identities as congruent with being Puerto Rican, experiencing a sense of blackness, and searching for Afro-diasporic connections. I then draw from ethnographic work with an anti-racist community organization in the Piñones sector of Loíza (Puerto Rico's township with the highest concentration of Black

Puerto Ricans) that stylizes blackness as a valid form of political subjectivity within a national context that has historically denied such subjectivity. In addition to environmental conservation and anti-poverty relief efforts, this community group utilizes the folkloric musical genre of *bomba* as a form of anti-racism and diaspora building with other Afro-diasporic communities. These local political efforts seek to transform Piñones into a site of anti-racist resistance that is rooted in the community's long history of subsistence and maroonage. This stylized form of community anti-racism within Puerto Rico stands in stark contrast to the place of Puerto Rico as a racialized US colony, demonstrating how race politics must account for local and global processes.

In the Spanish enclave of Ceuta, I combine life histories and ethnographic work in Ceuta's Local Assembly to explain the emergence and struggles of a political party of Muslim persuasion. This party is unique in liberal democracies, especially in Western Europe and the United States, because it has strong, ethnically Muslim leadership and composition without Islamist ideologies. "Of Muslim persuasion" is a (sometimes pejorative) way for the people of Ceuta to describe a political party with no historically known space in a liberal democratic political spectrum. As a Leftist social democratic party, the members of this party fashioned a political style that gives an institutional presence in Ceuta's Local Assembly to everyday racial experiences, which I highlight through a close examination of Muslim people's life histories. The result is a naturally occurring experiment of what can go right and wrong when political styles bring racial experience to legislative bodies in ways that go beyond grassroots activism and civil rights protests.

The main theoretical concepts in this book—racial experience, styles for flourishing, and the racial niche—are packaged as a method of inquiry for taking us from everyday experiences to addressing problems of racial inequality in liberal democracies. There are, of course, many potential social scientific approaches to racial inequality. Even for my lines of research, I could have focused on my community-based research in US boxing gyms or Puerto Rico. Or I could have devoted all my attention to the political efforts of Muslims in Ceuta. However, I believe that sacrificing some depth in each topic and juxtaposing all three ethnographic sites has significant theoretical advantages.

All three cases present styles for flourishing as part of survival stories in a racial niche. However, each case has different cultural, organizational, and political possibilities for the styles to effect social change through governmental political ideologies and action. The boxing gym was a community organization functioning within the amateur and professional boxing world, and it had no time or resources to engage in governmental political advocacy. At-risk youth were reached one at a time, albeit often effectively and within the context of deep interpersonal care. Afro-Puerto Ricans are similarly restricted when engaging in anti-racist politics because national politics in Puerto Rico do not recognize blackness as a legitimate source of political ideology and action (a legitimate source of political subjectivity). Nevertheless, Afro-Puerto Ricans have community organizations trying to fill the public policy void in their communities that was created by centuries of anti-blackness.[20] Moreover, established forms of expressive culture, like dancing the bomba, become alternative sources of educating audiences about anti-racism and Afro-Puerto Rican community struggles. Finally, although the Muslim community of Ceuta did not gain full citizenship until the 1980s, demographic patterns and racial experience led to the rapid rise of so-called parties of Muslim persuasion. These political parties, which at first varied considerably in ideologies, led to the rise of the Ceuta's

Democratic Union (UDCE in Spanish), a party of young Muslims whose communal experiences in Ceuta led to a particular form of leftist and anti-racist political ideologies.

Additionally, the three examples of styles for flourishing (boxing, dancing, and political practice) show that politically addressing racial inequality can take different paths. However, scholarly characterizations of race and racism often present confounding accounts of how racialized worlds have come into being and what political solutions are possible relative to those racialized worlds. For example, scholars do not commonly see boxing gyms in the US Midwest and bomba dancing in Puerto Rico as something that sparks anti-racist political imaginations. Meanwhile, the presence of Muslim politicians in Ceuta's Local Assembly has not guaranteed popular and broad political recognition of how racism is embedded in traditional Left-Right political ideologies. On the contrary, parties of Muslim persuasion in Ceuta demonstrate that anti-racist politics need more than political representation in governing bodies; it needs the sort of styles for flourishing that is less visible in boxing gyms and in a community organization's expressive culture.

STRUCTURE OF THE BOOK

This book begins with an intellectual historical approach to the question of race as a prism for anthropological theorization, followed by theoretical frameworks for racial experience, the racial niche, and styles for flourishing. I then present three ethnographic studies to examine how the racial niche can be a site for flourishing, and then I conclude with political, philosophical implications for anti-racism and coalitional politics in liberal democracies.

I do not envision the arrangement of chapters as moving from theory to ethnographic data. Instead, the intellectual historical exercise in Chapter 1 is meant to approach the history of ideas to critically assess present theoretical frameworks. I take this approach to be contiguous with the anthropologist's narrative of positionality that often frames their ethnographic study, for concepts are also products of the multiple positionalities of those who proposed and reproduced them in the past. In addition to the anthropologist's own sociocultural background, they are anchored by the concepts available to them, which are the results of previous entanglements of positionalities and concepts.

Readers should keep in mind that niches and styles vary significantly in the presented ethnographic studies. Therefore, I have arranged the order of ethnographic studies according to an increasing scale of organizational complexity for what might be considered political and governmental; the politics of the boxing gym are personal and immediately relevant to the boxers from surrounding communities in the gym, anti-racist politics in Puerto Rico are situated in an Afro-Puerto Rican community organization and activism, and anti-racist work in Ceuta is in a governmental assembly. The point of this arrangement is not to move from the seemingly more popular lower-case "p" of interpersonal and bodily gym politics to the more formal capital "p" politics of governmental politics; instead, my point is to demonstrate that racial niches are fertile ground for many styles for flourishing. Some styles find their way into governmental assemblies, while others remain at the community level. Furthermore, I outline how liberal democratic worldviews and governmental organizations are important when considering the limits and possibilities of anti-racism. As such, rather than take anti-racism in everyday lives, community activism, and party ideologies as tasks for different social scientific branches, this book highlights how styles for flourishing in the racial niche are all efforts of survival that can spark the imagination for new anti-racist political paradigms. This is why the book concludes with political, philosophical propositions for incorporating anti-racist politics at the community level into governmental coalitional politics.

Chapter 1 addresses the conundrum of recognizing how racial experience can reify negative notions of race and inspire tackling racism as a social problem. Drawing on the words of W.E.B. Du Bois and Lee Baker's intellectual history of anthropology, culture, and race, I delineate the conundrum as being particular to how racialized peoples were historically approached as a social problem as opposed to a source from which we could learn valuable cultural differences. This intellectual, historical legacy had a long-lasting effect on contemporary theorizing of race, culture, and society. To rebuild a holistic theory of racial experience, I closely examine and analyze a debate in the late 1990s regarding the origins of race. Although the scholars debated the proposition of racial thinking being rooted in human cognition versus being a byproduct of historical and structural racism, I suggest that neither side is correct because they fail to examine racial experience as a serious subject of cultural-theoretical inquiry. The chapter then proceeds to flesh out the theory of racial experience as aesthetic and biocultural. Finally, the chapter proposes that a theory of the racial niche can be used to interpret racial experiences and styles at multiple levels of analysis that range from the individual psyche to immediate surroundings to society and the global.

Chapter 2 formulates the theoretical concept of styles for flourishing, which I argue are performative, affectively scaffolded and habituated, and anchored by embodied social difference. I demonstrate how racial experience is developmentally acquired and reconfigured. This reconfiguration happens multiple times throughout lifetimes and in different parts of the racial niche. This analysis leverages Henrietta Moore's theory of gender and subjectivity and Patricia Hill Collins' intersectional Black feminism to articulate how racial experience is a form of embodied social difference that can be differentiated only from other forms of embodied social difference in direct reference to the racial niche in which a social difference is embodied. Concepts that are meant to demarcate social differences, such as race, ethnicity, nationality, indigeneity, or class, should be theoretically differentiated relative to their experiential location in the racial niche and the political possibilities for ameliorating racial inequity.

Chapter 3 presents a specific racial experience in the world of sport: the Mexican boxing style. Through life stories, the chapter examines how youth embracing boxing styles is a form of resistance to negative ideas about Mexican bodies and a way of developmentally flourishing through self-pride. I contextualize these forms of survival within the niche of US racial hierarchies. The chapter begins by briefly explaining why ethnographic work in sports allows for a more precise examination of how people experience and talk about race. It then provides a detailed sensory description of punching and the painful effects of being punched on the body, a hallmark of Mexican boxing's idealized, gritty style. The chapter concludes with a reevaluation of how racial reification can hardly be reduced to negative reproduction of biological race. Instead, I argue that reification is more nuanced than accepting racialized bodies and should include considerations for how racialized bodies can be loci of flourishing through hope and liberation.

Chapter 4 questions how to best understand "Afro-Puerto Ricanness," arguing that defining the social problem of racism in Puerto Rico necessitates documenting racial experience on the island and attending to how racial niches are socially structured in Puerto Rico and the US. I argue that if the Puerto Rican nation is an example of modern historical colonialism and a racialized niche of US imperialism, then Afro-Puerto Rican communities are an example of an older, transatlantic colonial instance of anti-Blackness and racial domination. I then examine how Puerto Rican nationalism obfuscates the historical and contemporary experiences of race in Puerto Rico. Because being Black and Puerto Rican in Puerto Rico is not necessarily a form of experience that leads to political mobilization, Chapter 4 focuses on anti-racist styles of flourishing by Afro-Puerto Ricans in Piñones, Loíza, and examines the absence of anti-racist politics in most social spheres of the island (inside and outside predominantly Black communities). I suggest that people in Piñones engage in what I term "mangrove politics," a stylized form of political activism rooted in the role of Piñones's mangroves in the processes of maroonage, subsistence economy, and ecological activism. The chapter provides a concrete activist effort to stylize bomba for purposes other than showcasing African contributions to the Puerto Rican nation. Instead, members of the group Majestad Negra stylize bomba to break free of what Isar Goudreau calls "scripts of blackness," which relegate Black existence to a folkloric past.[21] Artists actively advocate against racism and build Black diasporic communities beyond the island.

Chapter 5 argues that the main reason why the political problem of racism is often incongruent with accounts of racial experiences is that liberal democracies are chronologically and conceptually secondary to the existence of the racial niche. Historically, liberal democracies are, in fact, illiberal. Therefore, contemporary democratic liberal goals of ameliorating racial difference through nonracialized means often miss the nature of how inequity is palpable in the racial niche. The chapter chronicles the modern history of Muslims in Ceuta through life stories in two periods: segregation from the Moroccan hinterland (1956–1980s) and civil conflict in Ceuta between Muslims and Christians (1970–2010s). The former is a period of statelessness, and the latter is marked by Muslim people's struggles to gain citizenship and develop political voices. In addition to these historical periods, I delve into the life stories of a woman named Karina to complicate Ceuta's social dynamics beyond the Christian-Muslim binary. I employ the late Fatima Mernissi's Moroccan feminist perspective on border transgression to examine how Karina's life transgressions are a precursor to how everyday life racial experience can inform stylistic innovations in anti-racist politics (i.e., a style of intersectional and coalitional anti-racist politics). These life histories demonstrate how Ceuta's Muslims were racialized in the Spanish Moroccan borderland before they became a political problem at the birth of Spain's liberal democracy in 1978. I conclude that these life stories expose the fantasy of how liberal political styles on the Right-Left spectrum precede the race problem.

Chapter 6 argues that the presence of Muslim political leaders in Ceuta's Local Assembly forces us to understand how racial experience can and cannot translate into liberal democratic styles for governance. Although not consistently successful, Mohamed Ali, the leader of Ceuta's most important opposition party from 2003 to 2017, was able to use his parliamentary forum to question why his politics were popularly labeled "of Muslim persuasion" while supposedly nonracial political ideologies were not labeled "of Christian persuasion," which would register elsewhere in Spain, Western Europe, and the US as White. Following philosopher Charles Mills, I argue that we should conceptualize liberalism as racial liberalism, which is a way of understanding illiberal democratic governance within the racial niche. Finally, I draw comparisons between political styles in Ceuta to styles in the US Midwest and Puerto Rico. Boxing gym and Afro-Puerto Rican community organizations present an opportunity to reconsider the nature and place of grassroots, anti-racist activism, as an example of democratic pluralism and a political redefinition of the nation and state as primarily racialized forms of social organization. Grassroots anti-racism is not a corrective to an exclusive society but an assertion of coalitions as foundational for democratic deliberation and governance.

1

THE RACIAL NICHE

Origin Stories of Race and Theoretical Resolutions

In this and the next chapter, I want to make a more profound theoretical intervention about how to conceptualize racial experience within broader sociocultural contexts of inequality. What I mean by "a more profound theoretical intervention" is a theory of race dialectically engaged with its intellectual history bridged with theoretical orientations that do not usually coexist in scholarship.[1] Such theoretical intervention is necessary because race, as a social problem, hangs over scholarship as a cloud that can obfuscate the what, how, who, and why of race theories. As far back as 1909, Du Bois observed,

> those who complain that the Negro problem is always with us and apparently insoluble must not forget that under this vague and general designation are gathered many social problems and many phases of the same problem; that these problems and phases have passed through a great evolutionary circle and that to-day especially one may clearly see a repetition, vaster but similar, of the great cycle of the past.[2]

Fast forward one hundred years, and we find ourselves unable to think clearly across disciplines about Du Bois's race problem when researching racialized, minoritized, and marginalized communities. To be more precise, when we find ourselves thinking clearly about race, it is because disciplinary divisions allow us to. For example, there is over a century of anthropology that teaches us how race is not biology, yet marginalized peoples strategically deploy biological and other forms of essentialization to resist hegemonic political orders.[3] Even if marginalized people are not ideologically strategic in their biological essentialization, we can still question what degree of biological essentialization is detrimental or advantageous in efforts to survive and move out of social margins. Similarly, the exploitation of and discrimination of racialized bodies through geospatial exclusion have measurable health and economic consequences; however, from maroon communities to barrios, favelas to arrabales, and to other geographic spaces marked by racial differentiation, practices and strategies for survival and self-worth emerge despite those spaces being at the bottom of social hierarchies.

There are, of course, more potential variations of seemingly contradictory approaches to Du Bois's race problem. I present these variations because these contradictory approaches highlight how the race problem shapes scholarship and, consequently, how we approach questions of race in ethnographic research. Are we aiming to document and give voice to resistance from below, or are we elucidating systems and structures of oppression that we aim to transform for broad changes? Analogous versions of this question have been raised in other areas of anthropological research. For example, Scott emphasizes how the subtle strategies that "the weak" use to undermine hopelessly exploitative labor conditions,[4] Wolf demonstrates how local people culturally respond and adapt to Euro-centric economic and political systems,[5] and Nash highlights how indigenous people formulate their own alternatives to international development.[6] Most of these works, however, tend to emphasize creativity and alternative worldviews from a class or indigenous perspective, and their analytic ethos celebrates shared class status even when racialization processes are intertwined with class formation. Regarding racial groups (particularly in the Americas) there is a long intellectual history that has resulted in the separation of race as an object of study for its cultural worth from the study of race as a social problem.

> During the first part of the twentieth century, anthropology in the United States became a successful and powerful discipline because it explained the culture of out-of-the-way indigenous peoples, influencing law and policy from the Philippines to Puerto Rico. Anthropologists had less success describing the culture of the many in-the-way immigrant and black people. That job went to sociologists committed to the study of assimilation and race relations. One of the foundational claims of sociologists and psychologists who studied race relations was that the races were neither inherently superior nor innately inferior to each other and that any aggregate differences between the races were the result of historical and environmental factors . . . While anthropology marshaled its nascent authority to describe the difference of exterior others, sociology marshaled its nascent authority to document the sameness of interior others.[7]

By the mid-twentieth century, the division of labor that Baker describes was undersigned by the social scientific rejection of racial biological differences, of which anthropology played an important part. However, "two different discourses animated competing racial politics of culture, and both are woven into the genealogy and history of race in America. One pivoted on the value of cultural heritage, the other on racial uplift."[8] Baker goes on to argue that the heritage-uplift divide continued to shape popular and academic discourses about race. There are important political implications to the heritage-uplift divide. Heritage, which was adopted in the anthropological study of what Baker calls "out-of-the-way indigenous peoples," calls for a politics of multiculturalism and acceptance. Racial uplift means ameliorating class-based economic inequality or, more often, some sort of assimilation or change in detrimental social behaviors of racialized people that are already partially assimilated into Euro-American cultures[9]—that is, racialized minorities, particularly Black folks, whose culture did not have anything distinctive to offer an intellectual project of celebrating cultural difference. Of course, there are exceptions, such as the political ideologies of Malcolm X, that embrace the cultural value of the Black race and the necessity for uplift but are not assimilationist and, in Malcom X's case, unpopular as a way out of 1960s racial tensions.

I want to focus on the nature of the heritage-uplift divide and suggest that what is more fundamentally amiss is a theoretical rift between racial experience and political theory. Despite the *longue durée* of racial fixity in the Americas, people experience race in all sorts of ways that span the cognitive, emotional, aesthetic, and corporal sensibilities;[10] however, the race problem tends to dictate what sort of racial experience is attention-worthy. Heritage is about cultural worth, and uplift is about achieving social equality, so why would anyone interested in solving the race problem care about a boxer's embodiment of race in a boxing gym? The potential answers from the heritage-uplift divide are not commensurable. In cases where scholars or public intellectuals care about racialized boxing styles, it is because these styles represent an enrichment of our understanding of Latinx, Black, and poor white culture and survival strategies. However, interest in these topics regarding sports has mostly focused on how racialized styles are hegemonic traps—a social construct—that reify racialized hypermasculinity as brute labor primed for exploitation. The heritage approach curtails an inductive approach to racial experience, and the uplift approach curtails political possibilities that correspond with the racialized lives of marginalized social groups.

In this chapter, I propose a theoretical approach to racial experience and the racial niche that presupposes no political solutions. Instead, we should assume that because racial experiences and niches vary, the possibilities for solving racial inequality through governmental politics must consider such varied experiences. Furthermore, ideologies and projects concerned with governmental politics have never existed in isolation. Indeed, these projects have been diasporic.[11] Therefore, political thoughts that emerge from diverse racial experiences should also consider comparative and diasporic dimensions, especially if diaspora is in the minds of people working from local contexts, which I highlight in later chapters for the US Midwest, Puerto Rico, and Ceuta. In short, I am proposing political possibilities for flourishing that emerge from the everyday lives of racialized peoples—possibilities that allow us to interpret or translate racial experience as sources of political possibilities; the same thing that, for example, in a more seamless and less contradictory heritage-uplift anthropological tradition, June Nash proposes for indigenous Zapatista rebels opposed to neoliberal policies and pursuing greater autonomy:

> The unique advantage of the human species in evolution is the plasticity we have shown in adapting to new conditions in our physical and social environments. We are now on a trajectory that threatens to eliminate the variety of plant and animal species in our biosphere and even alternative responses in our policy

making. More concern is expressed in international arenas on the loss of genetic variety in plants and animals than in people. Indigenous peoples still maintain distinct visions of their relation to the cosmos and to other living organisms that promote distinct responses from those advocated by dominant institutions in the global ecumene. They are the best custodians for the fragile environments that are now being invaded by development agents . . . By returning to our ethnographic base we can rediscover the sense of what people who experience the rigors of developmental breakdowns are formulating as they fight for survival. Only when we attend to their case can we appreciate how their alternatives might ensure the survival of the human species.[12]

My aim is to theoretically recast the "heritage" part of the heritage-uplift equation for some of the "in-the-way immigrant and black people" that box in Midwest gyms, fight for dignified lives as Afro-Puerto Ricans, and agitate in the Local Assembly in Ceuta.[13] Similarly to Nash, I aim to "rediscover" the "distinct visions" that emerge from racial experiences. In Chapter 3, I focus on the "distinct visions" of youth as they rediscover their bodily worth through boxing. And I celebrate the "best custodians" of people engaged in racial uplift in chapters 4, 5, and 6 as it pertains to the efforts of Afro-Puerto Rican community activists and Ceuta's Muslims in governmental politics. In this and the next chapter, I want to take a brief journey into the intellectual history of the theorization of race in anthropology in order to put forth a holistic theory of racial experience as pragmatic, aesthetic, and biocultural—that is, to theoretically recover racial experience as heritage. Furthermore, I argue that the racial niche is a necessary theoretical locus for understanding racial experience, thus providing one possible bridging of DuBois's conundrum of the race problem being "many social problems and many phases of the same problem."[14]

ORIGIN STORIES OF RACE AND RACISM

I want first to address how scholarship has presented an origin story for race and racism. By "origin story," I mean how race emerged in accounts of evolution, world histories, and human lifetimes. I am interested in exploring the intellectual ethos and political theories of origin stories. I do not want to present a full account of the arguments, theories, and sociocultural contexts for scholarship on race that span centuries (indeed, any attempt to do so would fall short). Instead, I want to focus on a debate that is instructive in helping us map out two distinctive ontological possibilities for an anthropological theory of race.

Is race easy to learn? This particular question is at the crux of a debate over Lawrence Hirschfeld's "The Conceptual Politics of Race: Lessons from Our Children," which appeared in a special topics issue of *Ethos*, the journal of the Society for Psychological Anthropology.[15] Hirschfeld summarizes the argument of his article in his reply to five commentators.

1. Race as a category of mind is distinct from race as a category of power. The distinction is logical (one cannot have a category of power without having a corresponding category of mind) and causal (e.g., it has been argued that race is a category of mind because of the role it plays in organizing power relations).

2. Racial thinking is intimately linked to essentialist reasoning. Most frequently, this linkage has been explained in the following way: essentialist reasoning emerges as a function of the fundamental support such reasoning provides the political use of race.

3. An alternative interpretation is that race is essentialized because human psychological endowment includes an innate tendency to organize information about other humans in a very specific way. This tendency includes an essentialist heuristic.

4. We can test between the alternative causal accounts by investigating whether race is essentialized because it is politicized or whether it is essentialized because it is organized around innate principles of reasoning.

5. Conclusion: Race is recruited as a category of power because of the properties it has in virtue of being a domain-specific category of mind.[16]

Hirschfeld does not present much empirical evidence in the article or reply to commentators,[17] but he does summarize over a decade's worth of developmental anthropological and psychological work. His research for the fourth point demonstrates that children as young as three years old form an idea of race that is essentialist, like that of many adults. However, because children lack an interactional context that is explicitly politicized, Hirschfeld concludes that race is a domain-specific category of the mind—a category of "human kinds"—that derives from a "human kind-making module" that is evolutionarily derived. Children "naturally naturalize" race and other types of "intrinsic human kinds," like gender and caste, when the "ambient culture" marks these intrinsic human kinds as salient. In the US, race is generally assumed by historical and social scientists to be one of the most salient social categories.

Anthropological counterarguments by Virginia Dominguez and Ann Laura Stoler allow us to see some clear theoretical differences.[18] Stoler agrees with one of Hirschfeld's principal claims that race relies on forms of essentialist thinking and that such essentialist thinking takes hold in particular ways depending on historical and cultural contexts. However, Stoler does not think that the essentialist (i.e., beyond the visual) component of race comes from an evolutionarily derived category of the mind; instead, "race gains its force . . . form the political effectiveness of a system of social classification that appears fixed, permanent, and commonsensical while it remains porous and pliable."[19] Stoler also questions the fixity of racial essentialism, asking, "why assume that the concept of race is unchanging simply because the term *race* is constant over time? Are not such terms constantly imbued with new political and cultural meaning?"[20] Finally, Stoler turns to the question of whether race is easy to think by pointing out the "inordinate amount of time" that adults, especially the "architects of colonial policy," spend teaching children racism.[21]

Dominguez counters that if there is something like a human kind-making module, then Hirschfeld should emphasize that racial systems are one of many that humans in a society can produce. This lack of emphasis means that Hirschfeld can only make his evolutionary claims "by referring to seemingly ahistorical properties" that make race easy to learn. Contrastingly, Dominguez believes that race is not easy to learn given the multiplicity of racial systems between and within societies.

> "Race" involves knowing when and how much to rely on phenotypic criteria, which ones to rely on more and which less when they coexist and seem to point in different directions, and how presumably different "race" is from "ethnicity" or "culture" or "class" or "region" or "nationality" or "religion." "Race" involves knowing what is "racial" and what is not, as well as when to stop racializing some named population and when to racialize another.[22]

Like Stoler, Dominguez believes that Hirschfeld's lack of attention to specific historical and sociocultural contexts compromises his claim about race being easy to learn. In addition, Dominguez argues that children experience politicized aspects of race in a "society in which life chances are deeply patterned by racial classification and differential access to resources."[23] Therefore, race cannot be learned outside an already racially politicized world.

Hirschfeld's response mostly restates his argument with some attention to the objections raised by commentators. He acknowledges that it is naïve to imagine "that children are outside the scope of American racialist and racist politics," however, "the question is whether children use race to organize those arenas of the life space *that they control*."[24] Hirschfeld argues that because race does not play a significant role in organizing (e.g., creating a hierarchy) an environment like the playground, it demonstrates that children can essentialize race without politicizing it. This argument allows Hirschfeld to indirectly address the question raised by Stoler of whether race is the same thing over time. In fact, in Hirschfeld's article, he leaves the question of how much race is always the same thing by calling for more studies elsewhere in the world that examine other cultural phenomena that might be similarly essentializing but called by a different name (i.e., it is possible that other studies could show that essentialism is at the core of racism, nationalism, or ethnicity).[25] Finally, Hirschfeld directly addresses the claim that race is not easy to learn by pointing out that Stoler and Dominguez assume colonial officials' efforts to promote racial order or the difficulty migrants have in learning new racial classification systems are similar to how children learn race. Instead, Hirschfeld argues that, like language acquisition, social reasoning and learning race are easier for children than adults. Hirschfeld adds another counterargument, stating that "just because the criteria for category membership is difficult to identify . . . this does not mean that it is difficult to acquire the category."[26]

The debate concerning the ease or difficulty with which we learn race is instructive because it demonstrates how theorizing race's origins can set the tone for the political ethos of anti-racist scholarship. In this case, it is sometimes difficult to clearly understand what each anthropologist is debating regarding race theory.

What, exactly, are the theoretical stakes of debating and weighing cognitive against sociocultural determinants of race?

What got lost in the debate over Hirschfeld's "conceptual politics of race" is that the ontological nature of racial being is put into a political balance before it can ever be considered central for anthropological theory. Racialism and racism appear as distinct phenomena that, as Hirschfeld presents them, facilitate an inquiry into their relationship; but racism is ontologically loaded as a political problem needing solutions, which leaves racialism as the only seemingly nonproblematic form of racial being. Dominguez makes a similar criticism, stating that "if the truly interesting question turned out to be what kind of attachment, commitment, or investment particular individuals and groups have in 'race,' it would not be methodologically appropriate to predetermine the outcome of research by conceptualizing racialism and racism as 'two distinct cultural practices.'"[27] Dominguez takes that criticism in a direction that casts doubt on the ability of something like racialism to not always be compromised by an unequal and racist society, yet she does not present a counterargument for the evolutionary nature of why humans essentialize social groups.

The nature of race—ontologically and experientially—in Hirschfeld's research is strictly delimited from the very first line of his article. "When thinking about race there is a tendency to combine into a single package two distinct cultural practices:

one racialist, the other racist."[28] This initial distinction allows Hirschfeld to set up the anthropological and greater scholarly problem as one between the relationship of the partition of humans into categories as the cognitive foundations of racialism and racial prejudice and inequality as racist. However, notice that part of Hirschfeld's distinction is a claim about the tendency to combine what he is distinguishing. Dominguez speaks past Hirschfeld on this point and, implicitly, argues for the combination that Hirschfeld is trying to tease apart. "Commitment, attachment, and investment [to race] are all likely to be a matter of degree, not either/or possibilities. And they all suggest the mutual implication and interdependence of 'ideas' and 'forms of mobilization'—and not a case of linear (logical or historical) causality."[29]

Dominguez and Hirschfeld are, in fact, not necessarily taking mutually exclusive positions because Dominguez is proposing a range of ontological possibilities for or dimensions of racial existence, while Hirschfeld identifies two ontological points on what I believe is a spectrum of forms of racial existence. In her comments, Dominguez does not disprove the ontological difference between racialism and racism; instead, she points to a complex historical and sociocultural account of racial regimes that cannot be fully explained with *only* the concepts of racialism and racism, which then allows Hirschfeld in his reply to double down on how racialism operates independently of politics for children in certain contexts (that is, he accentuates that racialism can be both a distinguishable phenomenon from racism and related to racism in a broader sociocultural context).

Although I agree with Dominguez that racialism and racism are not two distinct cultural practices, I think a distinction can be entertained—at least as a hypothesis, and also because there seem to be plenty of cross-cultural examples of people themselves making the distinction between something like racialism and racism.[30] Therefore, it is a mistake not to follow Hirschfeld down the theoretical road a little further before taking issue with his position by pointing out the complexity of racial ontologies across cultural contexts. By teasing apart racialism and racism and bringing children into the equation, Hirschfeld's research allows us to consider how multiple dimensions of racial existence can be critical in formulating a theory of racial experience. Unlike Dominguez, I do not believe there is necessarily a problem with identifying and treating two cultural practices as distinct, even if said practices are mutually implicated and interdependent. It is nearly impossible for sociocultural theory not to parse apart interdependent phenomena to clarify complex processes.[31] In fact, Dominguez is mistaken to suggest that "mutual implication and interdependence" are opposite or exclusive of "linear (logical or historical) causality," for interdependent phenomena can, even when found in a more complex system of relationships, be in a wholly or partial causal relationship (or none at all)—or, put differently, some variables in interdependent systems can have more causal weight than others.[32] However, I agree with Dominguez that commitments, attachments, and investments in race exist in multiple forms and should be ethnographically outlined before conceptually separating race phenomena into racialism and racism.

The theoretical stakes of debating and weighing the cognitive and sociocultural determinants of race are crucial in determining how one conceptualizes racial being or racial ontology (Hirschfeld's racialism) relative to broader sociocultural contexts. Hirschfeld's path leads us to an origin story for human kinds that precedes the politics of racism and anti-racism. Stoler, Dominguez, and a majority of cultural anthropologists studying race find the origins in sociocultural systems structured by power and inequality.[33] However, these theories are difficult to summarize and characterize because the location of racial experience and structural racism varies significantly within and between societies. If anything, Stoler and Dominguez are part of a broader group of scholars uninterested in de-historized and de-culturally contextualized explanations for the origins of race.

I sympathize with the lack of interest in de-historicized and de-culturally contextualized approaches to the origins of race. In Hirschfeld's words, "race is recruited as a category of power because of the properties it has in virtue of being a domain-specific category of mind." This domain-specific category of the mind, if truly rooted in evolution, takes the anthropology of race into a gray area of inevitability because even if being racist is not inevitable, as Hirschfeld clearly articulates, there is inherent essentialism in a domain-specific category of the mind. More-over, the passive voice in the phrase "race is recruited" has two consequences. First, as Stoler and Dominguez similarly point out, it deemphasizes the intentionality of people in positions of power in reproducing racial hierarchies. Second, it implicitly privileges an analysis of social power structures that are unracial-ized. This second point is, perhaps, an unintended second origin story in Hirschfeld's account, because if race is recruited, then the categories of power for which race is recruited must already exist (presumably in society, history, or evolution) before the social processes of recruitment.

Consequently, with Hirschfeld's approach, we are left some-what naked in politically theorizing racialism and racism outside the realm of governance, for the race problem must be inevi-tably solved with some governmental involvement. Arguing for such governmental involvement is most easily arrived at through the contextualization and historicization of systematic racism and inequality (a là Stoler and Dominguez). Instead, Hirschfeld sidesteps the political problem of race by claiming that labor and class "are more often the basis for institutional disadvantage and more often appropriately specify the dimension along which it lies."[34] I fully engage with the problem of class and race in Chapter 6 when examining governmental politics and ideologies in Ceuta and in the Conclusion as a political philosophical problem. For now, we can note that even if labor and class politics play an important role in ameliorating racial inequality, such politics have often failed. Political thinkers from racialized communities have been weighing the balance of class and race in political action since at least the 19th Century.[35] Moreover, it is unclear how labor and class ideologies are supposed to incorporate lessons from Hirschfeld's research. The only lessons seem to be about educating children—mainly white children—early and often to guard against the ease with which they learn race.[36]

Even though I sympathize with the lack of interest in de-historicized and de-culturally contextualized approaches to the origins of race, to Hirschfeld's credit, we are left with an unresolved theoretical problem: the conceptual nature of racial being is never theorized beyond emerging from cultural systems and history. Essentially, the racialized self and racialized Other are so intertwined with cultural systems and history that to think about race is inevitably to think about the social problem of racism. I believe the intertwining of racial being and racism is the same that motivated Du Bois's engagement with the question of "how does it feel to be a social problem."[37] To complicate matters more, within contemporary and historical intellectual circles (particularly within the anthropology of race), what constitutes politics gets mixed in with academic theoretical debates.

Hirschfeld appears to confuse politics with intellectual thought, stating that "what is contentious is the relationship between racialist and racist modes of thought, which might be called the conceptual politics of race."[38] I am not claiming that theoretical debates, especially about race, are not always embroiled in some form of cultural politics—Lee Baker, many other scholars, and myself have argued as much.[39] But we must at least draw some distinctions between scholarly politics and the political worlds that affect the lives of racialized peoples because scholarly politics and other political worlds do not always overlap and have their own social configurations (e.g., organizations, social patterns, and local knowledge).

I do not want to give the impression that Hirschfeld is limited in putting his work in conversation with anti-racist political theory. His work is no less conversational with political theory on race and governmental politics than most anthropological work on race since Hirschfeld's published his work in the 1990s. Anthropologists often point to structural problems without clearly laying out possible political processes as solutions. Yet even though not articulating political theories is a shortcoming of most anthropological research on race, Hirschfeld's absence from critical anthropological scholarship on race is noteworthy given that he is one of the very few anthropologists in recent history to (a) wholly reject that race is a valid biological category and (b) use scientific methodologies to ascertain the developmental origins of race and human kinds. In other words, the political ethos of Hirschfeld's work has, within the sociocultural world of anthropologists, made him not popular even though his political theoretical shortcomings or lack of interest in political theory is something he shares with other anthropologists.

Citations of Hirschfeld's work are absent or theoretically inconsequential in fundamental cultural anthropological works on race or completely absent from journals, like *Transforming Anthropology*, which are more concerned with the anthropology of race.[40] Even in a comparative and interdisciplinary journal, like *Ethnic and Racial Studies*, Hirschfeld is only cited in one article.[41] Although it is difficult to speculate on a scholar's motivations or thought processes for not embracing Hirschfeld, there are some clues as to why some might want to overlook him in works where his scholarship is directly criticized. For example, Rattansi dismisses Hirschfeld's "experiments and inferences" as "seriously flawed."[42] Similarly, Kromidas argues that Hirschfeld limits children's world to "unpoliticize" them; furthermore, the limited and unpoliticized world and the notion that race is easy to think are "obviously and patently fallacious."[43]

As evidence for Hirschfeld's seriously flawed research, Rattansi cites the debate I outlined above, which is a wholly inappropriate way to dismiss experimental research. More importantly, as I have shown, Stoler and Dominguez's disagreement with Hirschfeld is much more nuanced than Rattansi allows. Kromidas also cites Dominguez to substantiate the argument that Hirschfeld depoliticizes children, but this claim also exaggerates and misunderstands the very specific reasoning that Hirschfeld provides for saying that children do not politicize race. Hirschfeld argues that there is evidence that young children do not make playground decisions to include or exclude based on race.[44] Whether one accepts Hirschfeld's evidence as meaning children do not politicize race is one thing, but one cannot ignore the fact that race affects interactions for children differently than adults in the US.

From a cultural anthropological perspective, the problem with Hirschfeld has not emanated from a scientific refutation of his thesis. In fact, in the fields of biological anthropology and psychology, Hirschfeld is part of a serious scholarly inquiry into the evolution of human cognition vis-à-vis essentialism of social groups.[45] Interestingly, in a *Current Anthropology* article that includes comments from various scholars, we find a very similar argumentative ethos to Hirschfeld's debate in *Ethos*. Gil-White presents an evolutionary argument for the essentialization of ethnic groups that renowned social anthropologist Tim Ingold immediately dismisses as "so manifestly absurd that I cannot believe it is meant to be taken seriously" (Ingold deems Gil-White an evolutionary psychologist, although the latter is an anthropologist).[46] However, in this debate, other scholars, including nonanthropologists, engage with Gil-White's data, methods, and overarching theory (although not without disagreement). The problem with Ingold, Rattansi, and Kromidas is that Hirschfeld and Gil-White's scholarship holds little promise for focused criticisms of social constructs that damage real lives and social structures that reproduce social inequality, and, at the very most, Hirschfeld and Gil-White's scholarship naturalizes the human capacity to engage in social prejudice. The origins of race are a high-stakes debate.

Ironically, at the very beginning of race origins debate, Hirschfeld does a very good job characterizing and describing a division between psychological (i.e., race as an evolutionary outcome of cognitive prejudice towards out-groups) and comparative (i.e., sociohistorical approaches that locate race in systems of power) approaches to studying race, and he sees his research as bridging those approaches. This is what he means when he writes, "systems of power continue to make contact with and recruit race because it is easy to think."[47] Nevertheless, Dominguez questions Hirschfeld's attempt at paradigmatic reconciliation, "Hirschfeld . . . ends up effectively on one side of the divide [the psychological]."[48] In the end, the impasse concerning the origins of race is an impasse about articulating the ontological dimensions of racial phenomena. The political ethos of the various political perspectives further prevents moving toward a theoretical resolution or synthesis.

There are two ways of theorizing what race is and how racism ought to be addressed from scholarly perspectives. For Hirschfeld, the ontological distinction between racialism and racism points towards an anti-racist politics of early education and parenting interventions of racist ideas that could be easily accepted by children.[49] For Dominguez, Stoler, and most cultural anthropological scholars of race, racism is ontologically embedded in social structures (e.g., cultural, linguistic, organizational, etc.), and anti-racist scholarship is concerned with delineating such social structures and giving voice to racialized people as they meaningfully navigate racist worlds. The theoretical impasse between these two perspectives results from incomplete articulations of the ontology of race and racism. Hirschfeld highlights the essentialist component of racial thinking but fails to theorize how essentialism is made meaningful by people in their everyday lives—all we get is that racial thinking is prone to racist systems. Importantly, there is some ontological agreement between both camps concerning the embeddedness of racism in social structures, but Dominguez and Stoler fail to account for the fact that essentialist thinking is cognitively embedded to some degree, which plays a role in the racialized lives of people who navigate racist structures.

A PRAGMATIST AND BIOCULTURAL SYNTHESIS OF RACE AND EXPERIENCE

I stated earlier that my aim for this chapter is to theoretically recast the heritage part of the heritage-uplift equation for some of the "in-the-way immigrant and black people" that box in Midwest gyms, fight for dignified lives as Afro-Puerto Ricans, and agitate in the Local Assembly in Ceuta.[50] The origin stories of race that I highlighted are important for this aim because how we understand race as heritage depends on our ontological assumptions about race. I believe that that each previously highlighted perspective has much to offer.

In this section, I bridge the theoretical gaps and miscommunications I identified in the previous sections and draw on additional theoretical work on race to present a pragmatist theory of racial experience, which leads me to accentuate the aesthetic and biocultural dimensions of racial experience. In general terms, pragmatism is a theory that not only takes into account cognitive dimensions of race in addition to sociocultural dimensions, but also a biocultural process that includes a full range of cognitive and emotional experiences with physiological consequences. Furthermore, these physiological consequences affect the way we continue to think, feel, and behave with bodies.[51] This pragmatist approach is prefaced in the philosophies of Antenor Firmin, W.E.B. Du Bois, John Dewey, William James, and Franz Boas, among others, that are generally unconcerned with the ontological differentiation between nature and culture. They view culture as an evolutionary outcome of human nature.[52] Furthermore, pragmatism also refers to a commitment to philosophize or theorize by privileging human experience.[53]

A Pragmatist Approach to Human Experience and Racial Experience

Let us begin at the end of the previous section with human experience, since experience is the concept at the heart of pragmatism and a biocultural approach. In explaining and employing the work of John Dewey, philosopher Thomas Alexander takes great care to explain Dewey's "denotative method," which Alexander characterizes as "a method for aesthetic receptivity and openness."[54] The denotative method "is *philosophical* method; i.e., a way of preventing philosophy from succumbing to 'intellectualism'; it is a way of putting 'knowing' in context and making 'experience' serviceable for the real philosophical project: wisdom."[55] Denotation means pointing to experience to begin and end any philosophical inquiry. This approach can be anthropological since we now know that what Dewey is calling for is an approach to pointing to experience that is universal and culturally diverse, and he thought that anthropology was well positioned for such an endeavor.[56] Similarly, Alexander's eco-ontology is a philosophical call for a cross-cultural ethnography.[57] Dewey warns philosophers to be humble and not confuse "reality" with "what is known" or substitute a theory of experience for experience itself, "getting caught up in theoretical objects may 'convince many a student that the nearer he gets to the reality of experience, the further away he gets from all the experience he ever had.'"[58]

However, anthropologists cannot assume they occupy a privileged theoretical space for documenting and understanding experience because ethnography places them out in social worlds. Henrietta Moore reminds us that anthropological concepts are, like all social scientific concepts, concept-metaphors. "Concept-metaphors like global, gender, the self and the body are a kind of conceptual shorthand, both for anthropologists and for others. They are domain terms that orient us towards areas of shared exchange, which is sometimes academically based."[59] Experience is a particularly slippery concept-metaphor for a few reasons. First, like many concepts in the study of culture (and culture itself), experience has a folk meaning for people in their everyday lives and a theoretically informed meaning for social scientific disciplines. Second, social scientific meanings of experience vary. Third, in anthropology, it is unclear what the conceptual domain of experience is. Anthropologists can either employ the concept of experience in undefined ways that make it difficult to tell what is excluded by the concept of experience or employ it in carefully delineated theoretical frameworks.

However, the slipperiness of experience is not necessarily due to how anthropologists employ it because "the role of concept-metaphors, like gender or the global, is not to resolve ambiguity, but to maintain it. Their purpose is to maintain a tension between pretentious universal claims and particular contexts and specifics."[60] I agree with Moore, but there is another layer of complexity to the conceptualization of experience. Mainly, adjectives often modify experience, such as my usage of "racial experience." Alternatively, people are said to experience something social in nature, such as gender, queerness, ethnicity, or nationality. This additional layer makes the concept-metaphor of experience take a back seat to the social form that anthropologists aim to highlight in their work. For all these reasons, it is important to highlight the conceptual delineations drawn by anthropologists dedicated to theorizing experience.

Willen and Seeman propose that phenomenological and psychoanalytic approaches might seem polar opposite but demonstrate how anthropologists have been well positioned to account for both "the intersubjective lifeworlds that humans inhabit and the uniquely individual life trajectories that ethnographers encounter and seek to understand," respectively.[61] Although not mutually exclusive approaches, anthropologists have mostly focused on the intersubjective lifeworlds that humans inhabit elucidated by phenomenological approaches, and they have managed to do so without losing sight of how broader social contexts (e.g., political economy) inform habitually conditioned phenomenological experiences.[62] Douglas Hollan applauds these efforts but warns that psychoanalytic approaches are necessary to prevent the phenomenological tendency "to smooth out the differences between people and their experiences by referring to their purportedly common habitus or routines or practices; in some cases to presume that they are thinking and feeling and imagining the same things simply because they are overtly acting the same ways."[63] Ethnographically, this psychoanalytic focus allows "a careful, almost moment-by-moment experience-near exploration of a person's stream of consciousness and sense of awareness, noting what draws attention and expression, either verbal or non-verbal, but also what seems not to be expressed."[64]

Let us now consider what a pragmatist approach to racial experience can entail. First, the experience in racial experience should always serve as a conceptual vehicle for modifying what we might count as a racial experience. Racial experience cannot solely be equated with cognitive articulations of a racial experience as reported by interlocutors or anthropologists. Instead, knowledge of racial experience should be grounded by all the possibilities of noncognitive experience. This pragmatist approach prevents us from getting caught up in Hirschfeld, Dominguez, and Stoler's debate over whether race is easy to learn unless we open up the concept of learning to cognitive, noncognitive, and emotional forms of learning; but learning is difficult to conceptualize without the notion of knowledge, which is, in turn, associated with cognition.

Second, following Alexander and Dewey, I suggest that all experience, cognitive and noncognitive, is aesthetic. Alexander's understanding of aesthetics is not restricted to beauty, but rather it is closer to its etymological Greek root, "sense of experience":

> Our experience is pervaded with a *sensed* texture of order, possibility, meaning, and anticipation. The world offers itself to us through our capacity to be lured into its aesthetics orders, which in turn become lived meanings. Our immediate experience of even the simplest, most mundane objects resonates with memory and expectation which are directly embodied in the world.[65]

Alexander's philosophical argument resonates with phenomenological and psychoanalytic approaches in anthropology. Therefore, an aesthetic account of racial experience directs our attention to the myriad of instances when race is intersubjectively made meaningful and how the life histories of individuals and communities allow the racial imaginary to be reproduced and contested. This approach represents a tall order for ethnography, for the phenomenological conceptualization of an intersectional habitus inclusive of race must also account for the psychoanalytic life histories of racialized individuals and communities purportedly experiencing the same racial order.

Third and closely related to the second point, in ethnographic practice, the study of racial experience should be in conceptual tension with other forms of experiences that are assigned (i.e., categorized or conceptualized) to a form of experience of another social group. Concepts need to follow and be amended by experiences. As conceived by Patricia Hill Collins, the social science of intersectionality should shake the anthropological confidence of knowing what sort of ethnographic data belongs in the conceptual realms of, for example, gender, ethnicity, and nationality vis-à-vis race.[66] This is especially important to remember given the intellectual history of anthropological engagements with race that have been contextualized in his chapter. Racial heritage, then, constitutes lived racial experience as it relates to the culturally meaningful worlds of our interlocutors.

Fourth, an account of racial experience that incorporates phenomenological and psychoanalytic approaches requires us to reimagine how we placate race as a correlate of anthropological anti-racism. Since race as heritage must be ethnographically discovered, the problem of racism and racial uplift should drive only the ethnography of racial experience when, and only when, it naturally occurs in people's lived experiences. Moreover, the problem of racism cannot be a priori structure that informs racial experience. Concepts, such as structural violence and systemic racism, cannot serve as a prism for understanding racial experience. Although it is often difficult for some to imagine how systemic racism does not inform every form of racial experience, there are social and cultural structures that are racial in nature that empower rather than oppress. Therefore, to first approach racial experience from a prism of systematic oppression risks missing how racial experiences can be a source for navigating and resisting such oppressive systems. And even if we allow racial experiences to be oppressive and sources of resistance, we must have some way of conceptualizing and theorizing how different forms of racial experience can coexist for individuals and in sociocultural worlds.

A Biocultural Approach to Racial Experience

Anthropologists and other social scientists working at the intersection of biology and culture have explored the biocultural nature of racism by highlighting how race gets into the body in ways that are measurable by various biomarkers and sociologically measurable health disparity outcomes.[67] What makes these approaches theoretically biocultural is the delineation of pathophysiology that traces how manifestations of racism as sociocultural phenomena become biologically tangible as effects on the body in various forms. Manifestations of racism work at various social levels to cause biological harm. For example, racism can be an interpersonal expression of racism that leads to violence and bodily harm, or racism can be systemic racism that has led to unequal access to preventive care for racialized populations.

Moreover, researchers have increasingly recognized that the exact pathophysiology for many detrimental health outcomes is difficult to ascertain and is not a direct path between a racist incident and stress. Preterm labor and preeclampsia, for example, are linked to chronic stress, but chronic stress results from many societal and environmental factors that cannot be easily isolated in research.[68] In proposing a biocultural approach that includes genetic and social network analysis for explaining the incidence of hypertension in African American populations, Fuller et al. find that models that include genetic and social network data better explain incidences of high blood pressure.[69] This study is particularly relevant for the discussion at hand because they find that individuals with a high concentration of family members in their social network are more likely to have high blood pressure. "Although access to kin support may buffer social stressors and promote health, providing such support may itself be a stressor."[70] Given that social networks are proxies for more complex sociocultural processes, the research team in this study provides a possible explanation for their network analysis. Relying on a few citations, they first postulate that African American families in the US are large and extended,[71] and these family structures are a source of support.[72] However, that support can negatively affect the ability of African Americans to accumulate wealth and have upward social mobility,[73] and African American women are particularly mentally stressed by such family networks.[74] The contradiction between the stress and support of social networks has been observed in previous anthropological research, particularly in the foundational work of Leith Mullings and Alaka Wali, whose Sojourner Syndrome metaphor explains how working-class women embody resilience and resistance in the face of social inequality in Harlem, New York.[75]

There is, however, a theoretical challenge (or incompleteness) for biocultural approaches that account for how networks and life histories support and stress social groups. The challenge is not the theoretical validity of the concept, since both quantitative and qualitative data demonstrate at various levels, ranging from the individual to global networks, how support, resilience, resistance, and stress are simultaneously present in the lives of racialized peoples. The problem is that it is unclear what forms of experiences (specifically racial experiences) are differently, similarly, or simultaneously generating stress and support. If biocultural approaches are conceptualized as a summative or intersectional instance of biology and culture, then it becomes difficult to operationalize racial experience as biocultural in comparative and cross-cultural frameworks because the biological and cultural components in research design are selected on an ad hoc case study basis. To face this challenge, I suggest placing the existing biocultural approaches to race within Agustin Fuente's integrative anthropological approach to the human niche.[76]

Fuentes proposes a heuristic framework that aims to integrate evolutionary approaches with broader anthropological currents, including ethnographic accounts of human sociocultural complexity. "This framework emphasizes the roles of mutual mutability between agents, collective action, social perceptions, and the roles of experiences and institutions in structuring human behavior as well as encompassing what we know about evolutionary processes."[77] Drawing on Rappaport, Fuentes postulates that the human niche has three mutually influencing components: individual, group, and community.[78] The "individual" refers to a single human, the "group" refers to a core social network for the individual, and the "community" refers to "the spatial and social context that includes the majority of social partners and the primary settings and ecologies with/in which an individual interacts.[79] Fuentes acknowledges that these components are reductive, but the reduction is necessary to engage the quantifiable methods of evolutionary approaches. Furthermore, "because what constitutes the 'group' is defined by what questions are being asked of the system, it highlights the critical need for ethnographic and sociohistorical baselines at the start of any evolutionary modeling."[80]

Although it is possible to think about how racial experience has shaped microevolutionary processes, in this book, I do not aim to propose any evolutionary modeling.[81] Fuentes's intervention is primarily an argument for biological anthropologists to be more anthropologically integrative, but I propose that culture theory can benefit from engagement with a rich and complex evolutionary theory. Mutually influencing components of the human niche allow a clearer articulation of how experience is racial vis-à-vis each influencing component; as such, placing biocultural approaches to racial experience within this human niche allows us to conceptualize the experience in racial experience as being ontologically multifaceted.

These human niches are the context for the lived experience of earlier humans and their communities, where they shared . . . social and ecological histories, as well as where they created and participated in shared knowledge, social and structural security, and development across the lifespan.[82]

If approached from this human niche perspective, racial experience is not just biocultural in the sense that a social form like racism can affect the body. Instead, racial experience is biocultural because it occurs within the context of a history of communities' racialized existence. The human niche can then be quired for its racialized nature as long as "nature" is akin to what Fuentes calls a "moving assemblage." "All of the interfaces within and between the three core components [individual, group, and community] are highly dynamic and malleable, and the human niche is indeed a moving assemblage."[83]

THE RACIAL NICHE AS A
MOVING ASSEMBLAGE

As previously indicated, resistance and resilience should be accounted for in ethnographic narratives of racism and systemic oppression. However, we should also account for a broader range of racial experiences that are not necessarily conceptualized as reactions to racism. I neither want to question nor ignore the pervasiveness of racism and structural racism. Still, it is important to consider that experience cannot only be conceptualized a priori through oppressive social structures, which in the past has led to confusing the social problem of racism with the study of race and racial experience—the heritage-uplift conundrum. Furthermore, I believe racial experience is best understood as sensorially multifaceted (via pragmatism) and biocultural. But what does this approach to racial experience mean for our understanding of racialized social worlds or contexts where differentiated social bodies are unequal? Addressing such embodied forms of social complexity, Greg Downey explains that "behavioral variability leads to niche stratification when organisms can inhabit the environment in divergent ways depending on behavioral inventory and social access. As social complexity grows, individual members of a species may occupy distinctive behavioral-ecological niches with overlapping ranges and even complementary functions."[84] For these reasons, racial experiences are best ethnographically assessed when conceptualized as occurring in racialized niches. These racialized niches, in turn, function like moving assemblages.[85] This theoretical approach demands that racialization be ethnographically examined and interpreted relative to one of the many assembling components of the racialized niche. But how does one recognize a racialized niche when one sees one?

To recognize a racialized niche, I suggest that a niche be conceptually approached as racialized if any of the following three conditions are met: first, if the niche exists in a social context structured by Euro-American racial formations or racial assemblages that make racialized bodies seem biologically predetermined;[86] second, if the socially marginalized people see themselves as racialized people; and third, if the researcher or interlocutors are interested in examining their socially embodied difference within the scope of racialization as outlined in the previous two conditions. The first two conditions demand that ethnographic interlocutors (and researchers) understand the concept of race that they articulate as "race" and related linguistic variations (including variations in different languages). There is no need for researched populations or researchers to wholly agree that race is an adequate form of understanding the social group. Instead, the adequateness of race can be assessed through empirical research and cross-cultural comparison. Furthermore, the third condition is necessary for cross-cultural comparison to be possible. For if concepts like caste, ethnicity, and nationality are going to be distinguished from race, then these should be distinguished based on comparative data that is pragmatist and biocultural.

Human niches are not social agents, but human niches are also not a sum of individual behaviors or social groups at different scales. Niches are inclusive of individual and social behaviors, alliances, and shared ideas, and, in their totality, niches are contexts for understanding the possibilities of human agency. Therefore, racialized niches are contexts for racialized peoples to experience a broad range of racial phenomena like discrimination, material inequality, the banality of everyday life, desire, pride, resistance, and flourishing. To conceptualize the possibilities of agency and a broad range of experience in racialized niches, I employ the concept of styles and styling. If racialized niches are moving assemblages, then people assemble styles to navigate their existence within racial niches with meaning.

Navigating with meaning, in turn, is not synonymous with progress or uplift. Meaningful navigation is meaningful because it is means something to those who navigate their way through lifespans in racialized niches. Struggles to survive are not always successful, but they are meaningful, even when these struggles reify race or are politically ineffective. We need a fuller account of how racialized people craft styles for meaningfully navigating their worlds to discover possibilities for racialized styles to effect positive social change; that is, to craft styles of flourishing in racist worlds.

2

STYLES FOR FLOURISHING

Reconfiguring Selves Through the Racial Niche

ORIGINS OF FLOURISHING

To flesh out the concepts of racialized niches and styles, I return to the question of the origins of race, but, this time, I want to enter the discussion from a different disciplinary perspective. I already argued that unreconciled ontological articulations of racial phenomena could explain the impasse concerning the origins of race. Under Hirschfeld's account, "race is recruited as a category of power because of the properties it has in virtue of being a domain-specific category of mind."[1] But by "power," Hirschfeld only means something akin to structural racism. Let us take an alternative road to youth development and race, focusing on how race is recruited as a category of power for racialized peoples. My aim in taking this alternative road is to demonstrate that the concepts of the racial niche and fashioning styles within racial niches account for more experiential components in racialized worlds.

Mullings and Wali's Sojourner Syndrome takes us on a long, intellectual path toward grasping the complex interweaving of a strong sense of self and the burdens of resisting social marginalization.[2] In addition, a large and well-established body of literature in developmental psychology addresses the negative impact of racism on mental health and the positive impact of racial identification on mental health (this does not include Hirschfeld). However, most cultural anthropological and cultural theoretical works on race rarely address this developmental psychological literature in their research. I believe it is important to wrestle with this body of literature because it provides a conceptual guiding light for my ethnographic work in the US, Puerto Rico, and Ceuta. Theoretically, the literature allows us to re-approach the heritage-uplift rift, move toward a pragmatist and biocultural theory of racial experience suitable for cross-cultural comparison, and put everyday racial experience into conversation with political theory.

The relationship between reported racism and negative effects on mental health is well-established through decades of research.[3] The social processes for these relationships are also well known; racism is a manifestation of essentialized identities (racialization) that negatively affect the everyday experiences of racialized social groups, and those negative experiences lead to anxiety, depression, psychological distress, and lower self-esteem and self-worth.[4] These foundations of chronic stress contribute to detrimental physiological health outcomes, such as preterm birth and hypertension.[5] However, a relationship exists between racial-ethnic identification and positive mental health outcomes. For example, for both Black American and Latinx adolescents, Hoffman et al. found that racial-ethnic centrality (defined as the extent to which ethnicity/race is central to youths' self-identification) is important in youths' positive development of academic and peer support groups, which in turn "can serve as a more positive and beneficial outcome for youth of color."[6] In a meta-analysis of forty-six studies on positive racial-ethnic affect and adjustment, Rivas-Drake et al. argue that "meta-analytic findings overwhelmingly suggest that more positive ethnic-racial affect is correlated with more favorable psychosocial adjustment and reduced health risks."[7]

Making sense of these findings is not as easy as positing the impact of racist beliefs and behaviors against positive beliefs about one's racial group. As discussed in Chapter 1, there are complexities involved in understanding the detrimental effects of living in a racist society and exposure to racist beliefs and behaviors—detrimental effects well known in the social sciences.[8] Therefore, in this chapter, I want to focus on some of the intricacies of mental health and positive beliefs about the self, racialized self, and the self's socialized racial group.

Although research supports the positive effects of racial and ethnic identity throughout lifespans, most research focuses on the developmental role of racial-ethnic identification for youth. In a comprehensive article reviewing existing research, Stephen M. Quintana evaluates key assumptions in theories of racial and ethnic identity development.[9] Exposure to racism significantly triggers adolescents' exploration of ethnic and racial identity, but there are important caveats to what constitutes exploration. Quintana argues that exploration takes place over time, with periods of acceleration and deceleration. Most importantly, exploration does not necessarily lead to an identity crisis where an individual experiences a more "dramatic shift or immersion into one's racial group."[10] This is an important finding because it points to a more complex social ecology affected by discrimination but not defined by it.

After exploration, the role that racial and ethnic identification takes on within a social ecology does not seem to be governed by normative developmental processes. Other factors, like the context of discrimination and different elements of racial-ethnic identification, can have diverse outcomes in mental health. For example, Quintana concludes his review,

> Cultivation of pride in and identification with youth's racial-ethnic groups was associated with adjustment and development, but this general finding was limited to those contexts in which discrimination was infrequent. Analogously, racial-ethnic identity orientations associated with being vigilant of and prepared for discrimination were adaptive in contexts in which discrimination was frequent, but apparently not adaptive in which discrimination was infrequent.[11]

Cultivation of pride and preparedness for discrimination might be reductive of a more complex set of narratives that occur throughout childhood and lifespans, but just taking note of how, when evaluated in different environments of discrimination, the effects on mental health can vary should make us pause and take stock of how complex racial experience can be in sociocultural contexts.

There is more nuance in the developmental psychology literature. For example, ethnic identity affects Latinx youth differently, specific forms of African American parenting style intersect with racial identification to affect academic motivation and academic achievement, and Mexican mothers and fathers can cause different long-term effects in youths' long-term racial-ethnic socialization.[12] There are also known distinctions between personal self-esteem and pride in one's racial group. For African American adolescents, pride in their racial group "is an important correlate of their current depressive symptoms and changes in the depressive symptoms beyond their general feelings of personal esteem."[13] This explains why, in response to discrimination, young racialized people may respond in ways that are adaptive or maladaptive relative to their future success as measured through academic achievements and socioeconomic mobility, yet, regardless of being adaptive or maladaptive, self-worth can be high among at-risk youth and low among highly achieving youth.[14]

Research in developmental psychology cuts across the heritage-uplift dichotomy by demonstrating how cultural beliefs and patterns of racialized peoples that might otherwise be detrimental are equally, if not primarily, sources of human prosperity and well-being (what I refer to as flourishing). In addressing the protective role of ethnic identity for urban, adolescent males facing multiple stressors, Williams et al. conclude, "For Black and Hispanic males, popular stereotypes about criminal involvement are often accepted by society as culturally normative, thus culture becomes a risk factor when viewed from this deficit perspective. . . . However, our findings demonstrate the ways in which cultural group membership, affiliation, pride, and exploration, as elements of social identity, are an asset for youth."[15] The pragmatist and biocultural approach to racial experience outlined in the previous chapter simultaneously accounts for discriminatory experiences and how racialized peoples flourish mentally and behaviorally through racial-ethnic identification processes. At the same time, the debate about the origins of race is rendered moot since it is possible for discrimination to be a symptom of structural racism as well as for essentialism to be at the heart of structural racism and the psycho-social positive effects of feeling ethno-racial pride.

The disconnects between the two competing versions of the origins of race and their inability to resolve the heritage-uplift problem can be theoretically manageable from a racialized niche perspective. First, recall that the origins of race debate reveals an ontological uncertainty regarding the nature of racial being (i.e., the nature of racial social being, not the pseudo-scientific biological definition of race that most anthropologists dismiss). Second, ontological uncertainty was, nevertheless, accompanied by a political ethos of anti-racism, where Hirschfeld advocates for anti-racist education for children as a way to intervene in the way race is recruited as a category of power, and Stoler and Dominguez want to identify and denounce the racist social structures that reproduce racial hierarchies. Third, on each side of the debate, the political ethos is vague in addressing racial uplift because there is no direct path between the study of racial experience (either as a category of mind or informed by racist social structure) and strategies for political thought that emerge from racial experiences in any given social context. Contrastingly, developmental psychological literature demonstrates that there are precise (yet varying) junctures between racial experience resulting from prejudice in racist societies and senses of self-worth and flourishing through processes of racial-ethnic identification, which are, in turn, relative to various social contexts that include families, peers, and institutions.

Yet the racialized niche moves us beyond a positive racial-ethnic identification counterpoint to racial prejudice and into a framework that accounts for histories of adjustments and maladjustments, protests and acquiescence, exclusion and inclusion, self-worth and self-loathing, coalitions and segregations, laughter and anger, and an ethnographically infinite set of ways through which people make racial experiences meaningful. These endless possibilities, consistent with the framework for racial experience I proposed, are why I value Fuentes's comparison of the human niche to a moving assemblage. Anthropologists have theorized sociocultural formations as assemblages to highlight various forms in which the heterogeneous contexts of human existence are determined by multiple logics, through which different elements (e.g., material, organic, conscious) can reconstitute themselves in new, mutually constitutive orders. For example, in defining a global assemblage, Ong and Collier explain that "the temporality of an assemblage is emergent. It does not always involve new forms, but forms that are shifting . . . As a composite concept, the term 'global assemblage' suggests inherent tensions: global implies broadly encompassing, seamless, and mobile; assemblage implies heterogeneous, contingent, unstable, partial and situated."[16] Building on Ong and Collier's approach, Campbell argues for placing assemblages within a dialectical framework that allows "multiple logics to be read as internally related without this becoming a unified system-logic."[17] This dialectical approach relies on Li's examination of how social actors' governing practices hold disparate elements of assemblages together.[18] Campbell is concerned with alternative capitalist practices, like worker's co-ops and self-employment, which can be understood as resistance to global capitalist practices but also operate within a capitalist logic. These anthropological theoretical approaches to assemblages on broad scales are reminiscent of Bourdieu's more bodily focused habitus. "The conditionings associated with a particular class of conditions of existence produce *habitus*, systems of durable, transportable dispositions, structured structures predisposed to function as structuring structures, that is, as principles which generate and organize practices and representations that can be objectively adapted to their outcomes without presupposing a conscious aiming at ends or an express mastery of the operations necessary in order to attain them."[19] My partiality for Fuente's human niche as a dynamic, moving assemblage to theorize the racialized niche is based on his inclusivity of a biocultural approach, the potential for dialectical analyses implicit in the mutually influencing components of an individual, group, and community, and the openness to practice (and experience) at the center of ethnographic inquiry of assemblages.

The racialized niche, then, is the analytical entry point into the ethnography of racial experience. How racial experience is understood as racial is an empirical question relative to the particular assemblage of the racialized niche. Furthermore, the origins of flourishing for racialized peoples are also relative to the particular assemblage of the racialized niche. Therefore, flourishing can be assembled in many ways, so the sociocultural nature of flourishing may be momentary or long-lasting, politically translatable or a one-time policy intervention, organized or unruly, and so on. The concept of uplift is less helpful than flourishing because the former begins with the problem of social inequality and quickly moves to known public policies for lifting the disadvantaged group.

Alternatively, the concept of flourishing recognizes that in addition to necessary public policies to incentivize uplift, people are already always meaningfully navigating racial niches. The important point is that we take DuBois's warning seriously about the difficulty of pinpointing the nature of a racial problem. I suggest that if we are to think about the race problem cross-culturally, we exercise even more care in defining what might constitute a racial problem. Undoubtedly, the social inequality that characterizes all racial hierarchies is relevant to thinking about any racial problem, but such hierarchies are one of many important components in racialized niches, and the many political possibilities for tackling structural racial inequality begin with efforts to flourish in particular racialized niches.

STYLES FOR FLOURISHING

Berg and Ramos-Zayas provocatively and powerfully argue for a perspective on racialized effect, proposing "a more nuanced examination of 'racialization' that foregrounds political economy and historical context as inseparable from the subjective complexity of racialized populations and national and international projects."[20] My approach to racialized niches as moving assemblages follows their seminal proposition, and their work can be read as calling for what I have proposed so far. For example, similar to the biocultural dimensions of racialized niches, Berg and Ramos-Zayas explain that "an ordinary event in the lives of racialized populations is produced as an emergent historical environment."[21] Akin to my pragmatist and biocultural approach to experience, they argue that "collective intersubjectivity requires attention to everyday ways in which racialized ways of being are (re)produced, narrated, and embodied in tandem with political, economic, social, and moral structures."[22] Like Berg and Ramos-Azayas, I want to consider how these "racialized ways of being" are "(re)produced, narrated, and embodied" through the fashioning of styles.

The concept of styles explains various aspects of how people exist in racialized niches. Irvine conceptualizes sociolinguistic styles as ideologically motivated and aesthetic forms of distinctiveness.[23] By distinctiveness, Irvine is basically referring to styles as functioning in reference to a sociocultural system, but she also means "more subtle ways individuals navigate among available varieties and try to perform a coherent representation of a distinctive self—a self that may be in turn subdividable into a differentiated system of aspects-of-self."[24] By ideological motivation, Irvine means that "ways of speaking index the social formations . . . of which they are characteristic. But an index can only inform social action if it functions as a sign; and a sign requires an interpretant, as Peirce long ago pointed out."[25] Finally, by stylistic aesthetics, Irvine means "as concerning (among other things) not only distinctiveness, but also the consistency of the linguistic features constituting a style."[26]

Bourdieu's classic conceptualization of stylization of life and lifestyles also incorporates a theory of distinction. He employs his theory of habitus to examine how stylistic preferences constrict agency. "The agents only have to follow the leanings of the habitus in order to take over, unwittingly, the intention immanent in corresponding practices, to find an activity which is entirely 'them' and, with it, kindred spirits."[27] Here we can see a theoretical likeness of how styles can be conceptualized within the racialized niche. However, Bourdieu's aesthetic approach is compromised by his a priori commitment to class-based analysis, which leads him to characterize the lifestyles of working-class people as a "pragmatic, functionalist 'aesthetic.'"[28] Bourdieu and other approaches that are conceptually committed to style to delineate processes of class distinction tend to unnecessarily simplify the aesthetic quality of styles and their potential to play more complex roles in social processes and symbolic significance.[29] Alternatively, I favor a theoretical concept of styles akin to Aimee Meredith Cox's of choreography, which is more attentive to aesthetic creativity performed through racialized bodies and in racialized spaces (i.e., racial niches):

> Choreography is concerned in a very fundamental sense with the ordering of bodies in space. Choreography is shapeshifting made visible. Choreography is embodied meaning making, physical story telling, affective physicality, and an intellectualized response to the question of how movement might narrate texts that are not otherwise legible . . . Choreography suggests that there is a map of movement or plan for how the body interacts with its environment, but also suggests that by the body's placement in a space, the nature of that space changes.[30]

For the remainder of this book, I employ a conceptual framework for how people in racialized niches fashion styles (i.e., *styles for flourishing*). As described in the remainder of this section, styles for flourishing fashioned from racial experiences are performative, affectively scaffolded and habituated, and anchored by embodied social difference.

First, styles are performative and draw distinctiveness throughout lifetimes. The social processes of drawing distinctiveness are important because they involve imagining a racialized self against which individuals' fashion themselves through everyday and ritualistic performances. With regard to these processes of distinction happening throughout lifetimes, Henrietta Moore's psychoanalytical gender theory provides a useful framework.[31] In the early stages of development, the ego's body is first known through bodies that are already socioculturally meaningful in relation to gender, race, and other embodied forms of social difference. Ego's body is never known outside of its immediate cultural meaning. As an individual moves through life, they continue to reorient their bodies in relation to the previous sociocultural bodily orientation, which can be traced to the earliest orientation when "the map of the body ego allows little distinction between the material and representational, between the physical and the psychical body, because there is no lived phenomenological body prior to a psychic investment in the parts and surfaces of the body."[32] Furthermore, these early embodied forms of difference are always shaped by structures of power. These structures of power are, in turn, the same that many scholars have examined as political economic creation of social difference to exploit labor.

Second, racialized styles are affectively scaffolded and habituated. From a philosophical perspective, "the concept of affective scaffolding challenges the internalist assumption that emotions, moods, and other feelings supervene solely on intra-individual states and processes."[33] Affective scaffolding is key to understanding how styles emerge from the racial niche. Human niche complexity (the dynamic assemblages) are all potential sources of affective stimuli. Moreover, approaching racialized styles as affective scaffolding moves us away from a social science of race as identity. To be more precise, it moves us towards a concept of identity that is not centered on individual consciousness; instead, identity is habituated in relation environments (social, ecological, organizational, etc.). This environmental habituation is akin to Bourdieu's habitus but more along the theoretical lines of pragmatist social psychology.[34] Candiotto and Dreon elegantly articulate this pragmatist position.

> We suggest considering affectivity as both scaffolded by habits and scaffolding habits. On the one hand, we claim that affectivity is a permanent feature of the active human experience of the world, supported by habits. . . . On the other hand, we claim that affectivity gives rise and nourishes more or less standardized practices, consolidated ways of facing circumstances, socially shaped ways of praising and blaming that remain largely unreflective. In this way, affectivity is not just scaffolded by habits but it also scaffolds habits.[35]

The relationship between habits and affectivity lead Candiotto and Dreon to rely on the idea of affective habits as "ways of interacting . . . at once organic, and cultural, individual and social, pre-reflective and cognitive, routine, and transformative."[36] From this perspective, the ethnography of racialized styles demands no commitment to broad processes of prejudice, antiracist politics, or systemic racism. Instead, psychological prejudice or hegemonic racist structures should be ethnographically discovered through affective practices emanating from multiple spaces in the racial niche.

Third, racialized styles are anchored by embodied difference—because racialized styles are embodied in racialized bodies, racialized styles are synonymous with social groups whose collectively embodied difference is part of social hierarchies. In turn, those social hierarchies place a social weight on experiences associated with styles by always connecting stylistic performances to the marginalized condition of racial groups. However, it is critical that we not approach the anchoring of embodied difference to racialized styles as a burden or something negative. Anchors hold back as well as provide strong foundations for dynamic movement. For example, when writing about the theorization of racialized spaces, Karla Slocum concludes that Black towns in the US "sit at the nexus of the racialization of space and the appeal of a Black space. The nexus is important, which leaves one critical takeaway: to talk about a successful Black place does not have to mean only talking about the triumphs and the achievements to the exclusion of the challenges. . . . Experiencing marginality does not foreclose success, and experiencing extensive success does not exclude being marginalized."[37]

The concept of flourishing, then, becomes a necessary addition to the idea of styles fashioned from racial experience. Although flourishing has a positive semantic connotation, the concept of styles for flourishing points to the *possibility* of growth; but the possibility of growth does not guarantee positive social outcomes. Like a plant flourishing in a concrete gap in the middle of a parking lot, flourishing can occur in difficult conditions that eventually limit growth beyond hegemonic boundaries. And even when we recognize and learn from the limited growth in those hegemonic boundaries, flourishing may be limited across lifespans or intergenerationally.

CROSS-CULTURAL COMPARISON
OF RACIAL NICHES AND STYLES
FOR FLOURISHING

Historically, the three racial niches discussed in this book (the US Midwest, Puerto Rico, and Ceuta) existed before the emergence of liberal democratic governance or so-called liberal democratic forms of governance that were inclusive of racialized populations. The racialized styles that I highlight in each ethnographic study are quite different (boxing, dancing, and political work in an assembly); therefore, the comparison of these styles is not in form but in function. Each style functions as an effort to flourish, given the particular histories of each racial niche. After examining each ethnographic study, I argue that the function of styles for flourishing is translatable into political ideologies for liberal governance if and only if coalitional politics honestly incorporate styles for flourishing into what are otherwise transactional politics that privilege traditional Left-Right liberal politics. Specifically, I demonstrate how the racialized self can be a locus for reification and resistance in the US Midwest, how racialized political subjectivities are a necessary disruptive voice in democratic deliberation in Puerto Rico, and how liberal democratic governance can be pushed and limit the possibilities of racialized political subjectivity effecting social change in Ceuta. Thus, I conclude that coalitional politics need to be particularly sensitive and dynamic to community voices and styles for flourishing to achieve democracy as a lived experience.

Given the scope of my comparative aims in a single book, it is important to delineate the limitations of my approach. First, I cannot fully describe the nature of the racial niche in all cases. For the US Midwest and Puerto Rico, I assume that it is uncontroversial to presume the interrelatedness of nation-state formation, racial hierarchies, and racial ideologies. For Ceuta, I chose to articulate the formation of the racial niche (see Chapter 5) more thoroughly since it is a more recent historical phenomenon, and more historical nuance is necessary to demonstrate how the racial niche precedes Spain's 1978 liberal democratic constitution and is directly linked to Muslims' political activism.

Second, there are multiple and overlapping styles for flourishing in each racial niche. For example, racialized people obviously participate in liberal governance in the US and Puerto Rico, and Ceuta's Muslims engage in sports and aesthetic expression. A more robust account of styles for flourishing in each racial niche, which could then compare the same styles across niches, would seem like a more robust comparative project. However, I believe that comparison is not an end by itself but part of a more complex dialectic between thick description and comparison. Matei Candea proposes that we not "dwell in intensely think comparison forever, but rather that we first construct intricate comparisons, that we commit to spooling out the potential of the initial contrast or analogy which caught our eye, and then, having done so, struggle against these thick comparisons, sharpen them back down to a point to reach our aims."[38] For this book, the drive to document racial experience precedes the thickness of the comparative exercise in this book. And although this means that I consider this comparative project as incomplete, I am comfortable with how I have singled out each style for flourishing to reach my aim of imagining new paths for coalitional politics and governance for racialized people in liberal democracies.

Third, the conceptual elevation of racial experience to theorize styles for flourishing within the racial niche covers over a century of anthropological practices that privilege unracialized concepts (such as culture, habitus, and embodiment) as valid abstractions of human behavior and thought. Properly placing racial experience alongside these longstanding concepts requires more work of theoretical undoing than what I present in Chapter 1. Therefore, more comparative work is necessary to fully justify such displacements, but I believe it is worth beginning somewhere, and that somewhere is with the lived experience histories of survival of racialized peoples.

3

GOING TO THE BODY AS MEXICAN BOXERS DO

Fashioning Styles from Racial Experiences

n the spring of 2009, when I first showed up at the St. James Boxing Club looking to start a new ethnographic project, I had to explain to the owners, Larry and Eva, why I was there. Before I had a chance to make my research pitch, Eva asked me where I was from. "Puerto Rico," I answered. They both smiled, and Eva, with a playful smile, shouted to the few boxers wrapping their hands in preparation for practice, "You all better watch out. We got a Puerto Rican boxer! You know they can throw down!" Eva then turned to me and told me how much she loved Hector "Macho" Camacho, a famous Puerto Rican boxer from New York whose career peaked in the 1980s. Excitedly, she mimicked his signature rapid punch combination while describing how smooth and quick Camacho was in his heyday. She even had a picture of herself with Camacho. Without discussing why I was there, we kept talking about recent Puerto Rican greats Felix "Tito" Trinidad and Miguel Cotto. Practice began, and a good half hour passed with us talking about Puerto Rican boxers and some of the great fights we all recalled. Those great fighters from the 1980s, 1990s, and 2000s included African Americans, Mexicans, Mexican Americans, white Americans (including Irish, Italian, and Midwestern), Europeans (English,

Welsh, Polish, Ukrainians, and Eastern Europeans), Central
Asians, and East/Southeast Asians. That race and nationality
were organizing principles for the first conversation I had with
Eva and Larry made my research pitch much easier when we
finally got around to it.

I explained my purpose: "I would like to study how race,
nationality, and gender play out in the world of boxing." For
Larry and Eva, the question of race and nationality already made
sense given our initial conversation. The gender part of that
equation, which Eva understood as having to do with women,
was equally welcomed given that Eva had many stories from her
sporting careers that she wanted to share. Over the next seven
years, I became an amateur and professional coach, nonprofit
organization board member and grant director, and promotional
partner at St. James. I devoted much of my ethnographic attention to boxing styles, which people in the boxing world often
equate with various cultural notions of gender, race, and nationality. Out the three ethnographic sites discussed in this book,
St. James is where I felt most comfortable researching racial
experience and politics. However, for many scholars and outside
observers, boxing seems conceptually distant from politics.

When people in the United States have public conversations
about race, it is usually in the conversational frame of race as a
social problem. Conversations about race are usually about racial
prejudice, injustice, and inequity (racism). In the boxing world,
however, talk about race is often part of routine conversations
about the sport. These conversations are not just about remembering a great fighter from a certain race or nationality, they are
also about how boxers from social groups fight a certain way or
how fight fans from a social group understand and like certain
forms of boxing. These conversations are about embodiment,
though people do not necessarily know what the concept of

embodiment means. Another important aspect of these conversations is that they occur between people from different social backgrounds since many gyms (and the boxing world in general) attract a socially diverse group.

In the US, the diversity of groups varies by location. Most coaches and fans from the West Coast will generally paint a geographic picture that includes Mexicans, Filipinos, and Black boxers. People from the Midwest bring up Mexican, Black, and white boxers. And on the East Coast they mention Puerto Ricans, Cubans, Black, and white (particularly Irish and Italian) boxers. These general trends correspond with historical and contemporary US demographic patterns, and there is much more diversity than what people generally imagine. This diversity is evidenced by the gyms that have different national flags hung up on walls; it is also evidenced by the conversations about race and nationality that are not boxing related and a result of a diverse, leisurely place where everyone is part of the same club or gym.

Conversations about race are common in other sports but can be somewhat more polemic. For example, discussions about athleticism and Blackness are common in the US. In my anthropology of sports course for undergraduates, I have no problem getting my college students to admit that they subscribe to the notion that Black people are more athletically gifted (e.g., better speed, agility, reaction time, and explosiveness) in sports like basketball and American football. However, because they are in a college classroom and have many years of schooling on properly discussing race as part of multicultural education, students sound apologetic in speaking about Black athleticism because they sense something might be off about their argument. Some even preface their remarks with an "I know this is probably wrong." Of course, as the students articulate these arguments, their notions of the biology of Black athleticism are often mistaken. In my class, I address the anthropology of human biological diversity and the role of culture in athletic performance.[1] Compared to discussions about race in all my other classes, the students in my sports course have the easiest time engaging in meaningful discussions about race, biology, and culture. Although engaging race through the anthropology of sports does not preclude the hesitation and nervousness that comes with other public conversations about racism, it demonstrates that sports provide an accessible insight into what people assume about race and offers conversational frames to discuss and debate those assumptions.

The boxing world is not the only place where race is discussed without the hesitations of embarking on a touchy subject. Stand-up comedy, for example, is another public forum where racial joking mostly occurs without tension. Many other places of leisure (e.g., parks, barbershops, or bars) also lend themselves to relaxed conversations about race. However, many of these places are not socially diverse, which is why people feel comfortable having these conversations. Moreover, the content of conversations about race in these places is often not directly informative about why racialized bodies think and behave in certain ways.

Contrastingly, talk about race, nationality, and bodies occurs naturally in boxing. Because discussing boxing involves people's explanations of why the mentality and physicality of certain social groups manifest in how boxers fight, one can ethnographically access folk theories or intuitive theories about the intersection of biology and culture.[2] Folk theories are most evident in conversations about boxing styles, which are interrelated sets of fighting techniques and combative characters. Techniques are the athletic execution of boxing: punching, getting out of the way of punches, foot movement, and overall strategy. Characters refer to ethos, traits like emotion, intellect, and spirit that boxers demonstrate during training and competition. As bundles of techniques and characters, styles have names that are generic to boxing, a social group, or both. Regardless of the scientific validity of folk theories about the biology and culture of boxing styles, boxers experience these theories as they engage in boxing. One can tangibly relate to, say, the raw power of a Black boxer when that boxer hits you or the relentless attack of a Mexican boxer. How punches are fashioned into racialized boxing styles is one ethnographic entrée in the US racial niche that is configured in the Rust Belt region of the Midwest.[3] In this chapter, I examine the processes through which Mexican-American youth adopt racialized boxing styles to make meaningful sense of their racialized existence—that is, to flourish. I first provide a detailed sensory description of punching and the painful effects of being punched in the body, a hallmark of a Mexican boxer's idealized, gritty style. Then I tell the stories of boxers Samuel, Smiley, and Ray. Their stories demonstrate how Samuel and Smiley (brothers) entered the boxing gym with preconceived ideas about fighting and being Mexican. We see how Miguel, a young but experienced Mexican-styled fighter, served as a role model for Samuel and Smiley to fashion themselves as "Mexican warriors." Ray's trajectory is experientially different, yet the Mexican boxing style similarly informs the self and social perception of the fighting body.

Through these life stories of boxers in the St. James Boxing Gym, I examine how youth stylize hope in their racialized bodies as they embrace boxing styles. Because this stylization of hope resists negative ideas about Mexican bodies in the US, I argue that racialized styles are a way to flourish in societies structured by racial inequality. Finally, I conclude the chapter by presenting what I call the "paradox of reification." This paradox arises when we recognize the problems of what happen when people embrace what they might perceive as a racial stereotype and what happens when those so-called stereotypes are loci for resistance and flourishing.

FIGHTING, BODY PUNCHING, AND THE MEXICAN BOXING STYLE

In popular culture, like in cartoons, films, or colloquial idioms, violent aggression is mostly visualized as a punch to the face. Around the world, aggression in interpersonal conflicts often involve strikes and injuries to the face and head.[4] The fiction and actuality of face-punching are related, but the relationship is not innate. For example, Brickley and Smith found a correlation between culturally specific patterns of violence and the rise of professional boxing at the end of the nineteenth and beginning of the twentieth centuries; professional boxers propagated the idea of face-punching, and men started face-punching in their everyday brawls and domestic abuse.[5] Regardless of how life imitates sports, the cultural idea of getting punched in the face differs from reality, which is different when executed by trained professionals than when it happens in a street brawl.

While working in boxing, I often notice how newcomers misjudge the nature of a punch because in movies punches make a sound akin to a wet towel slapping skin; the actual sound of a punch is often misrecognized. In reality, punches usually make a low thumping sound. For those trying out boxing for the first time, the weight of the punches also comes as a surprise. In fictionalized fighting, fighters hit each other in the face many times with "clean punches" (i.e., an unblocked, direct hit) that continue for an improbable amount of time to make a good action movie sequence (think *Rocky* from 1976, starting Sylvester Stallone), but in boxing, few boxers can stand more than two or three clean punches in a row. Many boxing matches, especially at the higher weight classes, involve both fighters trying to figure out for rounds how to land one clean punch to the head to score a knockout.

The reality of a punch to the body is even more obscure than the reality of a punch to the face. Even boxing fans and many sports participants do not truly appreciate the nature of a body punch. Legal body punches can land on the front or side of the torso, and in a traditional boxing stance where the arms guard a good portion of the torso, it is not easy to land a clean body punch. When body punches do land, the effect can range from a bit of discomfort to paralyzing the body. The latter occurs with punches that are felt by internal organs, particularly the liver, in such a way that the brain goes into "shutdown mode." Body punches are difficult to identify as a spectator, and viewed from a distance, they are very often difficult to assess for severity. Ringside commentators, journalists, coaches, and judges often figure out how hard a body punch landed after the effect is evident in the boxer who got hit. Sometimes the fighter who delivers the blow does not truly know the effect until they can see a delayed reaction from their hurt opponent.

Going to the body strategically presents a series of risks for the boxer throwing the punch. A traditional boxing stance has boxers holding their hands by the side of their face. To deliver a body punch, one hand has to leave a side of the face unguarded and travel toward the front or side of the abdomen, which is usually the furthest legal target from the aggressor's hands. Additionally, the aggressor must at least slightly dip their bodies to land a punch to the body more effectively. Leaving the face open and lowering oneself gives the target of the body punch an opportunity to attack the aggressor, who is now in the disadvantageous position of coming closer, lower, and unprotected.

The rewards of going to the body are not usually immediate. On the one hand, even the slightest discomfort accumulates whenever a boxer receives a body shot. Even the most fit boxers will start to exhibit fatigue as they accumulate body shots over rounds. Over time, taking body shots leads to decreased mobility and poor defense. A boxer hurt from the accumulation of body shots will have to make a tough decision: heavily guard your body more and risk taking a heavy blow to the head or continue to leave the body exposed and risk a debilitating knockout punch to the body. On the other hand, a boxer who commits to body punching throughout a fight can be neutralized or dominated by a skilled opponent. Going to the body can lead to taking too many bruising punches to the face, and an ineffective attack on the body very often results in lost rounds (in amateur and professional boxing, each round is scored independently and tallied at the end).

In today's boxing world, especially in the United States (the global mecca of professional boxing), going to the body is embraced by most competent trainers as good technique; but going to the body is also most commonly associated with the Mexican style of boxing.[6] The prototypical Mexican warrior, as the lore in the boxing world claims, is a relentless boxer who moves forward, attacking their opponent's body, willing to take some punches in their quest to take their opponent's soul. The soul, which is presumably well-embedded in the body, can be snatched by a Mexican warrior who depletes his opponent's stamina, making the body heavier and heavier as rounds pass, which ultimately leads to the most despairing feeling one can have in a ring: not being able to breathe and defend yourself as your opponent hits you from every angle.

Although the quintessential Mexican boxer has a masculine-nationalist genealogy (Allen 2017),[7] the Mexican style has no superhero quality, no punching superpower, no lighting-speed athleticism, and no immediate one-punch-to-the-head knockout satisfaction for the crowd. In other words, going to the body is not a prototypical hypermasculine act in US sports.

Therefore, how youth encounter the Mexican boxing style provides an excellent opportunity to think about how Mexicanness is racialized—that is, how Mexicanness is embodied as a broader form of social difference in the US Midwest racial niche. More importantly, beyond being able to probe the cultural nature of a racialized style in the boxing world, how young boxers learn about boxing techniques and going to the body is relevant for thinking about how racialized styles serve as a source of resistance and flourishing in societies structured by racial inequality.

SAMUEL, SMILEY, AND RAY

Smiley and his older brother Samuel came into the gym because someone told their mom that this could be a good place for Samuel to learn discipline. Samuel, a fourteen-year-old half-Mexican and half-Salvadorian, had problems at school and home. He would throw and break things in reaction to authority figures, was unwilling to talk to school counselors, and started disrespecting his mother during arguments. Samuel came to the gym with what the coaches perceived as a bit of confusion over why he was there. On the one hand, boxing was being presented to him as a remedy for wrongdoing. On the other hand, he walked in with his chest up, proud of having the opportunity to celebrate his violent outburst through a violent sport. At eight years old, Smiley was put into boxing to be there with his brother since their mother, being single and working until practice was over, could most easily have both boys in one place.

The gym transformed Samuel in a matter of weeks. We saw his demeanor change in the gym, but his mother and school counselor later said Samuel had calmed down significantly. What we saw in the gym, however, was that Samuel quickly gained humility and confidence. He was a scrawny kid work-ing alongside considerably bigger and much more skilled adoles-cents and young men, so it was difficult for him to continue with his big man persona. Around the two most experienced boxers, Black men in their mid-twenties with calm and joking person-alities, Samuel was shy and quiet; he even seemed a little scared. He would later watch them in competition with excitement as a teammate, but he was never outspoken around them. Samuel was less shy and more talkative around Miguel, a rising teenage Mexican American star in the regional amateur scene.

Samuel was a below-average athlete. His coordination was off, he was not explosive, and it took him a long time to learn combinations. It was obvious to us coaches that Samuel was there for reasons other than the promise of being a successful competitor. But Samuel was bright-eyed about competition. Within a month of training, he traveled to an amateur boxing tournament with the team. Two of our boxers won their weight division, which the whole team celebrated as their own. Samuel was visibly excited on the way back home from the tournament. He shared pictures with friends of himself posing with his vic-torious teammates. In those pictures, Samuel and other boxers held their fist to their chest, a traditional pose for boxers taking pictures. He was part of a winning team and starting to feel like a boxer.

Yet Samuel had not yet sparred (i.e., practicing fighting against an opponent with protective gear), so he took on a boxer persona before crossing the first Rubicon to become a boxer. Almost everyone who quits their initial efforts to be part of a boxing gym quits shortly after their first sparring section. Spar-ring short-circuits the notion that fighting and boxing are the same thing. Athletically gifted or not, the first time an inexperi-enced boxer spars against an experienced boxer, they are forced to reckon with the fact that, as far as the boxing world is concerned, they cannot actually fight. Like all skilled activities, practice is necessary. Most first-time sparrers feel humiliated, which is one of the main causes of early attrition in a boxing gym. Those who find humility in their first sparring experience can stick around, learn, and become boxers.

Samuel sparred for the first time after a few months in the gym. Letting him spar took longer than usual since he was so limited in his abilities. We put him in with Ryan, one of our most experienced fighters, since we knew that Ryan would not hurt Samuel and would act more like a teacher than a competitive sparring partner. Like most first-timers, Samuel struggled in the ring. He looked uncomfortable and tense and could not avoid punches or get close to landing punches, yet he was not demoralized. It was another week before he got back in the ring, and again he struggled. He struggled for months. During punching practice, others and I encouraged Samuel to calm down and be brave. Samuel would try hard. His courage was visible in his grunts, the widening of his already large eyes, and his leaning, almost jumping, when punching, which is the wrong way to throw a punch (the body should rotate along a steady vertical axis) but demonstrates a boxer's eagerness to reach their opponent.

As months passed in Samuel's training, he increasingly identified with his Mexican heritage. Several factors can account for his identification. He learned about the culture of the Mexican boxing style and the Mexican warrior through common conversations about the most recently televised fight. These conversations often refer to Mexican fighters, their techniques, and their strong fanbase. And coaches and boxers would express admiration for Mexican fighters and their fans. Of course, the social identity of "Mexican," which Black and white folks in the

Midwest often utilize as a way to understand Latino or Spanish, also influenced how Samuel's mixed Latin American heritage became homogenized in the social groups at St. James. This was a homogenized group that also included me, a Puerto Rican coach. Of course, this homogenization was not a mere abstraction; it was evident in, for example, the way in which parents, coaches, and boxers from various Latin American backgrounds spoke or recognized Spanish, from correctly pronouncing Spanish names to having conversations in Spanish.[8]

Miguel's continued recognition as the gym's Mexican boxing star was also important in how Samuel increasingly identified as Mexican. First, Miguel was seventeen and handsome. Other boxers would sometimes tease Miguel of rumors about him dating several beautiful women. They would even tease him by calling him the "Mexican pretty boy." Samuel was somewhat awestruck around Miguel. Trying to be cool like Miguel, Samuel would sometimes make awkward comments to Miguel, but Miguel never embarrassed Samuel and treated him like a little brother instead. It was natural for Samuel to admire Miguel. Second, Miguel's training and fighting strategy included pressuring opponents and going to the body—the prototypical Mexican boxing style described above. Samuel started trying to imitate Miguel's style. Samuel would lower his head and lean over his front foot like a bull rushing into a matador's muleta, but this was not the correct way to apply pressure. The most skilled boxers who adopt a Mexican style use their feet to stalk their opponents, and they keep their head behind their front foot. Samuel's approach to training reflected his poor overall athletic talent, but it revealed his passion for boxing as a way to envision and transform himself.

"Listen man, bend your knees, squat if you need to, but stop standing tall when you move your feet!" I said to Samuel with frustration. I usually consider myself a patient trainer. Not even in a corner during the heat of competition would I raise my voice in anger or excitement at a boxer, but Samuel was particularly frustrating to train. I explained to Larry and Eva after practice, "This kid enjoys rushing in [to his opponent] like a fool. He's not listening. He gets more pleasure rushing in than disappointment in doing it wrong." Larry laughed at my complaints and said, "He can't help it, Gabe. It's that [Mexican] warrior spirit." Eva and I both laughed. Larry was joking about bad technique, and he would never seriously imply that a Mexican warrior would rush into his opponent like a fool. Still, he was not wrong about the Mexican warrior spirit. Samuel was chasing an idea of who he wanted to be, and getting the right technique was, in fact, not as important as embodying the Mexican warrior spirit that everyone praised in Miguel.

Again, a boxing gym often becomes unappealing to a newcomer after they realize that their "I can fight" idea meets the sparring threshold that reveals "I actually can't fight." From a training, sparring, and competitive standpoint, Samuel had little chance of ever finding that he could fight if he learned proper technique. Instead, Samuel was satisfied with envisioning himself as a Mexican boxer. He did get into great physical health, as one would expect with the weekly conditioning routines, so he looked like a boxer. It took longer than anyone who has come through the gym for the coaches to allow him to compete in a tournament. When he did dress up for his first amateur bout, he wore a boxing helmet with Mexican flag colors. He put on the toughest face he could muster for the picture his mother took of him before the bout. He lost that first bout and every bout after that one, and although his eyes watered after that first loss, Samuel always stuck out his chest with pride before and after a fight.

Whether the fantasy of who Samuel wanted to be was a far-fetched delusion of how much he could improve as a boxer or whether he possessed the most positive attitude toward competitive losing, he was emotionally fulfilled by the idea of the tough Mexican warrior he embodied. The fact that he lost often meant that hyper-masculine domination of his opponents was not more important to him than his performance as a Mexican warrior. Furthermore, not only was he not dominating, he was losing by wide margins. Although boxing amateurs, especially those who are younger and compete at the lower weight classes, do not experience brutal knockouts, Samuel had the unfortunate experience of getting hit so hard that he was concussed on the floor for almost a minute. The event venue was packed with several hundred people, and the initial "oohs" of an exciting knockout turned into silence as Samuel lay on the ring canvas, barely moving. His eyes were open and staring at the ceiling. The ringside doctor checked his eyes, asked him a few questions to gauge his senses, and then Samuel gently sat up. The crowd clapped. Then a coach helped him stand up. As soon as his feet were flat on the floor, Samuel sprung his arms up in the air, and the crowd did not hesitate to turn claps into louder claps and cheers. He was not victorious over his opponent, but he had beaten the supposed shame that comes with such a devastating loss. Samuel was, indeed, a Mexican warrior.

Samuel's little brother, Smiley, traveled a similar road as his older brother. Although Smiley was skilled, he was not into boxing as much as Samuel. Still, he stuck with it. I will probably never enjoy holding training pads for a kid as much as I did for Smiley. His pseudonym here stems from how he smiled as he threw combinations. Everyone at the gym wondered how he could grin through a full workout.

It was not long before the day came for Smiley to enter the ring for competition. Amateur matchups are usually negotiated between coaches from different gyms. The ideal goal is to have even matchups, which is considered best practice when developing athletes in boxing and any sport. I was the only coach with our amateur team for a competition near Chicago. Most matchups had already been arranged by phone, but Smiley's was still up in the air. Enrique, a coach from a local gym and a former prominent professional boxer, approached me about Smiley boxing his son and said, "My son just has a few fights. I'll tell him to take it easy if it gets out of hand." I agreed to the bout.

Smiley approached his opponent as soon as the bell rang and received a barrage of punches in perfectly timed combinations. Enrique's son had more than a few fights, and if Enrique had instructed him to "take it easy," his son was not listening. Enrique encouraged his son, and the mostly Mexican crowd came to life with cheers and hollers as the two little Mexican warriors fought each other. But it was not much of a fight at all.

I was furious. Not a minute of the first round had passed before I stepped into the ring and stopped the fight. The crowd started booing. Smiley was in tears. I embraced and assured him he was a warrior for stepping into the ring. I told him that he was a champ. We walked off the ring to some sympathetic smiles, but I could not help but stare at a few people who had been shouting in excitement minutes earlier.

Enrique fooled me. "You have to watch out for that guy Gabe. He's bad news," Larry said when I spoke with him hours later. The rest of our amateur team had won all their bouts that day, but I was not in a celebratory mood. How could Enrique and that crowd do something like that? These were kids! Yet Smiley returned to the gym two days later for the Monday practice.

He appeared to have gotten over his loss and followed his older brother and Miguel as they moved from one routine to the next.

My experiences with Samuel and Smiley were not exceptional. They were not good boxers, but plenty of other youths tried the sport without much success. Like all athletic skills, there is a broad spectrum of talent. Of course, boxing, being a combat sport, discourages those less skilled from sticking around. Sometimes, the trajectory of young fighters is very different. For example, Ray came to the gym as a skilled nine-year-old boxer. His father, Rolando, had been training him in their garage. Ray had room for improvement, but his fundamentals were strong. I did not train Ray, but I observed other trainers help his dad, who was quickly welcomed into the gym as an assistant trainer since all coaches volunteered their time and there was always a need for help. It was not long before Ray competed and won all his fights by broad margins with Ronaldo in his corner. As months passed, Ray began to do what few young boxers were willing to do: go to the body, then go "upstairs" for the head.

Fight fans from all backgrounds easily appreciated Ray's skills. Near Ray's tenth birthday, the gym held a big boxing event and invited boxing clubs from hours away. The place was packed, and more than half of the of attendees were of Mexican or Mexican descent. The hot dogs, nachos, and candy were selling well, and the cheap beer flowed through a happy crowd. It was a family event, but it was also an event full of people who love boxing. Ray was scheduled to fight another son of Mexican immigrants living in Chicago. When Ray entered the ring, the crowd erupted. His family alone would have made enough noise to be noticed, but Ray had the whole community behind him. As soon as the bell rang, Ray jumped on his opponent and began a dedicated attack, landing punches to the head and body. Unlike previous bouts, his opponent was hardy and skilled, but not nearly good enough to threaten Ray's victory by points. Ray was superior, and he had the whole crowd behind him. Every punch combination received massive cheers, and both fighters received a standing ovation when the final bell rang.

MEXICAN BODIES AS LIVED EXPERIENCE IN THE RACIAL NICHE

At St. James, I constantly got ethnographic snapshots of how fighters from different social backgrounds and ages picked up boxing styles. The stories of Samuel, Smiley, and Ray all illustrate some developmental paths in experiencing Mexicanness. Their paths also demonstrate the uneven terrain that individuals navigate when they view their bodies in relation to others in the gym and their broadly existing forms of social bodily difference. Thus, when children and adolescents take on something like the Mexican boxing style, they demonstrate the openness of life courses towards those racialized styles and the propensity of those racialized styles to homogenize diverse life experiences. The homogenization of life experiences through styles, interestingly enough, is more experientially immediate through boxing than the cognitive sum of what might constitute a Mexican identity (e.g., "My parents are from Mexico" or "I have a Mexican family"). To put it differently, a homogenizing experience can bring experiential order to cognitive ideas about the self, even if, as I argue below, the experience of a boxing style is not much different, technically speaking, from the experience of another style.

Mexicanness already exist out there in the world, structured in the moving assemblage of the US racial niche. Kids who come into the gym are already exposed to a racialized existence. Where that Mexicanness comes from and its relation to the embodied Mexicanness of a boxing style is an important question. It is relatively easy to point to historical and sociocultural processes, ranging from the economic to the ideational, that paint a picture of racial niche complexity in how Mexicanness came into being historically and in particular social contexts, such as the US Midwest.[9] This complexity makes the Mexican boxing style as an iteration of broader phenomena structured by inequalities produced by capitalism and colonization. This approach stands on solid anthropological approaches to examining the reproduction of race and racism, which I agree with because such iterations are indeed at work in the boxing world.[10]

However, the significance of Mexicanness as a boxing style is experientially tied to conceptions of the body that are tied to multiple developmental moments in Samuel, Smiley, and Ray's lifetimes. When these kids experience Mexicanness through boxing, they locate in their bodies Mexicanness as it exists in the racial niche. This process of locating Mexicanness in their bodies is simultaneously psychological and sociocultural. The embodiment of Mexicanness in a boxing style bridges cultural experience with the palpability of exercise, punches, and competition. The cultural experience that is out there in the racial niche and the scholarly literature that documents it seems infinitely complex and presents a problem for the present method of inquiry. How much and what kind of Mexicanness in the racial niche did Samuel, Smiley, and Ray locate in their bodies?

To answer this question, a quantitative measure is not very useful. There is so much cultural meaning that it is difficult for children, let alone adults, to reflexively interpret with regard to their sense of belonging to a community and embodying a people. Nevertheless, a qualitative take on "how much" is not impossible.

I lean towards an answer that assumes that a lot of the Mexicanness in the racial niche is located in bodies, not because a Mexican boxing style is a natural or essential prism for making sense out of broad sociocultural phenomena, but because broad sociocultural phenomena are what inform an ideal type of Mexican self. Furthermore, the Mexican self is summarily evaluated against the fittingly Mexican body. What culturally counts as a lot varies for individuals, especially children, who have different working ideas about Mexicanness generated through facets of social life. Yet these varied ideas about Mexicanness can be similarly located in the more disciplined—literally through the athletic, disciplined boxing body—Mexican boxing style. For the three children in question, we see the various intersecting life pathways in which they come into the boxing gym to embody cultural forms of Mexicanness from social worlds outside the gym.

When Samuel, Smiley, and Ray walked into the gym, others in the gym identified them as Mexican, and they had a sense of their Mexican identity. As I explained earlier, it is impossible to ascertain the many identities that boxers might have embraced or rejected before they entered the gym. One can assume with some certainty, however, that developmental processes of identity formation are culturally patterned, as developmental psychological research demonstrates (see Chapter 2). For example, according Umaña-Taylor et al., Smiley (age eight) and Ray (age nine) should, in the US, have ethnically-racially differentiated themselves in early childhood from others young children and understood the content of ethnic labels and some knowledge of ethnicity.[11] By middle childhood (before adolescence), they should be aware of bias, understand social hierarchies, understand the importance of their ethnicity-race relative to how they relate to others, and have affective sentiments towards in- and out-groups. Therefore, the Mexican boxing style is encountered by children and adolescents who already hold a sense of Mexicanness.

Of course, from an ethnographic perspective, identification (specifically ethnic/racial identification) is but one aspect of social existence in the racial niche. Identification processes vary in relation to other parts of the niche assemblage that range in scale from household to global. In the case of Mexicanness, it has been broadly construed as part of processes of labor, colonialism, schooling, aesthetic expression, and immigration.[12] In the case of the Mexican boxing style, children cannot fully comprehend and appropriate style content until they master boxing techniques and can differentiate a set of techniques as Mexican. However, the idea of a Mexican boxing style and a Mexican boxer can be known relative to their understanding of Mexicanness.

Since Smiley knew nothing of boxing when he came to the gym, he learned that he "could become the next great Mexican champ," as trainers often jokingly said to motivated young athletes. So Smiley understood the idea of a "Mexican champ" in relation to his broad sense of Mexicanness outside the boxing world. Ray came into the gym with a clear idea of a Mexican boxer since his father had already emphasized Ray's Mexicanness in the sport through training and watching fights on TV. But even Ray's notion of being a Mexican boxer was limited at his age since he needed more experience in the boxing world against good opponents that presented distinctive sets of styles. Ray, therefore, also did not have a full grasp (or the bodily orientation) of Mexicanness through boxing, although he certainly had the ability to perform Mexicanness every time a trainer encouraged him to fight a certain way or a crowd celebrated his athletic execution.

Once immersed in boxing culture, all three children reoriented their bodies based on the Mexicanness in the racial niche that, throughout their young lives, oriented their sense of self. In the gym, they found different kinds of proximal bodies to locate Mexicanness in their own bodies. Samuel found it in Miguel, Smiley in Samuel, and Ray in the ideal collective bodies of Mexican fighters, which he learned from his father. Samuel and Smiley's sense of what it meant to be Mexican was not all that clear when they entered the gym; their mixed Latin American heritage, limited daily contact with Mexican kin, and living in a neighborhood with few other Mexicans meant they had a sense of Mexicanness, but it was mostly relative to broad understandings of social differences in the Midwest. When Samuel was fourteen, he was at a developmental stage where his need to define his social identity was much stronger than his brother's, so it made sense for Miguel to serve as a role model and ideal version of who Samuel wanted to become. In turn, Samuel and his attachment to Miguel became a reference of Mexicanness for Smiley, who in the future could reevaluate his embodied difference relative to his earlier stage of development.

I knew much less about Ray's family and home life, but while in the gym, it was clear that his father had provided him with a broad set of Mexican boxing bodies through which Ray could reorient himself. His father was the most immediate reorienting body because training a young fighter requires many demonstrations of how to properly do a technique. In addition, Miguel and other Mexican and Latino boxers in and outside of the gym (with whom Ray already identified as being "of my kind") were easily available bodies for reorientation given the weekly routine training, before and after practice conversations, and performances of Mexicanness (e.g., eating, joking, and listening to music) that seep into the gym. Also, since Ray watched boxing on television with his father, he was well aware of the Mexican boxing culture that existed beyond St. James. Unsurprisingly,

Ray and other children from diverse backgrounds often look up to boxers who look like them.

The professional boxers that children look up to are not masters of a Mexican boxing style that is objectively discernable by a set of techniques. Although many Mexican and Mexican American boxers fight in ways that conform with the aggressiveness and body punching that characterize the Mexican boxing style, there is significant overlap between styles. Furthermore, many Mexican boxers do not conform to the Mexican style, and many non-Mexican fighters have fighting techniques that incorporate the same elements of the Mexican style. Therefore, a major factor in maintaining the popular image of Mexican boxers for young boxers is a boxing industry that capitalizes on boxing styles, race, and nationalism to promote boxing events, which is a key component of the US racial niche that capitalizes on sporting racialization.

When referring to the "boxing industry," I mean professional promoters, television networks, advertisers, event venues, gambling businesses, and the consumers of these. In addition, Olympic competition also foments the identification of athletes with nationalities, and the Olympics are also a big business.[13] As I have explored in my other work (Torres Colón 2022),[14] these economic forces play an important role in how fans identify with social bodies and consume boxing and other sports. In the US, the boxing industry plays an important role in fomenting the Mexican boxing style since Mexican Americans represent a distinct consumer base that boxing promoters and advertisers target. Our small promotion company at St. James was aware of these dynamics, and we often considered the Mexican audience when making decisions about what boxers to seek out for our shows, what order to schedule matches (later matches are deemed more important), and what brand of beers to sell.

Most importantly, boxing events that capitalize on the Mexican boxing style fulfill their capitalistic prophecy when the audience experiences Mexicanness through a boxer's performance during these events.

Beyond the boxing industry, and as I have already explained above, there are historical, political, and economic forces steeped in global capitalism, colonialism, and racial orders that more broadly maintain Mexicanness and other forms of boxing style racialization as culturally viable ways for boxers and boxing audiences to identify with. Yet as important as these broader political, economic, and cultural forces are as driving forces for the US racial niche assemblage, they cannot fully account for how a particular form of Mexicanness (the Mexican boxing style) is reconfigured by children in relation to earlier forms of Mexicanness. In fact, given Smiley and Samuel's lack of talent, the boxing industry—a racially capitalizing force—was uninterested in them. Boxing gyms cannot be reduced to production factories for the boxing industry. Boxing gyms, especially St. James, are often a place of communal refuge and play for youth living at the margins of society. The Mexican boxing style is one of many ways in which children, adolescents, and young adults continue to make sense of the racial niches from where they come.

BOXING STYLES FOR FLOURISHING

During my ethnographic work, I have encountered many occasions when young Latinx and Black boys enter the gym with expectations of not getting beat by a "white boy." Mostly between the ages of eight and eleven, these boys brought ideas about how superior aggression is differently inherent in Black and Brown bodies, especially in relation to assumed inferior aggression in white bodies. These expectations about aggression are also present among adolescent and young adult boxers, although I want to be clear that not everyone who comes into the gym demonstrates, verbally or otherwise, that they have these expectations. This lack of explicitly stating bodily expectations might mean that they do not exist at all, that they might exist but not want to be verbalized, or that the expectations exist in a confused or subconscious form.

Young boys, adolescents, and young adults that engage in competition come to see themselves as representing their social groups (Black people, the hood, Mexicans, Puerto Ricans, Filipinos, etc.); but those expectations are also expectations about superior aggression that create a sense that representing is contingent on not losing to a white boy, someone from a group that is not supposed to be as tough as yours, or overcoming expectations of athletic inferiority. Given how I documented these statements by young boxers, adolescents, and young adults about inherent aggression and representation over the years, we can conceptualize the ideas of "not getting beat" and "representing your people" as being along a developmental spectrum. "Not getting beat by no white boy," for example, is at one end of early development and tends to be a more naïve idea about who should win in a fight. Although I never asked young boys and adolescents about losing to a white boy, I heard it a least a dozen times over the years.[15] The notion that one should not lose to a white boy was most evident when I casually asked young boxers who would win an upcoming amateur (not involving someone from our gym) or televised professional fight between a Black boxer and a white boxer. The universal response over several years was that the Black boxer would win. "Representing your people" is an idea that is not necessarily tied to the inherent superiority of one group over another, but at the very least it recognizes that one's racialized social group has some expectations that losing to a white boy is not good.

Evidence for the cultural idea of representing your people is easy to come by as young adults and adults, including boxers, trainers, and fans, often articulate such sentiments. Nevertheless, it is important to emphasize that the inherent nature of "not getting beat by no white boy" is always ambiguously present among young adults and adults who voice that a racialized boxer should represent their people and not lose to a white boy. The ambiguity results from life experiences when, in fact, expected fight outcomes do not come to fruition. Still, even some of the most cautious in predicting fight outcomes can, in a different conversation, seriously engage in a discussion stating that, for example, "Mexican boxers are tougher" or "Black boxers are slick." In short, the proposed spectrum between "not getting beat by no white boy" and "representing your people" is one in which the former always lingers, intertwined with the latter as life experiences change cultural ideas.

It is also important to note that I have worked with white boxers who were successful at the amateur or professional levels. For them, their family, friends, and their fans, a cultural inversion of the spectrum validates its shared cultural nature. Once a white boxer proves his toughness—and toughness is usually the perceived best quality by the boxing world—then all sorts of linguistic utterances yield to a narrative that "this White boy" will beat you. "Don't mess with that white boy," "You better think twice about stepping to that white boy," or "Don't sleep on that white boy" are all examples of what boxers say when advising other boxers who are entertaining the notion that beating a white boy is automatic. People in the boxing world immediately categorize a "white boy that can fight" as the exception to the rule. However, when it comes to representing your people, the inversion does not work as neatly in the Midwestern US. Instead of whiteness being represented, hometowns and neighborhoods stand in for race, usually as symbols of Midwestern working-class toughness. On the East Coast, an ethnic Irish or Italian background might become the group that the fighter represents.

Nevertheless, the idea of the Great White Hope is part of US boxing folklore precisely because whiteness has not been consistently associated with excellence in boxing since the mid-twentieth century.[16] Representation of racialized people in boxing and other sports, like basketball, is tied to normative cultural ideas about self-worth as expressed through the domination of the sport. How much these ideas are tied to racialized notions of masculine violence is a more difficult question to answer. Historically, there is evidence that representing your people is congruous with not getting beat in the sports arena.[17] However, the emergence of mixed martial arts and the rapid growth of women's boxing has demonstrated that masculine violence in combat sports does not explain the persistence of how combat athletes represent their people. Effective forms of violence are increasingly associated with a more socially diverse and global combat community. In light of the increased gender, global, and social diversity in combat sports, it is very important to note how the cultural idea that certain people fight in certain ways persist. The persistence of boxing styles, particularly the Mexican boxing style, is tied to the political economy of sport.

On the US national sporting stage, which is much more of a public domain, these attitudes about White boys are less explicit. But on August 21, 2020, Dallas Maverick basketball star Luka Dončić (a Slovenian who registers as white in the US) got into an argument with LA Clipper Montrezl Harrell (who is Black). Harrell called Dončić a "bitch-ass White boy" during the heated exchange, which made national news. The highest-rated sports talk TV show on ESPN, *First Take*, where issues of race and sports are often discussed, prompted the discussion with the following question: is it fair to let Montrezl Harrell off the hook? Stephen A. Smith, the show's star (and one of the most prominent Black sports commentators in the US), argued that it was fair to let Motrenzl off the hook because the incident happened in the heat of competition, that he apologized, and that a double standard in racial epithets is justified given overall inequity between whites and Blacks in American history and society. In addition, Max Kellerman, the show's white costar at the time (who often publicly identifies with his Jewish heritage), explained that white Americans do not need access to racial epithets just because some African Americans might occasionally use demeaning language against white. He argued that Dončić should be more offended by the "bitch-ass" portion of the insult than the "white" portion because the latter is no more than a way to refer to a white person in the mostly Black social space that is basketball. In this nationally televised event, sentiments that associate whiteness and weakness were suppressed to address the potential racist harm of expressing such feelings, even though these feelings about White boys are learned from youth.

Mexican boxers and the Mexican boxing style have come into performative existence within this US racial imaginary of aggression and masculinity and whiteness and blackness. However, I want to be analytically careful and specify that the racial liminality of Latinidad in the US varies through time and geography.[18] Black and White have historically structured the main demographic-geographic divisions in St. James and the immediate Midwestern region. Several generations of Mexican migrants, many arriving via Chicago or nearby farming regions, have become a significant main racial group in the area. For many of the self-identified Mexican, Black, and White boxers in St. James, race is affectively scaffolded and habituated through the complexities of relationships that exist in a gym where everyone is on the same team, regardless of racial background, and through the racial hierarchies and divisions looming inside and outside the gym. Outside the gym, the way aggression and masculinity were presented by the Harrell-Dončić controversy is one way in which blackness and whiteness frame Mexicanness as masculine aggression that resists notions of Mexican inferiority and asserts bravery through sport, albeit in a manner that can also reduce Mexican masculinity to a problematic form of hypermasculinity. Inside the gym, white boxers are accepted as teammates, but Mexican youth often see themselves as tougher than their white counterparts. Furthermore, Mexican boys see Black boxers as naturally stronger and faster but beatable through the aggressive perseverance that is the hallmark of the Mexican boxing style.

US racial imaginary, therefore, cannot be simply understood as a set of abstract and ranked-ordered social wholes that are the historical products of white supremacy. Instead, both racial imaginaries and the hierarchies of race in the US are made tangible, in part, through a multitude of racial experiences that are immediate to people's daily lives. In St. James, boxing styles are one form of racial experience, and it is important not to take such instances of racial experience as peculiar articulations of US race relations. Instead, these forms of racial experience are holistically important for the development of boxers because they are a way of rearticulating through the body the cultural significance of social identity that already exists in an individual's world. Going to the body as Mexicans do is a way of stylizing meaningful significance in racialized bodies that are already anchored by embodied difference in broader social worlds.

THE PARADOX OF REIFICATION IN RACIALIZED STYLES

So far in this chapter, I presented developmental snapshots of how racial experience can lead youth to reconfigure their racialized bodies by fashioning styles in relation to social identities and within a broader context of racial inequality in the US. For many boxers, going to the body as Mexicans do becomes the most performative, palpable experience of race through which they can make some meaningful sense of the racialization they experience before and after they enter the gym. Although the omnipresent social scientist sees the systems and hierarchies that structure racial differences, people in their everyday lives do not experience race in a way that obviously resonates as a form of social difference or evidence of a social hierarchy. Instead, racial experience, when stylized, is most immediately relevant to how a style is aesthetically in sync (i.e., affectively scaffolded and habituated) with an immediate social world. Samuel, Smiley, and Ray experienced Mexicanness in boxing even though they were children attempting to master a boxing style that, even when fully mastered, is still just boxing. Nevertheless, the particularity of a racialized style is anchored by socially embodied difference, which is a social whole that we, as scholars, can assess as structural racism or racial hierarchy.

Racial experience is the most immediate manifestation of both a meaningful sense of being in the world and an inequality based on embodied social differences, which I refer to as the paradox of reification. Anthropologists and other social scientists usually employ the concept of reification to point out how social forms that should not be biologized, such as gender and race, become hegemonic tools for oppressing the group whose reified traits place them lower on the social hierarchy. On one hand, going to the body as Mexicans do is a form of reification that is a significant aspect of identity formation. On the other hand, going to the body, by drawing on cultural phenomena from the racial niche, reifies traits aligned with the hierarchical racialization of Mexicans in the US. However, the paradox of reification is paradoxical not because of an inherent contradiction in the processes of reification out there in the world; instead, the genesis of the paradox is in how we, as social scientists and interdisciplinary scholars, come to know racial phenomena. In other words, the paradox emerges in the epistemology of race. Consider the following two questions that we could ask about my work in boxing:

- When thinking about racialized boxing styles, do we emphasize the biologization of race in the body, or do we highlight how socially depreciated, racialized bodies are empowered through sport?
- Is the boxing gym a site of racialized exploitation that is part of the hierarchical and systemic exploitation of racialized bodies at the margins of society, or is the boxing gym a place of refuge given the failure of the state and political ideologies to protect young and racialized bodies in the US effectively?

Again, the answers for both questions are not mutually exclusive. Yet as scholars, we walk a fine line when we focus on, say, how racializing notions of disposable working Mexican bodies are reified through a boxing style and, along the way, implicitly suggest that it would be best if we educated young Mexican Americans to not do that. In fact, the line is not finite. The line exists because an intellectual tradition, particularly in North America, created the epistemological line that creates the appearance of a reification paradox. As I detailed in Chapter 1, the intellectual tradition, like all intellectual traditions, is socioculturally conditioned, which means that political ideals about what we should do about race and racism affect social scientific theorization about race.

Notice that in the questions, the political implications are essentially driving the analytic content of the questions. If reification of non-biological things is occurring, note it through education and resist such ideas. If empowerment through the embodiment of a social identity occurs, note it through education and facilitate multiculturalism through social organizations and government. If exploitation is demonstrably tied to racialization, note it through research and come up with a social policy to eradicate the exploitation. If empowerment occurs in racially homogenous safe spaces, note it through research and develop policy (or private donations to nongovernmental organizations) to allow such places to exist.

From the intellectual historical perspective I explained in Chapter 1, if we return to answer the seemingly contradictory questions about the Mexican boxing style in the US, a project influenced by racial uplift would have us emphasize, maybe even lament, the biologization of race in the body as an articulation of hegemonic notions of race in the US.

We would also approach the boxing gym a site that is part of the hierarchical and systemic exploitation of racialized bodies at the margins of society. A heritage-influenced project would have us celebrate how socially depreciated, racialized bodies are empowered through sport and how St. James is a place of refuge given the failure of the state and political ideologies to protect young, racialized bodies in the US effectively.

To clarify, I do not want to present historical strawmen as a preface to a theoretical proposition, and I am not asking the reader to choose sides on the heritage-uplift divide. Recall that my aim in presenting theoretical concepts of the racial niche and styles for flourishing is to recast the heritage part of the heritage-uplift equation for "in-the-way immigrant and black people" and challenge the historical, intellectual invisibilization of racialized practices and styles.[19] I want to challenge those who might question the wisdom my boxing interlocutors provides for the human condition.

* * *

The forms of discrimination that many boxing youth experience outside the gym cannot be seen as the most relevant forms of racial experience for political thought, not because discrimination is not relevant to how people reimagine themselves relative to a system of exclusion, but because a boxing gym and the forms of racialization that exist within them are a more relevant example of community building and growth.

My research with boxers demonstrates that some of the most relevant forms of racial experience are not discoverable via identity assessments. Instead, racial experiences through which youth construct their racial subjectivity are particular to social spaces through which the self experientially fulfills itself through a racial imaginary, which may not register to social scientists as a positive life outcome. However, as the growing literature on Black placemaking argues, places like boxing gyms are the most important content for the survival of racialized lives.[20] Therefore, staying in the gym, regardless of whether it occurs through the pursuit of going to the body, is an immediate, positive life outcome for at-risk youth. Even though the whole endeavor of utilizing youth sports to keep them out of trouble is doomed in a society characterized by de facto racial hierarchies, going to the gym and going to the body is an instance of self-worth and a culturally dignified way of living.

A boxing style is not an instance of Mexican masculinity, sporting hypermasculinity, Mexican nationalism, working-class masculinity, identity performance, or US racial distinction from whiteness or blackness—a boxing style is all of these. All of them are socially recognized (including by academics with the established significance of intersectionality as a theoretical concept[21]) as different phenomena, but they are intersectional from early childhood. To reiterate Henrietta Moore's formulation, fantasies of embodied self "are linked to fantasies of relations and identifications with others. The earliest representations of significant others are caught up with forms of gendered difference that have no realizable expression outside their relations with other forms of difference, such as race, class and ethnicity" (2007, 123–24).[22] Indeed, intersectionality falls short as a concept metaphor given that intersections are more like bundles than intersections if these intersections are indistinguishable from the earliest stages of life.

Of course, if we place racial experience within a framework of lived experience that is attentive to lifetimes, social relations, intersectional embodiments, difference, and inequity, then it is still necessary to articulate the relationship between these aspects of racial experience. It is also necessary to recognize that there are ontological differences between an intersectional embodiment and inequality, particularly with material inequality. For now, it is important to explain that inequality is palpable in the boxing gym, primarily through means of self and social awareness and through the material inequality that affects boxers' experiences at home, school, and even in a gym that looks nothing like a for-profit gym or a fancy exercise studio. In other words, the grit of a boxing gym resonates with the material, social marginalization that many young and old boxers experience. However, these forms of material inequality are no more relevant to understanding racial groups than the tangibility of racialized bodies through sport. In fact, the sequence of bodily projections that boxers encounter throughout their lifetimes includes material inequality, yet bodily projections are rearticulated through the boxing body. The point here is not to knock the importance of historical and racial hierarchies but to understand that these broad, social forms are, for boxers, made culturally significant as a particular form of racial experience.

How boxers realign their bodies in relation to boxing styles is a process that can be traced back to the earliest stages of development, which is shaped by intersectionality that varies by sociocultural context. During the early stages of development, ego's body is first known through bodies that are already socioculturally meaningful in relation to gender, race, and other embodied forms of social difference. Ego's body is never known outside of its immediate cultural meaning. As an individual moves through life, they continue to reorient their bodies in relation to the previous sociocultural bodily orientation, which can be traced to the earliest orientation when "the map of the body ego allows little distinction between the material and representational, between the physical and the psychical body, because there is no lived phenomenological body before a psychic investment in the parts and surfaces of the body."[23] Furthermore, these early embodied forms of difference are always shaped by power structures. These power structures are, in turn, the same that many scholars have examined as political economic creation of social differences to exploit labor.[24]

Because of research timeframes in my boxing research, I am limited in tracing these bodily realignments over an individual's life course. Still, an ideal method for projecting how these bodily realignments take place from childhood to adulthood is to compare realignments between boxers at different developmental stages. Via such comparison, we can better understand what aspects of that realignment are influenced by the different variables at work for different age groups. Over the years, I found that although young boys and young men have different understandings of boxing, social groups, and identities, there are very similar ways in which social bodies are the most important reference points for understanding the bodily self.

Newcomers to the sport already have ideas about fighting and racialized bodies. These preconceived ideas point to a fundamental fact about race and social bodies: bodies are already racialized before entering boxing gyms—bodies are already part of a racial niche. Note that ideas about fighting and racialized bodies are not the same as boxing styles; in fact, understanding boxing styles in the world of boxing does not depend on these preconceived ideas. Most social scientific work about racial embodiment examines how particular social contexts reify race. But a process of reification must be relative to some previous form of reification, and the nature of reification between different stages is important for placing theoretical weight on some sort of reifications at different stages of life. Otherwise, how can we ascertain if a reification is an embodiment of an idea, an idea of an embodiment, or some combination of both? The answer is not theoretically trivial, for how we experience difference affects how we do or do not politicize race.

Race and ideas about race regarding fighting bodies exist in different parts of the racial niche, and they affect how an eight-year-old, fourteen-year-old, seventeen-year-old, and twenty-five-year-old from similar neighborhoods think about their racialized bodies in relation to others. I want to raise the question of why young boys and men would have similar basic ideas about fighting bodies, especially when developmental theories of how racial enculturation demonstrate a significant difference between these ages in racial awareness and forms of identification.[25] The possible answers to this question are as extensive as existing theories of racial formation in the social sciences. For example, suppose we were to follow Golash-Boza's sociological theory of race and racism.[26] In that case, there is little doubt that a racist ideology and racist structure in the US produce life conditions of prejudice and discrimination that shape the identities that affect how boxers adopt racialized boxing styles. Racist ideologies and structures, however, do not tell us the entire story of how ideas about fighting come into being; in fact, Golash-Boza's model preconceives the nature of racial processes as prejudicial and inseparable from racism.

Unless we are prepared to accept every racial experience as prejudice and racism prima facie, then we cannot keep pushing the "how" to its limits. Specifically, how early are these ideas about race and bodies acquired, and how mutable are these ideas about race and bodies throughout lifetimes? I understand Golash-Boza and other scholars' need to align race scholarship with anti-racism, which is a fundamental tenant of theories of intersectionality.[27] This book is ultimately in support of that alignment. However, the overwhelming presence of race due to historical racist ideologies and structures does not address how human agency is experientially defined by those structures and how people challenge those structures as they experience them. An early life experience of racial embodiment might be years away from the realization that race and racism are structural and derived from history, so how people experience race cannot be politicized from theoretical paradigms. Instead, processes of racialization have to be theoretically outlined with full knowledge that race is structured by inequality but without committing to how inequality structures racial experience.

4

BOMBA STYLES

Surviving Anti-Blackness in the Racial Niche of Empires

S even months after massive protests led to Puerto Rico's Governor Ricardo Roselló's resignation on July 24, 2019, I sat with Maricruz Rivera Clemente, a friend and community leader, discussing the aftermath of the massive popular uprising on the island. I was telling her about my ethnographic work documenting those tumultuous days. "Did you go to the protest? I didn't see you there!" I said in a teasing tone. I was guessing she had not attended. With a broad and dismissive smile, she rolled her eyes and teased back, "Oh please! What, me? Show up to that mess? Darling, we have enough problems here [in Piñones]."

I knew from years of knowing Maricruz that she opposed Roselló's administration and political party ideology (favoring Puerto Rico becoming a US state). Still, I wanted her to say more about this topic, so I said, "But in all seriousness, why not participate in a popular uprising like that?" Maricruz, who knows when I am turning on the ethnographic spotlight and often teases me about it, settled into her seat, took a sip from her Diet Coke, projected a broad smile, took a deep breath, and explained.

A long time ago, when Maricruz was finding her place in social justice protests in the 1990s and early 2000s, particularly in causes that aimed to protect the encroachment of big hotels from constructing near Piñones and subsequent environmental dangers, she questioned her mother about not participating some of the protests. Her mother responded, "Oh, sweetie! I have been protesting all my life when we had to defend our right to be here, to live on our land," and she explained that it was Maricruz's turn to defend what her mother's generation had secured.

That conversation humbled Maricruz. "I never questioned my mother's political activism ever again. She slapped me without laying a hand on me." Maricruz explained that from that time forward, she was mindful of participating in political protests for the sake of being an idealistic revolutionary. "I have chosen to focus my energy on the problems that we have here." If there are other political causes to which she can contribute something meaningful, she continued, "then I will do what needs to be done in the general interest of Puerto Rico." However, "the general interest of Puerto Rico has never been the interest of *la gente negra, la gente de Loíza.*"

According to herself, Maricruz is unquestionably Puerto Rican. However, her mother brought into focus the finite nature of politics over a lifetime and generations. To protest for everything, Maricruz has argued on multiple occasions, can lead to protest for nothing. Her mother's activism was the last generational stance on securing the land that maroons, self-liberated Black and indigenous people, and free Black people had occupied before, during, and after colonial times. Once the land was defended, it was Maricruz's turn to defend the beaches, the environment, and the question of equality for the Black people of Puerto Rico. Of course, the political status of Puerto Rico vis-à-vis the US deeply concerns and shapes her politics, which is why she was in complete agreement with Roselló's resignation. "But I'll go protest over there [San Juan], when they come protest over here [Piñones, Loíza] with us." This chapter focuses on how some Afro-Puerto Ricans experience race, particularly how they talk about and imagine their blackness, practice and perform anti-racism, and take political positions in a racial niche shaped by racial hierarchies within Puerto Rico and US colonialism over Puerto Rico. For many of my Afro-Puerto Rican interlocutors, blackness is unquestionably inherited from a concrete past that is tangible through ancestors and the history of the transatlantic slave trade. However, the sociopolitical place of blackness in the present is more ambiguous.

I argue that Afro-Puerto Rican politics are liminal within their racial niche, and this liminality is multifaceted and must account for:

- Puerto Rico's relationships and place within the US and the Americas
- The geopolitical exclusion of Black communities around the island
- The precariousness of blackness within Puerto Rican political ideologies
- The everyday grappling with what Isar Godreau has called "scripts of Blackness" or the place of Afro-Puerto Rican folklore in popular culture[1]

Somewhere between these layers of political liminality, many Black Puerto Ricans strive to find a meaningful place in the world where they embody difference, which is palpable as racial experience but has no proper place in the island's body politic.

By navigating between collective identities, political movements, exclusion from the body politic, and imagined belonging, some Afro-Puerto Ricans in Loíza are seeking political autonomy on an island nation that lacks autonomy, is marked by anti-blackness, struggles with thinking of itself as being in a racist relationship with the US, and does not acknowledge any need for racial politics within the island.

Maricruz's lifetime experiences are illustrative of a person that is both certain of her and her community's blackness yet uncertain of how anti-blackness figures into a broader political framework. Maricruz identifies and celebrates herself and her community as Black. Although not all people in her community embrace blackness as part of their identity, Maricruz and other like-minded people in her community have sought to have more people embrace their blackness. For Maricruz, being Black is more than color. Blackness is about the history of her community as a place of Black survival, ways of thinking, aesthetic expression, spirituality, environment, and ancestry. The concreteness and stylization of this multidimensional sense of blackness is distinguishable from other forms of social being in Puerto Rico, which is why Maricruz, taking after her mother, has a clear sense that her community stands apart from the people participating in "national" protest.

However, the stylized distinctions rooted in blackness between Maricruz's community and the people participating in the national protests against Roselló also point to how blackness is caught up in a liminal political space. Maricruz has a political affiliation to a national party and certainly opposed Roselló on the grounds of party-political ideology; and she has in the past participated in national protests because she has no doubts that her community is, fundamentally, Puerto Rican. Yet Maricruz has a clear sense of how national outrage can fail Afro-Puerto

Rican communities. In the case of protests against Roselló, the problem for Maricruz was that the political problem, if fixed (i.e., Roselló was removed from office), would not affect the future of her community's well-being. Therefore, the liminality of blackness in Puerto Rican politics is not necessarily ambiguous. There is a local logic through which people like Maricruz and her mother weigh how they should invest their political efforts based on their experience.

Therefore, in this chapter, the notion that blackness exists nowhere in the present refers to nowhere in the dominant forms of political ideology. Yet, Afro-Puerto Rican politics can be located somewhere: in a sense of place, in diasporas, in projects of social activism, in political protests, and in the vibrant exchange of ideas and awareness of what it means to be Black; these are the seeds for flourishing. Most importantly, I demonstrate throughout this chapter that the "nowhere in the present" is liminal in nature—hence actually somewhere—and forward-looking as part of an ancestral journey that has not yet been realized. Whatever the political future may hold for Afro-Puerto Ricans, a sense of that future reverberates in diasporic experiences of blackness that are sometimes fleeting and often difficult to imagine in relation to Puerto Rico's political economy. Yet diasporic experiences of blackness intertwine the local and the global through a sense that the political, economic, and ideological brutality of the transatlantic slave trade has yielded a common dialectic between anti-blackness and maroonage.

After a brief discussion of methodology and ethnographic context, this chapter is structured by the four aspects of the Afro-Puerto Rican racial niche I previously outlined. From my interlocutor's perspective, what it means to be Black or the idea that blackness is an unquestionable aspect of their ancestry and lived experience will be elucidated throughout each section. My approach aims to demonstrate that the blackness from somewhere (flourishing) is inevitably intertwined with being nowhere or the liminality of Afro-Puerto Rican politics in their racial niche. As my colleague and I have argued elsewhere, a people's sense of their past is illustrative of how they conceive of themselves in the present and project themselves into the future.[2]

This chapter first examines how blackness in Puerto Rico must be understood as a product of Puerto Rico's relationships and place within the US and the Americas, a place that is layered by various overlapping histories of coloniality. Then I examine how the geopolitical exclusion of Black communities around the island has marginalized blackness in relation to national political ideologies. This is followed by details of some of the concrete ways in which Afro-Puerto Rican popular culture is reclaimed and deployed by artists and community activists to express the relevance of blackness to Puerto Rican politics and the African diaspora. I conclude with the proposition that we imagine people like Maricruz and others in their community as part of living maroon communities that are vibrant sources of political thought and imagination.

METHODOLOGY AND ETHNOGRAPHIC CONTEXT

I have a long-standing working and intellectual relationship with my biological anthropology colleague and wife, Jada Benn Torres. We have collaborated over the years at different times during our careers, mainly when it was convenient for raising our kids and when our research interests properly aligned. When we left the maroon community of Accompong Town, Jamaica, around 2012, we talked on the airplane as we flew past Cuba. "Santiago!" I said pondering out loud where else in the Americas one could think of a Black community as being maroon. Our thinking at the time was that the sociocultural strategies for survival we observed in Accompong Town surely had to have other forms of articulation in other places where Black folks are otherwise thought of as marginalized, segregated, and oppressed. More importantly, we wondered if oppression masked collective strategies for survival and resistance that we could define, not solely as a social reaction to oppression, but as a form of flourishing and survival.

We tried to work in Santiago, Cuba, but Jada's genetic work would have proven too complicated regarding funding and moving biological materials from Cuba to the US. "What about Puerto Rico?" I asked months later. I initially thought I would focus on life histories of national political ideologies while helping Jada with community outreach, sample collection, and interviews in Afro-Puerto Rican communities. In turn, Jada was excited to expand her work in the Anglophone Caribbean into Puerto Rico.

After making initial contacts with various community leaders and people whom I found through friend and family networks on the island, we began work in Loíza and other scattered communities in the West and South of the island. Our interviews with research participants reflected our collaborative approach to ancestry work. This approach envisions genetic interpretations of the past as intersubjective and in the interest of the communities with whom we work.[3] Therefore, interview questions are inevitably longer and often lead to new friendships and collaborative relationships beyond the immediate research goals of the genetic ancestry project. In working with Afro-Puerto Ricans within an ancestry project, I also began talking about different aspects of racial experience and politics in Puerto Rico. These conversations, which always took place in people's homes or community centers, immediately created a point of contrast for any other fieldwork related to my questions about how political ideologies had evolved over lifetimes. The contrast was initially characterized by my perception that I was probably working with people that had different worldviews and experiences of being Puerto Rican. However, how different that worldview was and whether such a worldview had consequences for thinking about Puerto Rican politics was not clear from the outset.

Therefore, the methodology for this chapter is specific and adaptive to how I got involved in the collaborative cultural and genetic ancestry project while I aimed to establish a national project about political ideology. However, my initial assumption of a contrast between national and Afro-Puerto Rican politics is unacceptable, as I argue in this chapter. This contrast assumes an ontological differentiation between national politics and Afro-Puerto Rican politics that is differentiated from the perspective of non-Afro-Puerto Ricans. From a racial niche perspective, national politics can be questioned against the racial experiences of Afro-Puerto Ricans; therefore, I take as an empirical question what is "Afro" and what is "national," and I examine race, nation, and politics as they materialize in people's everyday life and meaningful sense of social existence. Consistent with the theories about the racial niche (Chapter 1) and styles for flourishing (Chapter 2), I epistemologically privilege the voices of my Afro-Puerto Rican interlocutors in outlining their racial niche, and I then consider the political implications for when the purportedly nonracial political ideologies are exclusive of Afro-Puerto Rican experiences and social concerns.

I have conducted over fifty structured and twenty-five unstructured interviews with Puerto Ricans who identify as *negro, afro-puertorriqueño, afro-descendiente, moreno,* or some other aspects of their blackness. These interviews mainly probed their sense of identity, racial experiences, and generational changes in identification and racial experience. I also engaged in participant observation around the neighborhoods where we carried out work, where I often talked with people about Puerto Rican politics and current affairs, the politics of race and anti-racism, and the role of Black aesthetics in Puerto Rico (since many of our interlocutors are artists). Artists and community leaders comprise almost a third of all interviews. However, although more than half of the interviews took place in Loíza, we interviewed people around the island in what we call "pockets of Black people." In fact, finding Black communities (that is, mapping and establishing lived presence through scholarly documentation) became an ongoing collaborative project with community leaders looking to expand their Afro-Puerto Rican networks and sense of community. This project resulted in multiple driving trips around the island that led to dozens of unstructured interviews and conversations.

Finally, there is an important aspect of my research that emerged from participant observation outside of Afro-Puerto Rican communities. Because I have family and friends on the island with whom I interacted with daily, I often found myself tuning my ethnographic ear to how people outside the research communities reacted to my research project. Puerto Ricans who do not identify as Black or live in the Black communities where we worked had ideas about Black Puerto Ricans, which provided an immediate point of comparison and context for the racial experiences I was documenting with Afro-Puerto Ricans. In addition, I could directly contrast my personal and social spaces with those of Afro-Puerto Ricans. My children's summer camp, for example, was in a wealthy section of the metropolitan

San Juan area, and the contrast between their camp and our field site often became a critical point of reflection. For as I return to at the end of this chapter, if Afro-Puerto Ricans' sense of blackness was socioculturally shared, then what are non-Afro-Puerto Ricans? White? Mixed? "Regular" Puerto Ricans? The realization that whiteness is at play in Puerto Rico was not surprising, but the political implications of an Afro-Puerto Rican polity in relation to a Puerto Rican polity have had a profound impact on how I reconceptualize my sociocultural and political thought about the island and how I began thinking about Puerto Rico in relation to the boxing gym (Chapter 3) and Ceuta (Chapters 5 and 6).

OUTLINING THE MACRO-LEVEL ASSEMBLAGE OF THE AFRO-PUERTO RICAN RACIAL NICHE: PUERTO RICO'S PLACE WITHIN THE US AND THE AMERICAS

Throughout my life and my recent research in Puerto Rico, I have read, overheard, and conversed about colonialism in Puerto Rico. I recall being thoroughly confused about postcolonial literature and theories as a young graduate student not because there was something inherently confusing about those bodies of research, but because I could not easily place myself (living in the US since adolescence), my island, and my people within global contexts of coloniality.

Puerto Rico became a US colony in 1898. Puerto Ricans have been US citizens since 1917, although those living on the island have lacked congressional representation and the ability to vote for presidents. Today, most self-identified Puerto Ricans live in the United States. Since the 1970s, nearly half or more of all Puerto Ricans have supported the pro-statehood New Progressive Party, and the other nearly half supported the status-quo Popular Democratic Party. Yet throughout the twentieth century, the US violently suppressed the Puerto Rican pro-independence movements whose supporters, since the 1970s, usually receive single digit percent support in elections. In the US, Puerto Ricans have historically been a marginalized and minoritized racial group, yet they have also occupied an ambiguous and liminal racial space in relation to whiteness and blackness. Therefore, if nowadays Puerto Ricans are colonized, they are colonized while most on the island consent to a relationship with the US, and those in the US mainland are a minoritized and racialized social group.

Puerto Rico is also a poor and unequal island, albeit in the manner that modern, liberal democracies have sustained poverty and inequality since the late eighteenth century. In order to maintain a functioning capitalist economy and prevent revolutions, the vast majority of those at the bottom of the socioeconomic ladder receive government assistance for housing, food, health, and unearned income.[4] This sort of assistance significantly increased over the second half of the twentieth century and reduced inequality;[5] nevertheless, the *U.S. Census Bureau, 2015–2019 American Community Survey 5-Year Estimates* shows Puerto Rico's median household income at $20,539. This median is less than half of Mississippi, the poorest state in the US at $45,081.

Relying on World Bank data, economists have used the Gini coefficient to estimate that wealth disparity in Puerto Rico is one of the greatest in the US and the world.[6] However, this inequality within the island is where we might first question the racial niche in relation to the place of blackness, anti-blackness, and political subjectivity. Where does being Afro-Puerto Rican figure into

Puerto Rico's socioeconomic and political profile as a colonial territory of the US? We can answer this question by examining how identification processes create social and fictive kinship ties within and beyond the island. Self-identified Afro-Puerto Ricans are, from a cultural perspective, registering their blackness and Puerto Ricanness in ways that defy dominant ideologies of the Puerto Rican nation as a US territory and part of Latin America.

The complexities of Black identity in Puerto Rico have been well-documented.[7] I do not believe that too much insight into racial experience can be gained by examining self-identification alone;[8] however, how people talk about identity and the contexts for those conversations was very insightful when examining how Black identity is an important component of what I would call an "Afro-Puerto Rican colonial subjectivity." Through my structured and unstructured interviews, many previous findings regarding the volatility of Black identity are mostly confirmed. That is, I found variation in Black self-identification and that awareness of the identity *negro/a* (Black) is sometimes embraced and sometimes rejected.[9] There are also different forms of rejection. For example, someone may mark that they are Black on the US Census and feel awkward when socially identified by someone else as negro. However, the genetic and cultural ancestry project was explicitly designed to include only people who self-identified as negro/a or some variation of Black like *afro-puertorriqueño* (Afro-Puerto Rican). Therefore, we worked with people for whom identifying as Afro-Puerto Rican was unproblematic; and we were also aware that many phenotypically Black Puerto Ricans would be unwilling to either identify as Black or participate in our study. This sampling bias was unavoidable and desired on our part since our initial purpose was to have our research be instrumental to the communities and people with whom we worked.

Negro/a was the most common form of Black self-identification, with nearly everyone willing to embrace the identity. A dozen participants embraced "Afro-Puerto Rican" or "Afrodescendent" in conjunction with negro/a, with only a few exclusively embracing "Afro-Puerto Rican" and rejecting negro/a as a label that did not reflect how they felt. Nevertheless, in conversation with nearly all participants, I was able to confirm that they were aware of how, for other community members, Black identities were difficult to embrace. Indeed, quite often such awareness was expressed through sarcasm and jokes, "That [one] who is much darker than me . . . you can't call her negra!" Many of my Black-identifying interlocutors expressed that Puerto Ricans who reject their blackness are delusional, self-hating, or in denial. Some interlocutors explicitly characterized such self-denials of blackness as a form of colonization. However, as expressed by a couple of dozen participants, that colonization was perpetrated by Whites (*la gente blanca* or *los blanquitos*). Sometimes the whites were white Puerto Ricans, sometimes the whites were white people elsewhere; however, these references were never exclusively linked to white people from the US.

A sense of Afro-Puerto Ricanness is partially achieved through distinction from whiteness in and beyond the island. Nevertheless, people who identify as Black or Afro-Puerto Rican are unequivocal in asserting their Puerto Rican pride. "I am super proud of being Puerto Rican" and "Above all, I am Boricua of pure stock!" (*boricua de pura cepa*) were two slight variations of a common response to questions about social identity. Typically, such statements were volunteered, and they came after an assertion of Black identity. I have yet to meet someone who identifies as Afro-Puerto Rican whose "Afro-" or "negro/a" somehow conflicts or subtracts from "Puerto Rican." Being Black was one of the primary reasons all participants enrolled in the genetic and cultural ancestry project, but a common discursive theme of research participants was that they felt that Afro-Puerto Rican ancestry had not been properly recognized in popular discourse.

Some participants were even aware of previous genetic ancestry studies in Puerto Rico,[10] and they could specifically recall feeling left out of national news coverage that emphasized maternal indigenous ancestry. Furthermore, many of our community partners' interest in collaborating with us was in the potential of establishing, through genetic ancestry science, the presence of Black people in Puerto Rico. I had several conversations where participants recognized that science "carried weight," as one community leader in a western township put it. He continued to explain that whether he liked it or not, our research was necessary as part of a broader effort to establish "the reality of Black presence in Puerto Rico." Similarly, as researchers, we took the position that we were not discovering blackness through genealogies, interviews, and genetic technology; instead, we were studying what was already known in the community, that they were Black and Puerto Rican. Therefore, when in previous work we identified the discursive theme *pues negro porque negro soy* (well Black because I am Black), we were highlighting some Afro-Puerto Ricans assertion that blackness was desired, unescapable, and true despite tricultural national ideologies.[11]

Asserting blackness as unproblematically part of a Puerto Rican identity during an interview highlights Afro-Puerto Ricans' senses that their third of the Puerto Rican whole is unequal. However, this sense of inequality is deeper than a mathematical abstraction of three equal parts where one is devalued in relation to the other two. Instead, the Afro third is not like the others. First, the other two-thirds do not constitute either a social group or a social group with geographical delimitations

within the island. Unlike the town of Loíza or the neighborhood of San Antón, there are no delimited geographic areas that
collectively self-identify as Taíno or Spanish. Second, if the tricultural heritage supposedly belongs to all Puerto Ricans, then
my interlocutors do not feel like they can claim the other two
wholes the way that other Puerto Ricans can claim some aspect
of the other three. Third and most important, being Spanish
and being Taíno is not experienced as blackness is in everyday
life. These insights were most prominent during interviews and
informal conversations when discussing famous Black Puerto
Ricans. Ismael, a small business owner in his late twenties, asked
me during a conversation about athletes, "How can you [Puerto
Ricans] celebrate Roberto Clemente without celebrating his
blackness?" He would clarify that he did not mean "celebrating
his blackness" by calling attention to his black skin, but instead,
he meant "truly celebrating who he is as a man that comes from
a Black community." Ismael got very serious and admitted that
what he was about to say pained him. "And we [Afro-Puerto
Ricans] allow them to claim him without his blackness."

Ismael's lamentation that someone like Roberto Clemente is
celebrated as one of the island's best athletes but without any
particular emphasis on his blackness was a reflection echoed by
others I talked to. Puerto Ricans' recognition of Black athletes,
musicians, and other prominent popular figures facilitates the
hegemonic acceptance of the tricultural heritage while denying the possibility that Afro-Puerto Ricans' life experiences are
unique and not shared by everyone on the island. Many Puerto
Ricans recognize that a few Afro-Puerto Ricans have made
meaningful national contributions without acknowledging the
Black communities from which these popular figures come
from; and without Black communities, Afro-Puerto Ricans can
be assimilated as Puerto Rican. This problem is also, to follow

Ismael's argument, a way in which many Black Puerto Ricans differ in how they claim their blackness as properly belonging in public or civic life. Making claims to blackness in public and political spaces seems disruptive to the supposedly inclusive tri-parted Puerto Rican identity.

This question of belonging in public and political or civic life is parallel to how Puerto Rico does or does not belong to the US nation. Although the question of Puerto Rico's political status is more complex than I can deal with in this book, it is important to note that one of the most important points of controversy over Puerto Rico's political status is the question of what would happen to Puerto Rican culture and identity if the island became a state. Spanish language and the Olympic team, for example, have been two concrete points of concern. Asserting Puerto Ricanness in popular culture seems to contradict the belonging in the US nation, with many pro-statehooders asserting that a Puerto Rican national character would be preserved and others holding that national character would be lost. Yet the status question has been the key defining feature of political parties since the mid-twentieth century, whereas Afro-Puerto Rican communities remain popularly unrecognized and politically marginalized. If the Puerto Rican nation is an example of modern historical colonialism (i.e., US imperialism), then Afro-Puerto Rican communities are an example of an older, transatlantic colonial instance of anti-blackness and racial domination. These modern and older colonial eras are interrelated, but it is important to conceptually distinguish them because that distinction is important to many of my interlocutors. However, they do not always characterize that distinction through the lens of a dominated people; instead, their participation in our project is part of a broader effort to resist and survive the racial niche as *cimarrones* (maroons).

OUTLINING THE MICRO-LEVEL ASSEMBLAGE OF THE AFRO-PUERTO RICAN RACIAL NICHE: "POCKETS OF BLACK PEOPLE" AND THE GEOPOLITICAL EXCLUSION OF BLACK COMMUNITIES AROUND THE ISLAND

In this chapter's methodology section, I mentioned the beginnings of the collaborative cultural and genetic ancestry project about the maroon community of Accompong Town Jamaica. One of the most instructive aspects of the field experience was learning how maroons' sense of self and community is sustained by a gendered social network that is inclusive of the necessity of economic emigration to urban parts of Jamaica, North America, and the UK. Research has recognized how land and agricultural distribution, religious celebrations, and ancestry are extensions of a contemporaneous and diverse maroon worldview.[12] Although many maroons in Accompong Town are quick to defend their autonomy and unique culture, the everyday efforts to survive as a poor, rural community in a globalized world stood out to us as an exemplary form of Black flourishing.

Those insights from Accompong Town, a Black maroon community within a Black post-colonial nation, shaped how we approached our project in Puerto Rico. We did not assume that Black existence in Puerto Rico was inherently tied to and evidenced by traceable African elements in aesthetic expression, language, food, or phenotypes as we have extensively discussed elsewhere;[13] instead, we first assumed in our sampling methodology that if all things were equal in the idealized Puerto Rican tricultural heritage, then Black people could not exist as Black people in any communities. In other words, Black communities' evidence themselves as Afro-descendants. Second, whatever sociocultural processes held those communities together as communities constitutes an empirical question. As such, the most basic requirement for enrollment in the study was that participants identify themselves in some way that indexed their blackness.

We worried that identification with blackness can be dicey in Puerto Rico, even in Black communities. However, because our research counted on collaboration with community partners when we initially pitched this sampling strategy, it was much more well-received than we expected. One community partner in Loíza reasoned while laughing, "This way you'll definitely get many people in our community [a recognized Black area], and you won't get anyone looking for a free genetic ancestry test!"

As I started talking to my interlocutors about where to conduct interviews, I used a phrase that I borrowed from my friend Daniel Nina. Daniel, who is a colleague and public intellectual, once used the phrase "*bolsillitos de gente negra*" (little pockets of Black people) to describe places with concentrations of Black people that the public might not recognize as Black. No one I talked to as we set up the project objected to my use of the words. Our first three community partners and research coordinators all understood the phrase. One of them continued using the phrase in our conversation to the point where I got the sense that people might have been using the phrase all along. More importantly, the phrase "pockets of Black people" has been culturally consonant because many interlocutors immediately knew what we were talking about. The phrase ignited conversations about where in Puerto Rico one could find pockets of Black people. What began as conversations about pockets turned into discussions of more complex family and community histories,

yielding a historically rich, island-wide fabric. Historical richness came through as dozens of people told matter-of-fact stories about where family members used to live, what they did for
a living, personal characteristics, continued spiritual presence,
and migrations into, out of, and between pockets on different
parts of the island. This matter-of-factness also manifested as
all interlocutors spoke with enthusiasm when identifying a particular Black pocket. Linguistically, this enthusiasm was audible
when prefacing a discussion of a pocket with, "*Pues claro que si*,"
(Well, of course this is true).

Before adding ethnographic texture to the following stories,
I want to first provide a conceptual framework for how these
stories about ancestors also tell us something about the spatio-
temporal nature of the Puerto Rican nation. This framework
is supported through the possibilities of Black existence in the
past that our interlocutors presented to us in dozens of interviews and informal conversations. Black existence in Puerto
Rico has possible origins in stories of enslavement, free life
within the context of racial hierarchies, and maroonage. Beyond
Puerto Rico, Black existence has possible origins with African
ancestors and contemporary diasporas in the Caribbean and the
Americas, which have their own histories of enslavement, free
life, and maroonage. In contrast to dominant historical narratives in Puerto Rico, these possibilities of Black existence stand
on their own as a complete story that does not rely on a cli-
matic mixture with Taínos and Europeans. That is, interlocutors never present these stories about their past as one third of
a national tricultural heritage. Therefore, these possibilities of
Black existence are a backdrop to the locations (the pockets)
that our interlocutors informally and excitedly discussed during
our conversation.

In proposing a historical framework for understanding post-emancipation histories, Rebecca J. Scott explains the following:

> As one attempts to formulate a research design for work on the aftermath of emancipation, the question arises: what exactly should one do with this insight about [the complexity of former slaves' initiatives in the context of constrains placed on them] . . . this realization that slave emancipation was neither a transcendent liberation nor a complete swindle, but rather an occasion for reshaping—within limits—social, economic, and political relationships?[14]

Scott's question directs us to take a nuanced approach to how we orient our research and imagination towards the varied experiences of Black peoples across the Americas after emancipations. Scott is essentially "studying the meaning of freedom," which for a historian can lead to different foci on the lives of former slaves.[15] Should they be understood through their new economic relationships, citizenship status, or "wider range of social grouping"?[16] A stake in this historical inquiry is how scholarship parallels or diverges from dominant narratives about a nation and its peoples. If paralleling dominant narratives, then emancipation can be one historical stop along a longer narrative of a nation. If diverging, then emancipation can be a historical stop in the struggle of Black people seeking equality as citizens.

However, the historical reality is that after emancipation, Black people in the Americas were never given a fair opportunity to reimagine their citizenship and social status in relation to constitutions, polities, and their belonging in a nation-state. In places like Cuba and the US, questions of racial equality, independence, and citizenship were intermingled in the framing of new nation-states,[17] but some semblance of racial equality was not and has not been a premise for how the state guarantees the promises of equality under socialism (in Cuba) or individual liberalism (in the US). Therefore, the many historical realities of Black people diverge from national narratives. How we frame those histories has profound consequences for engaging contemporary debates about ameliorating racial inequalities.

It is difficult, if not impossible, to avoid being embroiled in the mess that dominant classes configured for sustaining their ideals of multiracial nations. These dominant classes include political leaders, the economic elite, military elite, revolutionaries, leaders of powerful social movements, and intellectuals. At the essence of this mess is a simple contradiction between the multiracial citizen and the historical inequality of multiple races. When anyone, especially Black people, tells stories about Black people in the Americas, a new historical and non-multiracial past begins to inform contemporary citizenship. For Puerto Rico, Isar P. Godreau outlines the many cultural and intellectual currents that affect how political leaders, community leaders, and intellectuals imagine and represent blackness.[18] Godreau's canonical research prevents us from jumping into a cultural inquiry of racial experience in Puerto Rico. Doing work on many analytic fronts, the metaphor of "scripts of blackness" accounts for "dominant frameworks that set standards, expectations, and spatial templates for what gets to be publicly recognized and celebrated as Black and Puerto Rican."[19] In the previous section, I addressed the congruity between being Black and Puerto Rican. Now I address Godreau's "spatial templates" vis-à-vis my interlocutors' pockets of Black people, which beg for a reimagining of the geopolitical landscape.

According to Godreau, the recognition of Black places in Puerto Rico constitutes an "emplacement of race" that "allows people to segregate these spaces and construct non-blackness as the normative mark of the nation."[20] In the Puerto Rican popular imagination, the emplacement of blackness is primarily restricted to the town of Loíza in the northeast or the barrio of San Antón in Ponce (in the south, where Godreau conducted research). Blackness is relegated to historical narratives of coastal towns with a history of plantation slavery. These relegations have political consequences since Puerto Ricans think of those towns through musical folkloric blackness that, relative to non-Black Puerto Ricans, lacks agency in representing the modern nation. Therefore, in Puerto Rico, dominant scripts of blackness reduce Scott's "meaning of freedom" to a caricature of a distant enslaved past. In summarizing this caricature, Godreau explains that national discourses have romanticized slavery as not harsh, emphasized the mixing of races, championed the Hispanic nature of Puerto Rican culture, and relegated blackness to food flavors and rhythms. Nowhere in these sociohistorical scripts of blackness is a recognition of how Afro-Puerto Ricans struggled to make a meaningful existence for themselves post-emancipation. Even when considering the high number of free Blacks in Puerto Rico prior to emancipation, there is no real sense of how blackness shaped communities and social existence.[21]

In contrast to a history of erasure, I propose that our Afro-Puerto Rican interlocutors in the cultural and genetic ancestry project hold a "folk ideology" that is very similar to Godreau's scripts of blackness.[22] Many of our interlocutors are aware of national narratives that delimit the history and contemporary presence of Black existence, and they possess discursive strategies to counter such narratives. Of course, I believe Godreau herself is engaged in a project of countering these scripts, which is why I have come to see many of my interlocutors as conceptually aligned with Godreau's powerful criticism of Puerto Rican scripts of blackness. Moreover, in locating and naming pockets of Black people and creating discourses of social life in those pockets, Afro-Puerto Ricans create possibilities of Black existence in the past, present, and future.

There are four aspects involved in how my interlocutors weave pockets into fabrics of Black existence. First, there are many pockets, and interlocutors can locate them enthusiastically and take a defensive stand about these places not being recognized in popular culture. Second, Black pockets exist in diverse island topographies. Although Puerto Ricans often imagine coastal places and their history of plantations as Black exceptions to a mestizo-Hispanic nation, interlocutors paint a more complicated topographic picture of coastal life and identify non-coastal locations for Black existence. Third, there is a history of migrations within the island and outside of Puerto Rico. Although interlocutors often go back three to four generations, there is no reason to believe that these movements are not always a part of Afro-Puerto Rican existence. Given late nineteenth century historical records, migrations are necessary to account for contemporary racial demographics. Fourth, pockets are alive (even if they no longer exist) through stories of remembrance of social life. These aspects constitute the micro level of Afro-Puerto Ricans' racial niche.

Many Diverse Pockets

There are layers to the geographical dimensions of Black existence around the island. The most immediate dimension can be found within the same spaces Puerto Ricans have historically envisioned as homogenously Black. The base for the cultural and genetic ancestry project has been in Piñones, a sector of the township of Loíza that encompasses all the land, beaches, and mangrove forest west of the Loíza River. One of the first lessons that I was taught when starting research was that the people of Piñones do not always speak of Piñones as just a sector of Loíza. There are also different neighborhoods within Piñones that are associated with families and with particular histories. Something similar happens in Loíza, where people often trace their ancestors to different neighborhoods. Residents characterized some of these neighborhoods by proximity to labor, displacement from nearby regions, and extended family. In Piñones, many residents make it a point in conversations to distinguish themselves and their neighborhoods from the strip of restaurants and bars that line the main beachside road. That road is the same one that most people in Puerto Rico, particularly in the San Juan area, associate with Piñones. This association adds another layer of misrecognition; instead of a series of multiple communities with a unique history of labor and survival, Piñones is equated with a party strip for weekend hangouts.[23] The vast majority of Puerto Ricans I have talked to around the island have no idea that there are neighborhoods beyond the party strip.

Another dimension includes places around the island that I first learned about as I talked with people in urban areas in the western town of Mayagüez and the southern town of Ponce. As we walked into neighborhoods within and adjacent to those towns, we learned about other nearby places that were usually tiny communities with no more than a dozen families tucked away on mountainsides or the southern coastline. We visited a few tiny communities but did not go to most because the people who told us about them did not personally know residents, or our attempts to contact people in those communities did not pan out. The existence of these communities and the stories about locating them became important aspects of our research before and beyond any cultural and genetic ancestry results. The way participants identified communities and located other spaces of Blackness throughout Puerto Rico became a prism for interpreting any anthropological findings at the end of the project. Black pockets, Black places, and Black people are what shaped our and interlocutors' understanding of stories about the ancestors and the past (via interviews) and genetic ancestry (via lab analysis).

These Black pockets add up to dozens of communities scattered throughout the island, and I believe they can be usefully grouped into specific types. First, there are Black pockets within urban areas that most Puerto Ricans would not readily identify as Black. For example, in Mayagüez, five participants described their childhood neighborhoods as mostly *"de gente negra"* (of Black people). Although people (including three of the five participants) had moved away, they still identified those neighborhoods as Black because many Black people still lived there and because Black or Afro culture still influenced the sounds, religious practices, and feel of the neighborhoods.

In Loíza, most participants spoke of Santurce, which is large sector of the capital town of San Juan, as being historically Black and nowadays holding many Black families. The town of Carolina, which sits between Loíza and San Juan, also appears in ten transcripts as being, as a young woman put it, "practically Black, because that is what people [Puerto Ricans] are thinking even though they are not saying it." Nydia, a woman in her mid-forties who lives in an upper-middle-class gated community in Carolina, told us stories about how, growing up, most economically well-off Black families knew and interacted with each other. "We had to support each other" with information about education and jobs. Support also included socializing at each other's houses and visiting establishments where they could eat and dance without feeling awkward. These spaces were not exclusively Black, but most were around the areas of Santurce and Carolina, so concentrated social presence undergirded the sense of being in an area where the Black community could gather. It is important to note that Nydia was clear that calling places Black and identifying as Black growing up was not common; it was particular to certain family and community members who "just did not care." Nydia, however, sees herself as following the path of those who did not care, which is why she was willing to speak of being Black and Black places.

The second category of pockets is the places that provide a corrective to the idea that there were no Black people in the mountainous interior of the island. Manny Martin, an elderly participant in Loíza, mocked the idea that there were no Black folks in the mountains. "Where do people think my ancestors ran away from?" He retrieved a photocopy of an old newspaper ad about the escape of a slave from the Martin Hacienda (one of the few owned by someone with an English surname) and said, "I don't know for sure if that was my ancestor, but I chose to believe that is where I come from." With a proud laugh, Manny continued, "If not me, then someone here [in Loíza] comes from that brave maroon!"

However, the most common corrective was more matter of fact than Manny's story. Particularly, more than a dozen participants in the ancestry project identified a Black ancestor whose family came from a mountainous region of the island, and there was no geographic pattern. Towns like Cayey, Las Marias, and Naranjito appeared in our genealogies. A retired schoolteacher in Mayagüez explained: "What happens is that a lot of Black families remained in small compounds throughout the years." She continued to speak about her own paternal family. "They lived up there [near Las Marias and Lares], but even the people that live in those areas would not be able to find them . . . they would have just driven by." Similar stories about Black ancestors from the mountains came up when I met a couple of families north of Mayagüez in the town of Aguadilla, located on a highway that used to be a Black neighborhood in the past. A patriarch of one of those families explained: "The people who lived there came from Mayagüez, but also the interior of the island."

The final category of pockets is living communities, which overlap with corrective pockets. These communities include one I visited in a mountainous area and other communities that I did not visit along southern and northwestern coastlines. The mountainous community was the most enjoyable for me as an ethnographer who, after years of doing anthropology in places other than Puerto Rico, finally got to go home and experience an old-fashioned quest of finding a place by word-of-mouth instructions. I began the quest in the town of Patillas, east of Arroyo, along the southern coastline. There, three unrelated participants spoke about "Barrio Negro" (this is a pseudonym because the community consists of a few families), which is in a sector of Yaurel in the northern region of the town of Arroyo. The downtown area of Arroyo is on the coast, but less than a mile from the coastline, Arroyo becomes mountainous. The sector of Yaurel varies in elevation between one hundred and five hundred meters above sea level, with the lowest points located in the river valleys that travel to downtown and the coast.

Understanding this topography is important because in the three conversations that I had with participants, I could not help but ask, "Why is there a Black community up there?" My question was not about aiming to get around the notion that Black communities only existed along the coastline. Instead, I remembered how, when living in the maroon community of Accompong Town, Jamaica, one maroon had taken me to a mountain top from where one could see the Appleton Estate (perhaps the most famous rum-makers from the island). "From

there [Appleton], slaves could escape to [Accompong Town]."
The distance between the places of labor and freedom was a few
miles, but the rapid change in elevation and roughness of the
terrain made it difficult for British soldiers and slave catchers to
capture maroons.

I suspected that something like what happened in Accompong Town could have happened in Arroyo. The three first
participants and six others did not know about maroons in
Arroyo (and I have not found research that supports my suspi-
cion). However, I did hear two older people describe how they
remember how their parents and grandparents used to travel
down the valleys for work in town and up the valleys to go
home to their families. How far back those routes go is difficult to know. The 1860 and 1899 censuses indicate that the non-
white population outnumbered the white population in the
area surrounding Arroyo. Also, the area was being developed
for sugar production and has been a hot spot for contraband
since the eighteenth century.[24] The sector of Yaurel is just a few
miles from the town center where sugar was processed, but it
was not a convenient location for workers, especially when one
considers that many workers lived around downtown. My point
here is not to speculate about the maroon-like nature of Yaurel;
instead, I want to emphasize that Black communities, even
when near sugar production, cannot fully be defined by sugar
and labor. Yaurel cannot be functionally defined in relation to
sugar, and Yaurel is, in fact, in the mountains. Of course, one
only needs to browse the censuses since the eighteenth century
to understand that the "negros" or "colored" (depending on the
census) were always present throughout the island, including
the mountains. The current concentrations in the northeast and
southeast are results of post-emancipation migrations of former
slaves and free Blacks.

Migrations and Weaving of a National Afro-Puerto Rican Fabric

The idea for a discussion on post-emancipation migration came from participants in the cultural and genetic ancestry project. Four of the first ten interviews we conducted in Piñones, Loíza, are with people who live outside of Loíza and in the San Juan area, and a couple of young women live on the east coast near the town of Fajardo. During our interviews, all four mentioned their comfort when visiting Loíza. Speaking with confidence and leaning back, Magali put it plainly, "This is like home!" She then signaled with her hands towards her face and body, "I am most comfortable with being like this here." Magalis then explained that having traveled to us to participate in the research project was her pleasure. "I come back whenever I can for these sorts of cultural activities. They fill me with joy." Later in our interview, I learned about one of Magalis's parents who had moved out of Loíza after marriage. Because she had family in the area, coming back to Loíza was part of her family life.

Magalis's life experiences in Loíza are part of a broader pattern of movements of Afro-Puerto Ricans within the island today and in the past. Almost all of the fifty participants we conducted genealogies with as part of structured interviews revealed ancestors from a different part of the island. I do not want to generalize demographic patterns since our sampling strategy was not employed for generalization; however, there is no reason to believe that the fifty people in question would have unusual geographic kinship patterns because of our sampling strategy. Regardless of the overall historical residential pattern of Afro-Puerto Ricans, we know the pattern that exists today is not the same one that existed in the nineteenth century.[25] The significance of Magalis' coming back to Loíza begs us to reframe

Afro-Puerto Rican movements around the island as more than push and pull remnants of a legacy of labor or random moving from one place to another. These movements are migrations of a social group that, in the narratives of our interlocutors, can understand itself as moving through time and space.

"What are these people talking about? In the nineteenth century Mayagüez had more Black people than anywhere else in Puerto Rico!" Frustrated, Francisco, a community activist and artist in his late forties, shouted in exasperation as we drove south of Mayagüez along the coastline. In his spare time, Francisco dedicated decades to studying the history of Afro-Puerto Ricans in the Mayagüez. Francisco works for the city's sanitation department, but he is passionate about history and Black culture. The "people" Francisco cannot understand are scholars who do not recognize the presence of Black Puerto Ricans throughout the island. Demographics should not be this difficult to think about. If, as Francisco correctly claims, census data shows that Mayagüez had more slaves than the rest of the island, and if censuses show Black presence throughout the island since the eighteenth century, then how did we get to the current concentrations of Afro-Puerto Ricans?

"We move. Like everyone else, we move. My wife is from Yauco, and her parents are from Ponce. And my grandfather is from Mayagüez, but my father moved to San Juan, then he came back to . . . start a family." Francisco gave this explanation in a conversation with Roberto, another middle-aged man who participated in our research. Roberto leaned back on the sofa and nodded in agreement. Then he added, "People move looking for [work] opportunities, but they always remember where they came from." Weeks later, as we spoke to more people in the western and southern coasts, we realized how true Francisco and Roberto's assertion about movement where. Most participants in the south discussed their relatives in the west and northeast, and all participants in the west had family histories in the south, southeast, and northeast. In the northeast, slightly more than half of all participants had family that came from the south-east, south, and west. In our conversation with Francisco and Roberto, the discussion turned into an enthusiastic concentration of Afro-Puerto Rican history. For almost half an hour, they talked about the historical movements of their family, and they also engaged in a back and forth of "the Cepeda family," "the Linds," and other families whose origins are not where most Puerto Ricans would locate them.

Perhaps the most important moment in our understanding of Afro-Puerto Rican migrations came in a discussion with, José, an elderly and well-know bomba artist who lives in San Juan. "The barriles, I believe, tell our history." *Barriles* (barrels), the name for the bomba drums, are crafted with multiple techniques, especially with regard to securing the animal skin to the barrel. José explained that he believed that the history of Black Puerto Ricans could be traced around the island and back to Africa by examining the different crafting techniques for attaching dried hides to the drums. As José dove into his own family history, full of brilliant artists, he mentioned something that caught my attention: "and my [family name] came from Mayagüez through Ponce." The family name in question was the same as Roberto's family. I asked, "Wait, are you related to [Roberto's family] . . . from Mayagüez?" José answered that he is, and his family legacy has been one of taking up Black Puerto Rican music around the island.

These stories of migration demonstrate that Black Puerto Ricans have been attached to place today and in the past. The island's colonial processes resulted in concentrations of Black people around the island, and the social lives and rich histories of Black Puerto Ricans reshuffled what it means to be Black and in place. Today, even when not in Black communities, Black Puerto Ricans can identify with Black places, like Loíza, and Black social life through kinship and family histories. Although Puerto Rico does not have historically well documented migrations after emancipations, it is evident that diverse social processes—from maroonage to labor-related migrations to ideological efforts to promote Afro-Puerto Rican identity—have led to a vibrant understanding of Black place and belonging, which immediately opens possibilities for geopolitical questions vis-à-vis Afro-Puerto Rican political subjectivities.

TAKING OFF THE COSTUME OF SERVITUDE THROUGH BOMBA

"How do we mobilize as Black people?" This question, asked by Maricruz, might summarize the main questions raised in this book. This is a similar question that we asked in the boxing gym for Black, Latino, and disadvantaged youth; and this is the same question that *musulmanes* (Muslims), as you will see in the next two chapters, have asked of themselves in Ceuta. I have placed the question of Afro-Puerto Rican identity and political subjectivity at the heart of this book precisely because the idea of an Afro-Puerto Rican body politic cannot be clearly observed and described as fully formed. However, from a racial niche perspective, macro-, micro-, and sociohistorical factors yield a self-identifying racialized social group. Therefore, when we observe Afro-Puerto Ricans engaging in political activity as either explicitly doing Afro-Puerto Rican political work or more ambiguously coming together as an Afro-Puerto Rican community engaged in political activity, we can begin to ask questions about the racialized subjectivity in relation to the possibilities of flourishing within liberal democratic orders.[26] Moreover, if the liberal democratic order plays a role in the conditioning of the racial niche as a sociohistorical space of exclusion, then the question of racialized political subjectivity becomes a more profound question about the possibility of racialized styles as forms of anti-racism and flourishing.

In Piñones and other Afro-Puerto Rican communities, Blackness—as an experience and ideological concept—moves beyond national folklore and a component of dominant, national, tricultural narrative into a stylized community approach to advocacy, autonomy, community uplift, and aesthetic expressions.[27] Here, I want to highlight how Maricruz's community organization, the Corporación Piñones se Integra (COPI), educates through bomba and conservation efforts in the Piñones.

Traditionally, bomba is a musical form characterized by a playful game between drummers and dancers. Bomba has many subgenres that are characterized by different drumbeats and cadences, and dancers adjust accordingly to such variations. One of the most common and defining elements of bomba is the way dancers engage in punctuated movements, known as *piquetes*, that are matched by the smallest drum (called the *primo*). In addition, a call-and-response between singer and chorus is a defining feature of a genre that is diasporic and has origins in West Africa. Therefore, historically, bomba represents a musical tradition that is part of the many aesthetic expressions that gave meaning to Afro-descendant communities.

However, Webb explains that in the mid-twentieth century the genre became more standardized through stage performances, studio recordings, and how the Institute of Puerto Rican Culture "sought to institutionalize and standardize bomba in order to maintain its 'authenticity' and integrity, establishing certain performance standards designed to promote an 'authentic' style of bomba."[28] This institutional effort to entrench bomba as a traditional form has been successful because popular culture accepts bomba as a script of Blackness inside and outside Black communities. In the southern barrio of San Antón, Godreau found that although bomba is popularly associated with the barrio, while doing fieldwork, she hardly ever heard bomba in everyday life.[29] Even in Black barrios and towns, many residents see bomba as folklore and not modern. Even in the modern resurgence of bomba beginning in the 1990s, the genre is closely tied to an essential form of blackness, whether this blackness is experienced by musicians or perceived by audiences outside of Black communities[30]

COPI's *Grupo Folclórico Majestad Negra* (Black Majesty Folkloric Ballet, as the group translates it) has sought to rearticulate the meaning of bomba as a modern expression of Afro-Puerto Rican existence and anti-racism. The first time I encountered this effort was when I was hanging around the community center before conducting some scheduled interviews. "Why all the stress?" I asked the visibly troubled manager of the Majestad Negra. "The seamstress! She takes so long. She is good, but we are down to the last minute." I asked what the new dresses were all about, and the director proceeded to articulate an anti-racist philosophy of fashion. "We don't dress like servants. When I started this, I refused to accept that dressing like servants was the way that we did it in the past...I imagine us dancing in our clothes, without shoes." The image made sense to me, especially on an island were wearing sandals around the house and neighborhood is common. "Why wouldn't one take off their shoes!" I playfully exclaimed as one of the COPI's worker's toddlers ran by me barefooted.

Instead of the traditional colonial era clothing, which includes heels and multilayered dresses, the women of Majestad

Negra wear elegant skirts with two layers: a tight-fitting one that covers the body and a longer half-skirt that covers the backside that is used to accentuate dance movements. The outfits are colorful, and the headwraps resemble modern West African and diasporic styles instead of the colonial era. Yet how the group dresses reflects an even deeper philosophy of how bomba has been reappropriated by the people of Loíza and other towns that make up Majestad Negra. Where they perform and the content of their music stands apart from many other traditional and modern performances. As the group's manager explained to me over several conversations, the group's purpose is to "educate and fight racism through that education."

"We don't play in bars and informal places." Although the manager and director of Majestad Negra have no problem with the resurgence of bomba in popular culture, they want to strike a balance between not losing the historical significance of bomba and moving bomba out of culturally dominant folkloric parameters.[31] Playing informally in plazas and bars is something they appreciate and celebrate, but they also note, as the musical director put it, "what happens is that the cultural sentiment of bomba is lost." He quickly added that it is alright for people to enjoy bomba as music, but they should always remember that bomba "is Black music." Therefore, Majestad Negra performs in their home community center, at cultural events, in education venues, and theaters. Once in those formal spaces, which secures a sense of formality for their performances, the group proceeds to break various norms with regard to the norms of formality and authenticity for the genre.

Beyond how they dress, Majestad Negra often includes performers from various generations, so two or three children are often on stage during official performances. Even though youth might not perform with advanced skills, the lead singer often takes time to explain to the audience that they include youth to emphasize the living culture and passing down of traditions. Another element of performances unique to the group is presentation of traditional songs as part of a culture of a living Black community. The modern dresses do some of this work, but songs are often theatrically framed to place the audience in modern times. For example, a song about mourning the death of an infant or a woman whose husband will not let her dance are prefaced with a reenactment of a woman mourning and a woman trying to run away from her husband, respectively. The scenes are in the present, and there is no attempt to place them in a historical past.

Just like the past is framed in the present lives of Afro-Puerto Ricans, the group has made it a point to utilize bomba to engage contemporary issues. And although contemporary bomba compositions are not unique to Majestad Negra, the junction of community, politics, and musical expression is an innovative use of a so-called folkloric tradition. To be sure, the Afro-Puerto Rican musical genre of *pleana* has been used in popular protests,[32] but Majestad Negra uses bomba as part of efforts to build community and bring attention to problems facing the community. Moreover, the group has been actively involved in diaspora building efforts. They traveled to Cuba on two occasions to participate in the Carnival of Oriente and hold jamborees with a group that plays and preserves the musical genre of Tumba Francesa, a genre that traces its origins to prerevolutionary Haiti.[33] In October 2021, Majestad Negra hosted a "cultural bridge" event, hosting the Chief Joseph Chatoyer Garifuna Folkloric Ballet of New York, whose members, mostly from Honduras, practice and conserve their historical music and dances. And in August 2022, I traveled with Majestad Negra to document their journey to Costa Rica, where the group participated in Limon's annual Afro-Caribbean festival.

These trips are explicit efforts to build diaspora through exploring musical genres rooted in Africa. I have heard multiple conversations of musicians comparing their musical styles, the place (or lack of place for) of African-derived folklore within their respective national contexts (Belize, New York, Costa Rica), and the need to continue building alliances of Afro-descendant folkloric groups within the Americas and Africa. It is important to highlight that Majestad Negra travels as a representative of Puerto Rico, but musicians and dancers are always quick to remind that they also represent Black Puerto Ricans. As a result, when Majestad Negra performs in places around Puerto Rico that are not Black, they often speak to audiences as if they are educating across cultures. Contrastingly, when coming together with Afro-diasporic musical groups, conversations have an ethos of mutual self-discovery of a common past. This is partly due to the Majestad Negra's conscious effort to reeducate Puerto Ricans about bomba as an anti-racist practice and partly due to their understanding that bomba emerged from the same Afro-diasporic experiences that shaped Afro-Cubans, the Garifuna people, and Afro-Costa Ricans.

As taken up by Majestad Negra, bomba becomes more than a genre. It becomes a stylized aesthetic practice interwoven with public education, anti-racist affirmation, and political voice. Within the Afro-Puerto Rican community, Majestad Negra utilizes bomba to build community, transfer intergenerational knowledge, and foment Afro-centric aesthetic expression in a cultural space unattached to hegemonic scripts of blackness. Furthermore, because there is a geopolitical space (Piñones, Loíza) that is both the space for social processes of Black place-making and a place that is tied to a history of maroonage and community building, Majestad Negra is an expression of a particular pocket of Black people. In turn, this autochthonous expression allows us to approach ideas of Afro-Puertoricanness and pockets of Black people from a more heterogeneous perspective where blackness in Puerto Rico has multiple voices, with histories that are both local and interwoven with others in the island and the diaspora, and incomprehensible through the national tri-cultural heritage ideal.

Outside the window in the building where bomba lessons are taught in COPI, I stood with Marcos, Majestad Negra's musical director, as he told me a long story about how he and others were growing the dozens of tiny mangrove plants in front of us. "The biologist that came by was amazed by all this!" Marcos explained while laughing and feeling proud of his accomplishment when a biologist from Puerto Rico's Department of Natural Resources (DNR) had dropped by to learn about Marcos's operation. These small plants are part of a project that COPI administrates to clean up and reforest the Piñones Mangrove State Forest. Clean-up mainly involves clearing the channels that run through the forest. Channel clearing is done by trimming mangrove trees and removing dead wood and new mangrove growth. Clear channels, in turn, allow water to flow through the forest's lagoons, which clears up the water and allows biomass growth. Equally as important, clear channels mean that when storms hit the area, waters from the ocean can flow in and out of the forest, which prevents floods in the community.

COPI has been comanaging the mangrove forest with DNR since 2007. The agreement itself was a victory for the community, but it is also linked to earlier community efforts to prevent the state sale of public lands for hotel development. Since the land for sale is managed by the state, by establishing a co-management of the forest, COPI can prevent future attempts to endanger the mangrove forest through private development. The cleanup and reforestation efforts, which are supported with funds from the New York Times's affiliated Hispanic Federation, are part of a strategy to get people in the community invested in the mangrove forest. Historically, Juan Giusti examined the labor ecology of Piñoneros and the mangrove forest.[34] Workers harvested dead wood to make charcoal, and, along with fishing and other social relations with workers in adjacent cane fields in Loíza, Piñoneros experienced their blackness through their ecological intimacy with the mangrove forest. Giusti's analysis concludes by pointing out that this ecological dimension of blackness is necessary because it moves beyond the conservation of ecosystems as conceptualized without its human inhabitants; instead, Giusti argues that ecological conservation and stewardship is directly tied to the survival of a community and a Black community with historical and contemporary cultural formations of blackness rooted in the ecosystems. Piñoneros' efforts to stop development and ongoing efforts to clean up and reforest are a historical continuation of early processes of maroonage in the mangrove and later labor and subsistence prior to the rapid industrialization of Puerto Rico in the 1950s.[35]

On a sunny October afternoon in 2021, I kayaked with Marcos through the cleared mangrove channels and chatted with him about the broader impacts of the project. "I think we can create a lot of opportunities with this project. People see that this is theirs, and they take care of it . . . [and] people are already trying to use it to build their businesses, like those guys who tried to start their ecotourism operation . . . people can just care more about their community [when they know they are not alone in conservation]." I asked him a few questions about what people "caring" means. "When people understand their past, and learn about the treasure that this forest is, they can be proud of themselves, and stand up for themselves . . . don't you think?" The idea that caring for the forest could result in entrepreneurial activities and a sense of community points to how the mangroves continue to be part of an ecology tied to politics and self-worth, albeit as a revitalization effort.

Over the years, I have had many opportunities to sit for long conversations with Marcos, other mangrove workers, members of Majestad Negra, and other artists working with COPI, and I have noticed that narratives of anti-racism and community flourishing are essentially the same when discussing the purpose of Afro-Puerto Rican aesthetic expression and the conservation of the mangroves. Conservation, like bomba, becomes a racialized style of community activism that transforms experience in the racial niche into an affectively scaffolded and habituated political subjectivity. With the care of the mangrove and sounds of bomba comes the potential of local body politic, what I call "mangrove politics."

WHO IS IN CHARGE HERE? MANGROVE POLITICS AND THE PROMISE OF AN AFRO-PUERTO RICAN BODY POLITIC

Emanating from the macro and micro milieu of the Puerto Rican racial niche, mangrove politics is a multigenerational attempt to mediate racial experiences and Puerto Rican and US body politics. Through local public policy, mangrove politics fill the void created by Puerto Rico and the US's failure to recognize Black experience and politically conceive the necessities of Afro-Puerto Rican citizens. Contemporary communal efforts to educate through bomba and the mangrove forest co-management are expressions of Afro-Puerto Rican existence and enactments of a local public policy. Even the ancestry project is part of this local public policy. In fact, the very existence of this chapter is part of a mangrove politics strategy since it the reason many of my interlocutors in Piñones have explicitly acknowledged their wanting to collaborate with me.

Speaking on a radio show on March 23, 2022, and responding to a question on the lack of statistics that the Puerto Rican government collects on race, Maricruz explained that if the government does not recognize a problem, "then they do not have to work on the problem." She then cited the cultural and genetic ancestry project as a community effort to study and document "ourselves." The research project was a different way to understand how Afro descendants could be made visible outside the traditional tricultural heritage model in Puerto Rico. A few months before the radio show, I joked with Maricruz that COPI had weaponized anthropological research for an antiracist agenda. She laughed, but she laughed too much for one of my silly jokes. I noted, "You are laughing, but not denying." Maricruz laughed even harder.

Of course, it was never a secret between anthropologists, COPI, and community members that the purpose of the ancestry project was, in part, to affirm Afro-Puerto Rican ancestry in a way that participants could imagine their histories without the burden of being one third of a national discourse. There is also no doubt that Maricruz has used the social capital of being affiliated with an American institution of higher learning, such as Vanderbilt University, to play a political game with serious intentions. Affirming that a community engaged research project is a response to the government's inattention to racism and making that affirmation in a public forum, such as a radio show from the University of Puerto Rico, demonstrates that there are people in Piñones unwilling to just demand that government do more. Instead, they are choosing to act themselves.

In addition to anti-racist education through bomba, the conservation of the mangrove forest, and our ancestry project, communities like Piñones, elsewhere around the island, and beyond have historically taken many actions that are political in nature and fill the void left by governments.[36] These actions are in the political areas of anti-poverty, health care, disaster relief, and housing. For example, COPI helped organize food drives in the aftermath of Hurricane Maria in 2017, community members took to the street to inform others of vaccine availability during the COVID pandemic, and there have been successfully organized protests over the years to protect housing and lands from outside developers. Although many lands are now legally owned by members of the community, historically, many parcels were owned by someone outside of the community, and the state often considered residents squatters.[37]

Much has been written about Puerto Rican racial identifications. Whether scholars link changing racial identities to US imperialist projects or identify local forms of colorism and discrimination, why and how Afro-Puerto Ricans recognize their blackness is undeniably an act of racial self-assertion and self-worth relative to dominant narratives of whiteness and mestizaje.[38] However, I have tried to highlight throughout this chapter how cultural self-recognition and self-worth yield racialized styles of community activism that are seeds for Black flourishing in Puerto Rico and the US. The most fundamental premise of this body politic is that it is unquestionably Puerto Rican. Hilda Lloréns notes the same premise with interlocutors on the island and mainland US.[39] It is thus reasonable to conclude that communally active Afro-Puerto Ricans are moving towards political ideologies of empowerment and recognition of blackness within the boundaries of a Puerto Rican body politic, even when such political ideologies are Afro-diasporic.

However, the potential of a Black body politic in Puerto Rico immediately runs up against the ambiguous colonial space of Afro-Puerto Ricans within the island and of Puerto Rico within the US. There is no recognition by major political parties in Puerto Rico of racism or the unquestionable socioeconomic marginalization of Afro-Puerto Ricans. Although the question of poverty has been of concern to many public intellectuals and political figures, attention to poverty is mostly framed relative to the island's political status as US territory. Moreover, even though the enduring inequality faced by Black people throughout the diaspora is no secret, the vast majority of Puerto Ricans fail to even imagine the possibility that blackness leads to different experiences of poverty. For example, when I spoke to non-Black Puerto Ricans living in the San Juan area about the struggles against hotel development in the Piñones area, they do not view those struggles as having anything to do with race. Instead, they see the struggle as one that falls in the realm of environmentalism and anti-capitalism because of the power of influence that developers have on the Puerto Rican government. However, many Afro-Puerto Ricans I spoke with in Loíza frame political struggles against the hotels as one of many in a long line for Black Puerto Ricans to have their homes, their beaches, and mangroves to be recognized as their own.

The excitement and effort of recognizing the social existence of Afro-Puerto Ricans in dispersed geographical pockets points to the materiality of Black bodies occupying physical spaces that can be imagined as a racial niche, a precondition for an Afro-Puerto Rican political subjectivity. Of course, geopolitical presence need not result in Afro-Puerto Rican political subjectivity, and the only place I observed a direct link between an Afro-Puerto Rican community and an Afro-Puerto Rican political subjectivity is in Piñones (more specifically COPI). Still, the celebration of bomba as anti-racist and protecting the mangrove forest as a homeland is well understood and often shared by

Afro-Puerto Ricans elsewhere in Loíza, Mayagüez, Ponce, and other pockets where we worked around the island. As soon as Afro-Puerto Ricans understand the social nature of scripts of blackness and begin to rewrite those scripts to educate, conserve, and politicize community actions, blackness from nowhere and political liminality become blackness from somewhere and politically tangible (from the racial niche and the mangroves).

5

THE ORIGINS OF RACIALIZED CITIZENS IN THE ILLIBERAL STATE

Life Stories in the Spanish-Moroccan Borderland

INTRODUCTION

The ethnographic study of *musulmanes* (Muslims) in Ceuta, Spain offers another perspective on racial experience and styles in the racial niche. However, unlike the US boxing gym and community activism in Puerto Rico, in Ceuta, we find an interesting case of government political representation for musulmanes, a racialized group. This chapter provides a historical perspective on how musulmanes became a racialized social group in a liberal democracy. My purpose here is to illustrate how most, if not all, liberal democracies have anti-liberal or illiberal historical beginnings for racialized peoples, either within the nation-state polity or as colonial subjects. This approach to racialized peoples and illiberal democracies follows Charles Mills's philosophical proposition that we rethink liberalism as racial liberalism.[1] I do not ambiguously question how Western liberal ideals of citizenship, freedom, and democracy coexist with slavery, dehumanization, and subjugation of racialized peoples. Instead, I assume that those Western liberal ideals have and continue to function precisely because the equality of racialized peoples has not been at a sustained ideological core of liberal democratic deliberation.

This chapter examines the formation of Ceuta's racial niche before and during the current Spanish liberal democratic era, which extends from 1978 until the present. Three historical periods and life stories outline the moving assemblage of the racial niche and how this assemblage exists in tensions with liberal democratic promises, such as liberty, freedom, equality, and pluralism. In the following chapter, I examine the ideological political style of Muslims in Ceuta's Local Assembly. As we will see, governmental political representation in liberal democracies places serious limits on the ability of racialized people to fashion political styles for their flourishing. If Afro-Puerto Ricans struggle to have their communities recognized in Puerto Rico's body politic, the case of Muslims in Ceuta demonstrates that even when a racialized body politic gains electoral representation, liberal democratic orders resist. The historical background of this chapter suggests that, like Ceuta, liberal democratic orders resist racialized political subjectivities because the historical rise of the liberal citizen has always been sustained by racial orders.

HISTORICAL ODDITIES?

From the outside, Ceuta appears to be out of place. It is a roughly nineteen square kilometer territory located on Morocco's North African coast within eyesight of the Iberian Peninsula's southern coastline, yet Ceuta is a Spanish territory. Ceuta and its sister city Melilla, located further east along the same coastline, are the European Union's (EU) borders that extend into the African continent. Historically, Ceuta was one of the last vestiges of the Spanish Reconquest of the Iberian Peninsula during the fifteenth century. It remained a Spanish fortification for hundreds of years after that, guarding against military threats from Northern Africa.

Later, Ceuta was a launching pad for Spain's colonization of northern Morocco in 1912 and again in 1936 when fascist rebels, led by General Francisco Franco, initiated the Spanish Civil War. After Moroccan independence in 1956 and through the end of Franco's dictatorship in 1978, Ceuta remained Spanish with a civil and military population comprised of Spanish citizens and Moroccan noncitizens. Today, Ceuta's location at the southern end of the Strait of Gibraltar is an exception to Europe's symbolic geography that for centuries differentiated East from West, colonizer from colonized, and the familiar from the exotic. Ceuta is also a bridge, albeit a broken one, between the global North and South from where thousands of Maghrebi and sub-Saharan migrants desperately attempt to complete their journey onto the Iberian Peninsula. And like many other urban centers throughout Western Europe, Ceuta is now seen by some of its inhabitants as a place where a troubled Islam meets a progressive West.

Ceuta's internal boundaries and continuities also transcend the global and historical borders. Self-identified *cristianos* (Christians) and *musulmanes* (Ceuta's two major social groups) variously delineate these boundaries and continuities.[2] These identities reflect different religious beliefs and practices; however, they also reflect what people in Ceuta understand as ethnic, cultural, and racial differences, especially since not all musulmanes and cristianos practice the religions signified by their collective identities. These differences are mainly determined by historical origins: musulmanes in Morocco and cristianos in peninsular Spain.

There are perceived phenotypic differences through which cristianos and musulmanes differentiate each other. Musulmanes are said to have darker skin, darker eyes, darker hair, and "Arab features" (e.g., nose, eyelashes, curly hair). However, these generalizations do not always hold true, and there are many phenotypic features shared by both groups. Musulmanes are also distinguished by their language (including a distinctive accent when they speak Castilian), dress (both traditional and contemporary), and by proximity to other "marked" musulmanes. Occasionally, a musulmán will be mistaken as a cristiano, but rarely will a cristiano be mistaken as a musulmán. Most musulmanes speak Castilian Spanish and a local Arabic variant of northern Morocco (popularly known as Dariya), identifying with Arab or Berber ancestors. Most maintain family and social ties with Moroccans across the border. In addition, most musulmanes officially only gained Spanish citizenship in the late 1980s, even though many were born in Ceuta. Cristianos speak Castilian Spanish and do not see themselves as different from their Spanish/European counterparts in the Iberian Peninsula. However, many strongly identify with the regional heritage of the southern Spanish province of Andalusia, where many maintain family and social ties. Unlike musulmanes, cristianos in Ceuta have always been citizens of Spain.

Despite these differences, both musulmanes and cristianos call themselves *ceutíes* (people of Ceuta) and make use of a concept called *convivencia* (cohabitation, coexistence, or living together), which describes Ceuta's cultural landscape. Convivencia is a borrowed word originally coined by historians to describe a time during the Middle Ages when Christians, Muslims, and Jews lived peacefully, although not equally, in the Iberian Peninsula. The word convivencia also has mundane definitions that explain the coexistence of beings in different places. For example, it is common to speak of convivencia between domestic partners, coworkers, or political parties. However, since the early

1980s, ceutíes have specifically used it to describe the peaceful coexistence of four cultures or religions in Ceuta: Christians, Muslims, Jews, and Hindus. The latter two, although very small in numbers, have played a significant role in the historical and economic development of the city.[3] Musulmanes and cristianos do not always share the same definition of convivencia, yet the concept is significant because it captures how ceutíes communally remember the past, think about the present, and hope for the future. Most ceutíes understand that they should negotiate their intercommunity struggles lest they degenerate into feuding factions and jeopardize the future of the exclave as an integral part of Spain.

Nonetheless, starting in the mid 1990s, cristianos and musulmanes have been the protagonists of a political drama that resulted in them being on opposing political parties in the Local Assembly. This led to a situation that rarely occurs in Western liberal democracies. Marginalized cultural minorities in Western liberal democracies have sought to remedy their situation by integrating into established political parties, lobbying through nongovernmental organizations, protesting through popular political movements, or seeking autonomy; in Ceuta, musulmanes have formed their own political parties. Ceutíes generally refer to these parties composed of and voted for by musulmanes as *partidos de corte musulmán* (parties of Muslim persuasion). The appellative hesitancy by ceutíes to simply call them "Muslim parties," which is not always resisted, comes from the fact that Islam and Muslim ethnicity have not explicitly motivated these parties' political agendas.

Two parties of Muslim persuasion have served in the Local Assembly from 1995 to 2011: the *Partido Democratico y Social de Ceuta* (the Democratic and Social Party of Ceuta or PDSC) and the *Unión Demócrata Ceutí* (the Ceutí Democratic Union or UDCE). The PDSC was part of an executive government with the ruling center-right *Partido Popular* (Popular Party or PP) from 1996 to 1999, and it has been in opposition with other socialist and localist parties. The UDCE was the leading opposition party to the PP from 2003 to 2011 and worked closely with the PDSC and other socialist parties, particularly the *Partido Socialista del Pueblo de Ceuta* (People of Ceuta's Socialist Party or PSPC), led by Juan Luis Aróstegui. In 2011, the UDCE allied with the PSPC to form the Caballas Coalition, which lasted until 2021. Regardless of their various ideological positioning to other parties in the Assembly, the agenda of parties of Muslim persuasion is to improve the living and working conditions of musulmanes through infrastructural development in marginal neighborhoods, increase job opportunities, and attain a more equitable distribution of investments by the local government. Yet the political struggles of these parties have not only centered on achieving these goals but also on the very legitimacy of their political organization. Many cristianos see political parties that appear to exclusively represent and be represented by musulmanes as coming dangerously close to promoting ethnic conflict and as not genuinely Spanish or liberal democratic.

These peculiar internal political struggles and Ceuta's unique geopolitical location are historically intertwined and relevant in understanding the political present. Spain's colonial history in northern Morocco mostly explains the marginalization of musulmanes in the city's outskirts. Meanwhile, the Moroccan state claims Ceuta as part of its territory, making some cristianos mistrustful of the growing political influence of musulmanes. It also causes many musulmanes to distance themselves publicly from their Moroccan origins as they assert their Spanishness against cristianos' fears. Moreover, the Spanish government's unwillingness to embrace its African territories fully and equally (e.g., Ceuta and Melilla) since the 1978 Constitution has essentially relegated all ceutíes to the political margins of Spain.

Ceuta may seem out of place, but it is in the intersections of multiple boundaries and continuities where ceutíes, like all people, "fashion places." And as they do, "so, too, do they fashion themselves." [4] In this chapter, I explore how musulmanes' sense of community has emerged throughout the twentieth and into the twenty-first centuries, which led to the formation of a musulmán body politic with representation in the Local Assembly (i.e., how a political style emerged from a racial niche).

After the territorial continuity between Ceuta and Spanish Protectorate in Morocco gave way to an international border between Spain and Morocco in 1956, musulmanes experienced roughly thirty years of virtual statelessness. Following a period of civil turmoil in the 1980s, through which many musulmanes gained Spanish citizenship, a local sense of community began to congeal based on their previous experiences of territorial attachment to Ceuta and ambiguous citizenship vis-à-vis cristianos, Spaniards, and Moroccans. Whereas cristianos' sense of community creates a bridge of nationality between Ceuta and peninsular Spain, musulmanes' sense of community does not leave the confines of the exclave; it is Spanish with a Moroccan heritage, but above all, it is a sense of being from Ceuta. It is within this historical context that we critically interpret how parties of Muslim persuasion are a stylized outcome of social exclusion, racialization, and an autochthonous political ideology, which I argue is at the crux of understanding the possibilities and contradictions of liberal democracies remedying injustices for racialized peoples (see Chapter 6).

METHODOLOGICAL
NOTES ON LIFE STORIES

I am not aware of the existence of any documented history of Ceuta's musulmanes. Here I intend to make a small step in that direction by presenting the experiences that some musulmanes have had on their journey to becoming citizens of Ceuta, Spain. In 2004 and 2009, with the assistance of my friend Mohamed Mustafa Ahmed, who in 2022 began serving as a representative in Ceuta's Local Assembly, I recorded conversations over many days and long hours with Miriam, Karim, Rachid, Ahmed, and Karina. Their stories are the main source of information for this chapter. However, I have relied on many other formal and informal interviews with cristianos and musulmanes to structure historical content. Mohamed Mustafa Ahmed was instrumental in establishing contact with informants and conducting interviews.

Anthropologists have made theoretical and methodological remarks about the relationship between history and oral narratives. Their main concerns are with the utility and significance that one or a few community members can provide through extended interviews. First, there is a question of how well an individual's life experiences correspond with an "actual" history of their community. "There may be a correspondence between a life as lived, a life as experienced, and a life as told, but the anthropologist should never assume the correspondence nor fail to make the distinction."[5] Second, Peacock and Holland argue that social scientists have differently emphasized the "life" and "stories" in life stories. Peacock gives primacy to how the life of the narrator constitutes either a historical fact or a subjective experience, while Holland explores the structure of stories themselves within a broader sociocultural context.

However, other scholars stress the importance of approaches that simultaneously account for how individuals shape and are shaped by broader social processes.[6] My approach aims to examine how racial experience shaped generations of musulmanes and culminated in the cultural phenomenon of parties of Muslim persuasion.

From a theoretical standpoint, I take these life stories to represent an important part of the "actual" history of musulmanes who lived in Ceuta most of their lives because their stories are corroborated by multiple informal interviews with other musulmanes and cristianos and years of ethnographic fieldwork. Life stories provide an important qualitative richness to the moving assemblages of a racial niche, for people make sense of the junctures and disjunctures of such assemblages as they articulate and perform living memories of the past. Moroccans who arrived in the city since the 2000s might not relate so well to these life stories because they are not attached to the cultural memory of musulmanes who have lived in Ceuta for generations. The interlocutors whose life stories I present in this chapter are musulmanes who have lived close to cristianos with social, economic, and political ties to Ceuta. However, the factuality of these life stories is not my only concern. The telling of the life stories themselves indicates how musulmanes represent themselves and their community at the time Mohamed and I recorded their stories.

Telling a life story, "like other forms of talk or communication," is part of life as lived, for it is lived and experienced, at least during the moments of telling. Even if there is no simple, direct relationship between life as lived in the past and life as told, the very act of telling a life story is itself an experience—now, during the instances of telling (Lamb 2001:16).[7]

Lamb's perspective aligns with this chapter's objective of examining how musulmanes imagine and politically represent their community as part of Ceuta and Spain.

I have organized these life stories into three periods with significant overlap. The first is from the beginning of the twentieth century to the end of the Spanish Protectorate in northern Morocco in 1956; the second period stretches from the end of the Protectorate to the mid-1980s; and the third is from the late 1970s to the present. All three periods correspond to a change in the relationships of musulmanes, cristianos, and the Spanish and Moroccan states. These drastic changes shaped how musulmanes have projected their sense of community and how parties of Muslim persuasion practice politics. This sense of community reflects the dual and contradictory existence of musulmanes in the racial niche over time. On one hand, musulmanes are always musulmanes, bound in relation to the colonial dominance of the Spanish state and cristianos in Ceuta. On the other hand, Ceuta's musulmanes have emerged as a distinctive ceutí community amid ambiguous borders, citizenship, and contemporary political practices.

ENCOUNTERS AT THE
PERIPHERY (1912–1956)

Writing about the peripheral neighborhood of Benzu from fieldwork conducted at the end of the 1970s and early 1980s, Eva Evers Rosander (1991) gathered important accounts from musulmanes about what daily life was like at the beginning of the twentieth century. Spain's colonial incursion early in the twentieth century created a need for workers to build the infrastructure of Ceuta and other parts of the colony. The neighborhood of Benzu, which sits below a quarry on the northwestern coast of Ceuta, was a site where such workers came together. During the first half of the twentieth century, the quarry supplied stones for the new colonial infrastructures. Both cristianos and musulmanes labored and lived side by side in Benzu. Rosander describes how her interlocutors remember those days:

> Stories about the past have a common theme: the hardships at work and the poverty were compensated by the pleasant neighborhood and the friendly interaction between Spaniards and Muslims. In those days everybody was equally poor, the old [Benzu] men and women told me; this engendered a strong feeling of solidarity regardless of religion and ethnic identity. People used to participate in each other's daily activities and attend each other's parties. They even celebrated the major religious festivals together and shared the party food; something which does not happen spontaneously today (Rosander 1991:25).[8]

Henk Driessen (1992)[9] reports similar circumstances in Melilla, although tensions there between the Spanish military and nearby Berber tribes were higher because the latter often violently resisted the encroachment of Spanish mining companies onto their lands. Driessen explains that at the beginning of the Protectorate, during the 1910s and 1920s, a massive influx of poor laborers from southern Spain migrated to the Protectorate looking for work. However, there was not enough work to keep up with demand. As a result, "poverty hit the Spanish population almost as hard as the Riffians. In fact, the majority of Spaniards in Melilla and the Protectorate were only slightly better off" (Driessen 1992:47).[10] Although Driessen argues that ethnic loyalties were stronger than class affiliations in Melilla, in Ceuta, where violent conflict between Spanish forces and Berbers did not exist, musulmanes and cristianos enjoyed relative economic equality within the confines of poverty.

Driessen argues that Spain mainly used the Protectorate as a training ground for its military and for the extraction of iron ore in the mountains adjacent to Melilla. Consequently, "when Spain resigned its Protectorate in 1956, it left a poor infrastructure and an impoverished, largely illiterate population" (Driessen 1992:41).[11] This lack of development meant that by the 1940s, musulmanes in Ceuta were forced to find other forms of employment as mining slowed down. "Men found employment in construction projects in Ceuta, fished and sold the catch in Ceuta, smuggled tax-free cigarettes and liquor from Gibraltar or enrolled temporarily in the Spanish army" (Rosander 1991:26).[12] Women, on the other hand, began to take on a variety of seasonal employment or worked as domestic servants for Spaniards. As the end of the Protectorate neared in 1956, cristianos and musulmanes began to settle in different neighborhoods. This did not mean total segregation, but many cristianos no longer needed to live near the border after Spain abandoned the Protectorate. Musulmanes did not have many options aside from moving to Morocco, where economic conditions were no better or worse.

It is important to consider that most of the twentieth century musulmanes were not Spanish citizens, and their cohabitation in Ceuta with cristianos was structured by a colonial relationship. The average cristiano laborer would not have been able to exercise much power over his fellow musulmán neighbor. Still, a colonial elite clearly distinguished themselves from the Moorish Other (Balfour 2002:184–202).[13] Rosander's ethnographic account points to a continuity between the "Moors of Peace" and Ceuta's musulmanes. Historically, Spanish officials distinguished between friendly and unfriendly Moors. Until the nineteenth century, the Spanish military allowed the so-called Moors of Peace into Ceuta's fortified city limits to conduct business.[14] Some of these Moors of Peace in and around Ceuta later served in the Spanish military to pacify the Protectorate and fight in the Spanish Civil War under Franco. The very idea of a friendly versus unfriendly Moor points to a quintessential component in any ideology of colonial domination: divide and conquer. Far from a "friendly" relationship, the complicity of Ceuta's musulmanes and other Moroccans throughout the countryside that joined the Spanish military is better explained by the dire economic needs of young Moroccan males and/or an already fragmented and feuding Moroccan society (Balfour[15] 2002; Pennell 2000).

Not only were Ceuta's Spanish-speaking musulmanes different from those in Morocco, Rosander reports that in Benzu, musulmanes were differentiated by themselves and by Spaniards from musulmanes in other neighborhoods in Ceuta. For example, musulmanes in the borderland neighborhood of Benzu saw musulmanes in the other borderland neighborhood of El Principe as urban and more likely to take advantage of contraband across the border (Rosander 1991),[16] which is a perception still held by many ceutíes today. The segmentation and fragmentation that violently divided Moroccans during the first decades of the twentieth century appear to have persisted in Ceuta to a lesser degree.[17]

Karim is a musulmán in his late forties who has lived in Ceuta and Morocco, but mostly in Ceuta since the early 1980s. He is married, lives in one of Ceuta's peripheral neighborhoods near Principe Alfonso, and was unemployed during our conversations in 2004. I sat with him in a teashop in El Centro over many evenings, talking about his life and his take on musulmanes' history in Ceuta. I asked him about past divisions among musulmanes.

> The community of musulmanes comes from people that originated from Morocco almost fifty or sixty years ago. Musulmanes are either Berbers or Arabs. Many Berbers do not speak Berber, they speak Arabic. They are Berbers that are Arabized. And there are some Berbers that speak Berber in their house, and they also speak Arabic, and they speak Castilian.
>
> [Today], all neighborhoods are mixed. There are no Berber neighborhoods. Today, most consider themselves ceutíes that are Spaniards. They fight for their rights; they want to be part of this society and nothing else. That is the truth. Yes, they go to Morocco to buy some things. Their culture is of Arab descent. You understand? Their feasts and such things [are of Arab descent]. Because before they had not been granted citizenship, they were musulmanes with little: [they had an] identification card and nothing else.
>
> But before there were such divisions, before almost thirty or forty years ago. There was not necessarily an antagonistic relationship [between different groups of musulmanes], but one [ethnic group] did not like another because of residues of negative stories about another ethnic group because they did not get along over there [Morocco]. And they transferred those sentiments from there to here. The older folks did tell stories about certain tribes or tribal warfare. The young ones would hear that, and then when they grew up, they already had a prejudice against another ethnic group. In time, they started judging others, but as time passed, that is disappearing.

The Arabs that conquered North Africa in the seventh century were never fully able to control many Berber tribes in northern

Morocco. It was not until the establishment of the Spanish Protectorate and a difficult war between Spain and Berber rebels that northern Morocco was truly pacified. But the so-called pacification of Berbers in the Rif Mountains also entailed their subsequent marginalization from Spain and Morocco after Moroccan independence in 1956. In fact, northern Morocco as a region is still much poorer than the rest of the country. Only at the turn of the twentieth century did the Moroccan government heavily invest in northern Moroccan cities, although the countryside is still underdeveloped.[18] Karim's description of divisions among Berbers and between Berbers and Arabs is indicative of these broader divisions within Moroccan society. Karim concludes that whatever divisions existed in the past are no longer relevant. Today, politically active musulmanes think that these past divisions are an impediment to the political success of musulmanes in Ceuta.[19] Karim then continues to acknowledge past differences among musulmanes.

There are a couple of important aspects to how Karim develops this historical narrative. First, he places the origins of Ceuta's musulmanes near the end of the Protectorate. This is consistent with the migration of new musulmanes that arrived in Ceuta in search for work after the initial establishment of the Protectorate. Thousands came from the urban center of Tetuán and nearby rural areas in the Rif Mountains of Morocco.[20] These are not the same musulmanes with whom Rosander worked in Benzu, which is an older group of musulmanes who never amounted to more than a few hundred individuals that possibly lived in the village of Benzu centuries before the Spaniards expanded Ceuta's city limits in 1860. Today, the descendants of these old families make up a small percentage of Ceuta's musulmanes. I met two musulmanes whose families came from Benzu, and they both spoke of the history of musulmanes in Ceuta by referring to their family's heritage in Benzu. Contrastingly, Karim and his parents' generation moved to Ceuta during the middle of the twentieth century, when the Spanish-Moroccan border was beginning to be established and politically defined in its modern form. That border was not the physical barrier that it has been since the early 1990s. The musulmanes that came to Ceuta in the mid-twentieth century only knew the official Spanish-Moroccan border as a porous zone, not as a Rubicon that would transform them into immigrants.

Second, Karim remembers the stories of hostility and prejudice among various groups of musulmanes within the context of aspirations for political unity in the late 1990s and early 2000s. Later on in our conversation, he talked about the older group of musulmanes that had inhabited Ceuta for centuries. He mentioned them while arguing that cristianos should not treat musulmanes like immigrants, and therefore musulmanes have the same rights as cristianos to live in Ceuta. Karim never refers to musulmanes as immigrants or newcomers. Instead, Karim finds common ground between the old and new generations of musulmanes within his community's current struggle for equality. For him, Ceuta is borderless in relation to Morocco. Karim acknowledges that musulmanes "originate in Morocco," but this does not imply that they are foreigners. This is a radically different conception of territoriality than that of cristianos who emphasize the Spanishness of Ceuta exclusively in relation to the Iberian Peninsula.

The early neighborly relationship between musulmanes and cristianos in what today are peripheral neighborhoods came about at a time when colonialism, poverty, and the need for labor were greater than the need for a physical Spanish-Moroccan border. Whereas most cristianos historically represent the twentieth century when musulmanes arrived in Ceuta, musulmanes tend to see historical continuity between Ceuta's peripheral regions and Morocco. However, this continuity is not a matter of national territories; it is between the few musulmanes that inhabited Ceuta and a new generation of musulmanes. These encounters at the periphery are consistent with processes of state formation elsewhere.[21]

SEGREGATION (1956–1980s)

In time, the Spanish-Moroccan border played a role in structuring the relationship between musulmanes and cristianos in Ceuta. Moroccan nationalism and independence in 1956 forced ceutíes to reevaluate their relationships. Most cristianos that lived in the Protectorate left Morocco rather hastily. Their exodus was not violent since Franco handed the Protectorate over to Morocco without military resistance, but I heard many accounts from cristianos of the generalized uncertainty felt by Spaniards in northern Morocco in those days. This included cristianos in Ceuta who did not know if Franco would cede their land to Morocco. Many Spaniards migrated to the peninsula, but others settled in Ceuta. For the first time since Ceuta's civil society flourished late in the nineteenth century, a unified Moroccan state appeared across the border with an antagonistic outlook towards their former colonizers. Ceuta and Melilla were suddenly at the front of the Spanish-Moroccan postcolonial condition.

Musulmanes in Ceuta also found themselves in a difficult situation. Although religion was not the only driving force of Moroccan nationalism, it was enough of a factor that being a devout Muslim implied allegiance to the newly formed nation and vice-versa (Laroui 1997; Pennell 2000).[22] Musulmanes who stayed in Ceuta were potentially outsiders to both cristianos in Ceuta and Moroccans across the border. Rosander explains,

> the Spanish-Moroccan border that was established at Tarajal [border crossing point] . . . made the Ceuta Muslims non-Moroccans, not only in practice but also in theory. They now hurried to change their image and orient themselves towards the Moroccans, fearing that the Spaniards would not be able to keep Ceuta and Melilla once the Protectorate had passed to King Mohamed V of Morocco (Rosander 1991:29).[23]

The uncertainty of what would happen to Ceuta affected both cristianos and musulmanes for very different reasons; although at that time all ceutíes understood the fundamental polemic: cristianos cannot be Moroccans, hence Muslim, and musulmanes cannot be Spaniards, hence Christian.

Spain did not cede all of its North African territories. In Ceuta, musulmanes had to live with the condition of being stateless, and cristianos had to live with musulmanes in much closer urban quarters. The population increase of musulmanes in Ceuta occurred during the colonial period (1912 to 1956). Therefore, the geographic proximity between musulmanes and cristianos during the Protectorate was gradual from east to west. The old city enclosed by fortified walls was essentially Spanish, followed by mixed peripheral neighborhoods, and then the Moroccan countryside. After Moroccan independence, the Spanish-Moroccan border became relevant, and, for the first time, cristianos and musulmanes experienced their belonging to Ceuta strictly in relation to one another.

This new relationship was not equally negotiated. Cristianos felt genuinely ceutí and Spanish. Ceuta has remained an important military place since 1956. Christianity and military fervor combined to give cristianos a sense of belonging to an exclave that was still part of a single, unified Spanish nation (Driessen 1992;[24] Stallaert 1998). Meanwhile, musulmanes were genuinely out of place. Musulmanes might not have thought of the land they occupied as foreign territory, but the imposition of the border created an awkward situation in which they were not quite Moroccan and not Spaniard. As a result, musulmanes continued to live their lives with a simultaneous orientation: internally towards Ceuta and externally towards Morocco. This, coupled with their inability to integrate with cristianos politically and socially in Ceuta, led to a gradual urban segregation between both communities. Karim explained the relationship between musulmanes and cristianos years after Moroccan independence.

I do not mean to say that we did not live well before [in the period after the end of the Protectorate]. We lived well, and there was respect. But each community was separated from one another. *There was no physical contact like there is now.*

Before [the end of the Protectorate] there were many musulmanes in the army, in the barracks. Their religion was respected, their feasts, and their culture, one hundred percent . . . They could not reject the cultural and religious side of a human mass that formed part of [Spain's] state army. They could not. It would no longer be logical. Respect it and leave it in its place. It was a necessity that they [Spaniards] had at the time.

[In the years after Moroccan Independence] that social structure was lost. The barracks were emptied of musulmanes. People retired from the army. Only a few [musulmanes] were left in the Legion, but only a few.[25] Then began the civil phase of the population.[26] Not all musulmanes were in the military, but many were in the military class. With time that was lost. Then musulmanes became part of Ceuta's population, but only as civilians. I am not trying to say that there was no respect. There was respect. There were musulmanes who entered the house of cristianos during their feasts. *Now that is lost . . . That was not lost in an abrupt manner, rather over many years, over thirty years.* It was lost and people did not realize it until much later. People in their fifties and sixties remember that. Musulmanes and cristianos both remember it.

It is important to keep in mind that this process of segregation occurred under Franco's dictatorial regime. However worse life got for musulmanes, their ability to escape marginalization was curbed by the poverty that existed on the Moroccan side of the border. Leaving Ceuta was not an option, yet socioeconomic upward mobility was impossible with their exclusion from the Spanish state. Musulmanes were stateless in more than one way. They were not citizens of any country, but over time they also began to lose their more immediate citizenship as people of Ceuta. Since musulmanes were not socialized in Spanish schools (or any non-Koranic schools), they did not have a strong command of official Castilian, although most were still more familiar with the language than Moroccans across the border. These linguistic and educational differences contributed the distancing of both communities.

Karim makes several references (which I have emphasized through italics) that might appear contradictory. At first, he indicates that after the end of the Protectorate, musulmanes and cristianos became segregated, but he distinguishes that segregation with a "physical contact" that exists today between the two communities. Later, he states that the respect that existed between musulmanes and cristianos has been gradually lost over time. I asked Karim about what he meant by "physical contact," and he responded that it meant the ability or willingness of some musulmanes to come to El Centro (which is where we held our meetings). In the past, he explained, musulmanes would rarely venture into the city from peripheral neighborhoods. Nonetheless, even after years of democracy and the increased physical mobility of musulmanes around the city, respect is still lacking between many members of both communities. Thus, lack of respect is, for Karim, the most important element separating cristianos from musulmanes.

One of the most important factors in the marginalization of musulmanes in the twenty years following Moroccan independence was the ability of Spanish state agents to exclude musulmanes from participating in an already politically repressed nation. Ahmed is married with children, in his early fifties, and worked in public transportation for most of his life. Although he has not accumulated a lot of wealth, he has managed, since the 1980s, to ascend to an economic lower middle class like the majority cristianos. However, during his youth, he lived at the margins of ceutí society like most musulmanes. He recalls how the police would randomly enforce their power during Franco's dictatorship.

> One day I was stopped with my father's car in Hadu [midway between El Centro and the border]. And a policeman comes over, opens the door, gets in the car, and says, "To the police headquarters." And I thought to myself, "What have I done?" I got to the police headquarters, he got out of the car and said, "goodbye."

Like most musulmanes, Ahmed was once part of a stateless community. He described his experience with the Spanish police in a joking manner. He did not enjoy the experience, but he understood that he could not do much at the time.

Rachid, a close friend of Ahmed who joined our conversations over several evenings in Ahmed's living room, divulged stories that painted a complicated relationship between some cristianos and musulmanes. Rachid was born in Morocco and settled in Ceuta with his parents when he was young. He held various manual labor jobs throughout his life, although he has been unemployed on many occasions. Along with his family and relatives, Rachid lives near the brink of poverty in a neighborhood mostly inhabited by musulmanes.

Ahmed and Rachid remember that in the past, musulmán and cristiano men used to socialize in and around military hangouts, but they also remember the beatings that many musulmanes took at the hands of Legionnaires. Similarly, they spoke of a few neighborly relationships between themselves and cristianos that took place within impoverished neighborhoods, but they also recalled the open discrimination against musulmanes in public and professional settings. However, the increasing marginalization of musulmanes in Ceuta did not become a priority for Spanish officials. There was neither a need to create institutional mechanisms to exclude musulmanes (because they were not citizens) nor was there a threat from musulmanes (or anyone else in Ceuta) under a heavily militarized exclave and dictatorial Spain. Therefore, without institutionalized discrimination and organized resistance, the marginalization of musulmanes was normalized as Ceuta's social, economic, and political order.

Because there were no public struggles between cristianos and musulmanes in those days, most stories that musulmanes tell from this period relate to work. Life was work, and musulmanes served as the reserve labor force for a limited local economy. Karim described one of his work experiences.

Here in Ceuta there used to be fish factories where fish were preserved. There was a factory in the port [that] had its fleet of small boats. They went to sea and fished there, and they went all the way to Morocco. They fished tuna, bonitos, and other sort of fish. They would preserve [the fish] in aluminum cans and send it to the peninsula.

During the summers, I would come here from Morocco. In those days [1970s], I must have been fifteen or sixteen years old. One time they needed people to work. They went up to a neighborhood where musulmanes lived and started yelling to see if anyone wanted to work for the factory. They picked us up in a truck. I got in the truck and went with other men that were older than I was and other young ones that were still one or two years older than I was. I started the first day. I had to take the fish from the boat, put it in a basket, and give that basket to another man, and he passed it on to someone else until it got to the truck, they unloaded it, and the basket would come back to the boat. A lot of times the boats would come in the evenings, sometimes during the day, but most times in the evenings. We would start working at six in the evening and work until seven the next morning.

When we finished working, we would get in the truck and go to the factory where they would pay us. They paid about two hundred pesetas. Today that would be equivalent to about one Euro with thirty cents. I am talking to you about the 1970s, '71, '72, '73. It was low pay, but with so much need, we did it, but without job security or anything. You worked your shift, they paid you, and you went your way. But we did not work every day. With that money I bought myself clothes, and I saved a little money to buy books, paper, and pencils.

Even though they lived in Ceuta, there was little opportunity for musulmanes to study or gain professional skills that could assure them social mobility. Still, that was often much more economically promising than anything Morocco had to offer in those days, with the exception of an advanced education for those that could afford it. Karim received most of his education, including a university degree, in Morocco, but his case is rare among musulmanes in Ceuta. Most musulmanes from his generation, like Ahmed and Rachid, do not have a high school degree. Karim had to leave Ceuta for long periods with very little money to receive an education. The majority of musulmanes continued to work without the option of social mobility. Rachid and Ahmed explained,

AHMED: Before, [musulmanes] in Ceuta did not give their children an education, they would put them in school and by the time they were six they left it.

RACHID: Since we had the statistical identification card, even if we wanted to study, it was hard to continue. And besides, the majority of us here were here to work. But with the statistical identification card you could not go to college.

AHMED: You could not study if you could not leave this place.

The statistical identification card (SIC) amounted to an official recognition of musulmanes' statelessness from 1956 until the 1980s. The SIC is a part of musulmán history that often comes up in conversations about the past. I gathered that older musulmanes share stories with the younger generation about the SIC because musulmanes who are not old enough to remember it often mentioned it to me. The SIC was not a document with any guarantees. In fact, with Morocco increasing its claims over Ceuta, the treatment of musulmanes who frequently crossed the border by Spanish authorities worsened.

Writer Mohamed Lahchiri (1950-), born and raised in Ceuta and currently residing in Morocco, relates his story of the SIC in a published book. The following story took place during the time leading up to the Green March in 1975, when tensions between Morocco and Spain increased over the control of Western Sahara.

> Well, during all this time I would cross customs posts every vacation, every three months (during the summer months almost every day), because I first crossed them as a student, and when I started working, I did it as a professor . . . At the beginning there were no problems with passports or visas; I think that the guys from Ceuta would pass with school identification card or with the Statistical Identification Card. Later, one day, after the Green March, in the police station of Los Rosales [a peripheral neighborhood near the border], in my tiny fatherland, they took away the famous Identification Card while telling me that I no longer had a right to it because I was working in Morocco. That is, because I was working in Morocco, I lost the right to be from Ceuta, from my tiny fatherland. I protested by writing several times, but they did not pay attention to me. That decision launched me into an Odyssey-like race to find, with tooth and nail and everything at hand, a Moroccan passport if I wanted to see my own, I mean my family, my old friends, my street buddies, our bars, and an "etcetera" as long as the border that marks the tiny fatherland.[27]

What is striking about Lahchiri and other musulmanes' stories is not only the powerlessness that many musulmanes felt before state officials but also the apparent tranquility with which an increasingly segregated segment of Ceuta's society negotiated their political condition. As I mentioned above, the lack of migration alternatives and an oppressive Spanish state are mostly responsible for this. Musulmanes appear to have successfully negotiated state-imposed obstacles because their "statelessness" was secondary to their knowing that they were in their land. Consider, for example, this exchange between Rachid, Ahmed, Mohamed Mustafa, and me:

RACHID Almost everyone was like an immigrant. There was no document that could attest to us being from Ceuta.

AHMED And the document that we have did not give us the right to anything.

RACHID Nothing, nothing, no rights at all. Around 1969 . . . they made available to us a statistical identification card which gave us the right to work and social security, but nothing else.

AHMED Not even to catch a boat.

RACHID Not even to catch a boat. And if you wanted to do that, you had to go to the government and ask for a pass that would specify how long you could travel and where you were going. You had either a specific trip or fifteen days. If it was fifteen days, you would have to leave your identification card in the government. And if you had to go to Algeciras, then you could only go to Algeciras, if you are going to Cádiz, then only to Cádiz, not anywhere in the Spanish territory, only to . . .

MOHAMED MUSTAFA To the exact place, to your destined location.

RACHID Exactly. And let me tell you something. [That happened] to people that were born in Ceuta, people that were born here, with birth certificate from here, and not even them [could travel to Spain].

AHMED And [if you caused] any problems or [made any] false move, the police would pick you up and take you over there [Morocco].

MOHAMED MUSTAFA When exactly was this?

RACHID From '70 on up.

MOHAMED MUSTAFA Things have gotten better, no?

RACHID [ignoring Mohamed Mustafa's question] And with the identification card it was only enough to live and nothing else.

AHMED [responding to Mohamed Mustafa's question] The situation of musulmanes improved with the Socialist Party [PSOE].[28]

MUSTAFA Later on, in '79 or '80, they changed, instead of a statistical identification card, they gave us a residency card. And when they gave us that residency card, we had a right to go the peninsula, and then there was an obligation . . . a facilitation or obligation? I do not know . . . of the European community or of Spain [to give us the residency card]. Then they gave us Spanish nationality, papers to register locally, that was in the 1980s.

GABRIEL But what was your citizenship in those times? Before '85, '86? If someone said to you . . . say someone came from China and asked you "hey you, what are you Spanish or Moroccan?" What would you say?

AHMED I would say, "I am from Ceuta." I was born in Ceuta.

RACHID Or Moroccan, because how can you be Spanish and not have Spanish nationality. Moroccan because Morocco is the place of origin, because our parents are from Morocco. Originally, they were Moroccan.

The power of the state is again evident in this conversation through the limitations of mobility to the Peninsula, where presumably a musulmán might have had the ability to improve his marginalized condition. It is also interesting that Rachid, like Karim, also says that musulmanes were treated "like an immigrant." Rachid also believes that Ceuta is his land. He adds to Ahmed's response that not only are they from Ceuta, but also from Morocco because that is where their parents are from. Indeed, many musulmanes continued to arrive from Morocco throughout the years and made Ceuta their home because musulmanes' sense of community has, over the years, simultaneously accounted for Ceuta's geographical continuity with Morocco and its uniqueness as a Spanish/European territory in North Africa.

Given these experiences, it is easier to understand how "being from Ceuta" has different cultural significance for musulmanes and cristianos. This "being" is experienced in the particular assemblage configuration of Ceuta's racial niche. Furthermore, being within the racial niche generates intersubjective spaces where the embodied racial self can result in racialized political subjectivity (as I have documented for some Afro-Puerto Ricans in the previous chapter) or be subverted by an unracialized, liberal, egalitarian dream (as racialized minorities have experienced in the US Midwest).

It is also important at this point of musulmanes' life stories to flag the question of class. Musulmanes and cristianos coexisted in poverty. However, the concept of class cannot supersede the experiential nature of the same material conditions (or lack of). Instead, the experience of material conditions is intricately tied to collective forms of being from Ceuta and in the racial niche of Spanish colonization and interethnic hierarchical dynamics in northern Morocco. In Ceuta, different senses of belonging evolved in an increasingly segregated landscape between musulmanes and cristianos. The political situation would eventually improve for musulmanes, but not before they were once again treated "like an immigrant," this time quite literally.

CIVIL CONFLICT (1970S–2010S): THE PROMISE OF LIBERALISM AFTER LIFETIMES OF INEQUALITY

Economic development and political change in Ceuta and Spain impacted the relationship between musulmanes and cristianos. The overall economic marginalization of most musulmanes did not prevent a small group from achieving financial success.

With the closure of the border between Spain and Gibraltar in 1969, Ceuta's economy picked up the market for duty free goods (Gold 1994).[29] In addition, with the end of Franco's dictatorship in the mid-1970s and Spain's prospective incorporation into the European Community in the 1980s, the question of musulmán citizenship took a dramatic turn. The public debate over citizenship had a lasting effect on the social and political scene. Karim first explained the impact of economic mobility on musulmanes.

First, let us look at one thing. Let us look at the social process of Ceuta. From the 1970s . . . until the 1980s . . . and until recently.

First, the musulmanes of Ceuta belonged to very poor families. They went back to Morocco [periodically] and lived any way they could. Their acquisitive power was inferior, less than today. There came a time when the city enjoyed a commercial and economic expansion that translated into an openness of the musulmán collective that, at that time, lived [mostly] in the neighborhood of El Morro on up [midway between El Centro and the border].

Musulmanes did not come to El Centro with the frequency that they do today. Rarely would one see one or two in very small groups of musulmanes that were able to, in quotation marks, "integrate" within the whole of the cristiano community. Why [were they able to integrate]? Because they mingled with them in the bars. Drinking and alcohol enabled relationships. Some ate ham and drank like authentic Spanish cristianos. They dressed in the same manner, they spoke Spanish, and they did not usually respect the religious habits of their parents. To their parents, they were rebellious people. To themselves, they were free people. [This was] from the '60s, '70s, until the '80s.

Then, that small group was able to integrate themselves. A group of forty or fifty people, no more, people who had acquisitive power that was higher than other musulmán families. Why?

Because they had parents that were merchants, they belonged to families with money, and they could permit themselves the luxury of being around here [El Centro] all night, drinking, talking, in a car, in a motorcycle. But the rest [musulmanes] did not come here [El Centro] for any reason, only when they needed to deal with some bureaucratic document or buy some clothes for themselves, nothing else. They did not sit in cafeterias, in bars, or nothing because they did not have that acquisitive power, not because they rejected all of this.

Now, the cristiano community of El Centro with time . . . clashed [with musulmanes] because those were very fast contacts, not over a long time. It was very sudden, and [musulmanes] imposed themselves with their acquisitive power. [Musulmanes] would go into a business and buy many clothes. The owner could not reject money that came with such ease. One went out and another came in. Then an acceptance started to exist based on that acquisitive power of a people of Muslim origins . . . [correcting himself] it is an error to say "of Muslim origins," I mean "musulmanes." Some have their nationality documents, some do not, some with residency, but the vast majority now have their DNI [National Identification Document, i.e., citizenship]. They are Spaniards.

Let us say that it was a forceful acceptance because the merchant wants to make money, and the buyer has to buy . . . An acceptance, yes or no? It is still an acceptance, but if it were not because of their acquisitive power, then that contact would not have occurred so easily.

And then, with that same acquisitive power, many musulmanes began buying businesses in El Centro. Before, in the nineteen seventies, there were hardly any, only a few. Now there are more. The service workers are also now musulmanes. So we can say that the ethnic fabric of El Centro has changed. Before you could see the European element dominated almost ninety-five percent over the rest. Not now. One wanders the streets and sees that there are different races. Now you can see even blacks, not "blacks," [sub-Saharan] Africans. You can see Pakistanis with the phenomenon of immigration, Algerians, Moroccans. Before you could not see this mix. In the '70s and '60s you could not see so much mixture, today you can. Then there is slight contact. Just by seeing that there is ethnic diversity, that means that there is contact. In the '70s, there was none until the beginning of the '80s. I mark that [time as a] transformation . . . I see that transformation at a local level as a result of that acquisitive power.

Karim was not one of these early merchants, but he maintained close relationships with some of them. His narrative suggests that a small group of musulmanes in El Centro impacted the broader relationships between musulmanes and cristianos. In addition, it is interesting that Karim points out the different behavior some musulmanes with money undertook: "Some ate ham and drank like authentic Spanish cristianos." Economic class and religion were not only a divisive factor between cristianos and musulmanes, but also among musulmanes.

Rosander (1991)[30] explains that by the late 1970s she observed different criteria for prestige among musulmanes in Benzu. First, length of residence in the community distinguished the families that first came when the quarry opened in the 1920s from the more recent arrivals from Morocco. Rosander explains that older families were proud of the ability of some of their men to speak Spanish well and relate to Spanish traditions. Second, adherence to Islam mattered and was exclusive of many Spanish social practices adopted by some musulmanes. Third, musulmanes who accumulated wealth by taking advantage of Benzu's changing economy also gained prestige in the community. The last two criteria were characteristic of newer immigrants from Morocco, "thus, two sets of criteria for meritorious [Benzu] male behavior co-existed in [Benzu] in 1978. One set, beginning to be experienced as 'old-fashioned,' was Spanish-oriented; the other was more explicitly Morocco-and Islam-oriented" (Rosander 1991:36).[31] To this, I add that most new immigrants were not well off and were in a worse socio-economic situation than older families. One can imagine an emerging racial niche in which class, religion, geography, language, and tradition crisscrossed a community that, nonetheless, had to imagine itself against the Spanish Other. Also, it is important to note that not all musulmanes are equally bilingual. Those who had more interactions with Spaniards had a better command of Castilian.

Regardless of these internal differences, musulmanes confronted a civil crisis together in which the Spanish state threatened them with expulsion. After the transition to democracy and the establishment of the 1978 Spanish Constitution, Spain moved to join the European Community (EC). As a precondition for admittance in the EC, Spain agreed in 1985 to adopt a comprehensive immigration policy. Given that, at the time, Spain was not receiving large numbers of immigrants, the aim of the 1985 Immigration Law was to regulate the legal condition of foreigners already in the country (Arango 2000).[32] The new law did not consider the special circumstance of musulmanes in Ceuta and Melilla. Initially, the law left most musulmanes without any possibility of gaining citizenship. After many protests by musulmanes and counter protests by cristianos who wanted the law to be enforced as it was initially passed, the national and local government came to an agreement that allowed musulmanes to gain citizenship. These experiences shaped the way musulmanes currently imagine and represent their community in Ceuta. Karim passionately remembered the struggles endured by musulmanes in those days:

KARIM The musulmán collective felt the emergence and writing of the [1985 Immigration Law] like a bucket of cold water. I remember well how the collective felt a feeling of massive insecurity in a rapid manner. Everyone felt insecure. They thought badly about the future. Those that had the Statistical [Identification] Card—the famous Statistical Card—said that they would go to Morocco. The few that had [Spanish] nationality felt protected.[33] The rest were divided with many opinions, and no one knew what was going to happen. Musulmanes formed associations that were in the front of fighting for those rights. Some had a political discourse different from the rest. Some favored the nationalization of musulmanes. Those that had been born here had their rights, everyone should naturalize. [Others] defended the idea of receiving residence status. There were older people that thought that to naturalize would mean that they could no longer be completely musulmanes. That [thought] does not just come from the 1980s, that comes from many decades before in the 1950s, from the 1940s to the 1960s.

MOHAMED MUSTAFA Do you think that has a lot to do with the Protectorate?

KARIM [No,] not the rejection [of Spanish nationality]. [It was] the religious interpretation of certain faquíes[34] . . . They [faquíes] said that those [musulmanes] who had a Spanish nationality or had a nationality different from that of their [Moroccan] origin would distance themselves from Islam, it was haraam.[35] It was a sin to naturalize, it was illicit to naturalize. That is why a lot of musulmanes that were in the army did not opt for nationalization. And they went to Morocco. Some died there. Some stayed here and did not naturalize.

In those times, the system for nationalization was harsher than it is today. One had to meet many conditions to get a Spanish nationality. Not like now.

Then, from the end of 1985, 1986, some associations were formed. One of them went out to negotiate with the Ministry [of the Interior] in Madrid so that they could transmit to the [musulmán] collective the results of the negotiations. Later, another group came out that rejected the results of that negotiation.

In Melilla, a parallel thing occurred. An organization was formed called Terra Omnium, headed by the famous [Aomar] Dudu. Dudu was a man educated in economics, did not know any Arabic or [Tamazight[36]]. He only knew Castilian. He was eloquent, and he was the head of that organization and carried out the negotiations. Then there were problems, and he left for Morocco.

Here in Ceuta, there was an association of musulmanes . . . Then others were founded, and then others. But the first, the first was in the beginning of 1985 and was called La Comunidad Musulmana de Ceuta [founded by Ahmed Subaire]. And then came Mohamed Ali's [Asociación Musulmana de Ceuta], and then came La Comunidad Musulmana del Estado Español, and then another community, and then many came out. Today there are many. But the first was born like that. It was born in a historical context mixed with agony, fear, misunderstandings, rejections, a bit of everything. There was chaos, social chaos. No one knew what was going to happen.

Then, around that time, some ceutíes started to naturalize. A plan called El Plan de Dotaciones Básicas was drafted in Madrid to facilitate living conditions: remodel the peripheral neighborhoods where musulmanes lived. From that plan, not even twenty percent of the total volume of investments was put into the Muslim neighborhood. In that epoch, [musulmanes faced] the problems of nationalities and that plan.

In the years 1986, '87, '88, people started to naturalize. Starting from 1987 on up, with more ease. And now they [cristianos] blame the socialist party for nationalizing the people of Ceuta.[37] That is why many people that are cristianos see musulmanes that are naturalized as incomplete citizens, that there is no reason for musulmanes to have been naturalized, as if it was a political deception, as if it was a penalty. They [cristianos] wanted to see [musulmanes] with that little card [SIC] or something equivalent, but without all their full rights, and I am talking of civil rights, all of them.

Now, what good is it to have Spanish citizenship if there is no right to work? There is right of work, but there is no work. You have right to housing, but there is no housing. You have right to culture and education, but there are no facilities. There is immense social failure among musulmanes. People fear for the future of their society. And when there is social failure there is juvenile delinquency and there are [other] problems . . .

I had the same fear and the same preoccupation as the rest [of musulmanes]. That is why I also tried to do something about it. To see what solution they would find to the problem. Would people naturalize or not? Would people accept the nationality or not? If people did not accept Spanish citizenship, what would they do? Would they opt for other documents that guaranteed their rights? What rights could that card or document guarantee? Would all or some be in the same situation as the rest or not?

They [musulmanes] had feared that with a residency card they could be expelled if there was a problem. [Some musulmanes were expelled, and] from those expulsions . . . many have suffered. And there are people that still live in Morocco that were expelled in the 1970s. Expelled from here, people born here, their parents here, their grandparents here. They had that right to

Spanish citizenship and not be exposed to that social careless-ness. Expulsion, getting kicked out of your land is hard, to rip someone from their land is hard. Many people who left here in that manner did not know about Morocco, or they did not want to live there. They had their parents here, their brothers and sis-ters here, everything here. It is not easy for someone to be forced to leave his or her land, not in search of bread like an immigrant, but to be exiled. Not self-exiled, but an imposed exile. It is a good thing that there were not that many [that got expelled]. Few people [that were expelled] have returned. And some have returned and have only obtained a residency document knowing that they have the right to Spanish citizenship.

Karim's oral history progressed from a time when musul-manes felt utter confusion about their relationship to the Spanish nation and state, to a political self-awareness of a musulmán community in Ceuta. Note how Karim shifts his narrative from one of acquiring rights to one of fulfilling the promise of those rights when he states, "Now, what good is it to have Spanish citizenship if there is no right to work? There is right of work, but there is no work." Musulmanes like Karim who wanted to become Spanish hoped for a favorable outcome, but feelings of hostility between musulmanes and cristianos still linger. The massive counterdemonstrations by cristianos in the mid 1980s against the nationalization of musulmanes were a public testa-ment to the social, political, and economic segregation that had existed in Ceuta for many years. Although demonstrations were peaceful in Ceuta, similar demonstrations by cristianos in Melilla resulted in violent confrontations between civilians.

Karim continued to explain how the political experiences of the 1980s changed the way musulmanes thought of themselves as a community. The group of political and community leaders that emerged from the citizenship crisis allowed musulmanes to play down previous divisions within their community.

[Musulmanes] passed from an ethnic time to a political time. They analyzed their visions towards a political future, leaving in the past what had passed. Those negative [relationships] have softened within the community of musulmanes.

[Division among musulmanes] has changed for a better future of internal understanding. People do not have time to think about what has happened in the past. These young people do not know that history. They may know a little, but not enough to judge others. They are politicized. People understand their present situation. They want a job, a house, an education, they want to meet their basic necessities.

Karim's account reflects his political ideology, which primarily favors the attention to musulmanes' needs in Ceuta. The political and civic engagement of the musulmán population from the 1990s until the late 2010s has not been as great as Karim would have liked it to be. Although musulmanes like Karim speak of themselves as being part of a politically unified community of musulmanes, the reality of borderland life (especially criminal activities) continues to affect how musulmanes achieve civic unity.

In the 1990s, as sub-Saharan and North African immigrants began using Ceuta as an entry point into the EU, the Spanish-Moroccan border tightened. The EU financed a double-wired fence along the border, and Spanish state agents heavily patrolled the area, although Moroccan residents from the province of Tetuán (adjacent to the border) and ceutíes have special permissions to cross the border for commercial purposes (and thousands of Moroccans do so daily). This fortification of the

Spanish-Moroccan border is part of a wider phenomenon of Western European immigration control (Brochmann and Hammar 1999; King, et al. 2000).[38] However, because of increased security along the border and an increase in European demand for hashish, criminality along the peripheral neighborhoods in Ceuta increased dramatically.

> RACHID Many of our young people are bad. And because of a few, all, almost all are marginalized. People [cristianos] think, "This moor!"
>
> AHMED What has happened is that there came some years of drugs. And some people have, because of a scarcity of work, started to make easy money . . . A kid who is thirteen, fourteen, that sees his father making money that way [selling drugs] does not want to study anymore.

Many of these smugglers and drug traffickers also took up smuggling immigrants into Ceuta and the peninsula. The Spanish government's response to criminality along the border significantly reduced crime in Ceuta at the turn of the twenty-first century. However, part of the response to crime by the local government involved the formation of the Unidad de Intervención Rapida (Rapid Intervention Unit or UIR). The UIR often clashed with residents in peripheral neighborhoods, and that resulted in a rift between the local police and musulmanes. In addition, the arrest in December 2006 of eleven suspected terrorists in the peripheral neighborhood of Principe Alfonso fueled existing concerns by ceutíes and Spain's national government about Ceuta serving as a gateway for terrorists entering Europe. The arrested men planned to target different civil and military location in Ceuta. Some had previous criminal records, and that furthered stigmatized musulmanes' peripheral neighborhoods as possible breeding grounds for terrorists.

So far, I have suggested that three overlapping periods have differently contributed to musulmanes' sense of community within Ceuta's racial niche assemblage. Whether as colonial subjects, stateless noncitizens, or unwanted troublesome citizens, the sense of belonging to Ceuta has been a common thread to musulmanes through time. These identity shifts have been contingent on the changing relationships between cristianos and musulmanes. In turn, these changing relationships have yielded to various fragmentations within the musulmán community, which, in the last two decades of the twentieth century, had to come together to fight for their rights as citizens of Ceuta, Spain.

KARINA'S TRANSGRESSIONS: REMIXING MUSULMANES' STORIES

The preceding historical narratives detail the dialogical emergence of musulmanes' sense of community within Ceuta's racial niche, which is a different sense of community from that of cristianos. Although I have not claimed that these different senses of community have evolved independently of each other, I have not yet critically addressed the power dynamic between cristianos and musulmanes beyond the obvious colonial and political economic domination of the former over the latter. I now want to briefly explore the effects of racialization in shaping musulmanes' sense of community by considering a particular set of life stories that illustrate how a racial hierarchy that dates back to the Spanish Reconquest and colonialism in the twentieth century plays an important role in shaping how musulmanes give meaning to their interactions with cristianos. Most importantly, in this section I delineate intersectionality's nature within a racial niche assemblage. Karina's stories are the stories of many musulmanas, and whatever contradictions emerged in her narratives are contradictions that are often ignored in popular political discourses but are always a potential source of flourishment.

Theory and ethnographic practice came together when I began to make sense of my conversations with Karina. Her stories allowed me to make sense of a body of data that I accumulated during many conversations with cristianos, mostly in bars, about the sexual mystique of musulmanes. Similarly, although many of her life stories began with details of specific events, they often returned to domination of some cristianos over musulmanes. Again, these aspects of her stories also allowed me to make sense of the many racist comments that some cristianos made about musulmanes during informal interviews.

Fatima Mernissi's work (1994; 2001)[39] further influenced how I thought about the implications of crossing boundaries, including sexual ones, between Western European and North African peoples. I view the theoretical framing I have given to my work with Karina as a transgression, given my mishaps as a male anthropologist trying to include as many musulmanas in my sample to form balanced interpretations. Nonetheless, I have tried to maintain a balance between presenting Karina's life stories as a voice from within the musulmán community and my desire to place it within the broader context of this chapter.

Mohamed Mustafa secured a visit with Karina, a musulmana in her late thirties with five children. She had been married in the past to a cristiano (with whom she had children), lived outside of Ceuta for several years, and occasionally practices Sufi rituals that most musulmanes do not considered legitimate Islamic practices. As such, Karina is not the "normal" musulmana that Rosander (1991)[40] describes in her study. In fact, many musulmanes in Ceuta would not consider her a "good Muslim" because she has not respected culturally prescribed boundaries between men and women and cristianos and musulmanes (Rosander 1991:273).[41]

Immediately after we sat down to talk, I realized that her answers to some of the standard questions that I had were much different from previous life stories that I had recorded. I first asked Karina to talk about how the relationships between musulmanes and cristianos had changed over the years.

> Absolutely, everything has changed. Before the girls were more united, there were fewer secrets among [female] neighbors. Today, all I see is evil. They envy you for nothing. And if they talk to you, they talk to you [gesture implying doubt], I do not know. Before, we [females] were more united. I see that everything has changed. Friendships are not the same, the [female] neighbors are surlier. And if they come to see you, it is to take what you have, and to see if you eat more or if you eat less. And we were not that way before, that is the way I see it.
>
> Before the girls were more united, the [female] neighbors got together. Some kneaded, others brought flour, and we made meals between four or five neighbors. Now, I see that everyone does their own thing. They are very closed off.

It was clear to me that Karina had other "changing relationships" in mind than that of cristianos and musulmanes. My initial reaction to her response was to redirect her so that she would describe the changing relationships between musulmanes and cristianos. I thought that perhaps she had misunderstood my question.

> In this neighborhood it was mostly payos [i.e., cristianos],[42] there were a lot of payos. And we used to get along very well. If there

was a wedding, they would be the first ones to come. And if there was something else, they were the first. We did it very well, we have not had any problems. . . .

If my mother had to leave with my brother, who has always been sick, and had to take him out of Ceuta, a Spanish [cristiana] woman would stay with us. And she would stay with us during the night, give us food, bathe us. We used to get along very well. But now it costs me a lot of trouble to leave my two-year-old girl with someone. It is hard . . . The problem that we have is with our own people, our own race.

Karina had understood my initial question, but she felt that musulmanes have hurt her most. Still, she did talk about a past in which musulmanes and cristianos got along. Karina was referring to relationships that existed in the late 1960s and throughout the 1970s. The Spaniards that lived in Karina's neighborhood at that time were mostly low-rank military men, and other ceutíes described her neighborhood as a hangout spot for gambling and prostitution. Regardless, her neighborhood has been poor since Karina lived in it. The class similarities that brought musulmanes and cristianos together in the 1920s still bridged gaps within an otherwise divided society. Karina finishes her description of the good relationships between musulmanes and cristianos by again redirecting her narrative toward the problem being "with . . . our own race."

As Karina continued narrating stories from her life, I realized that her family shaped her initial negative posture towards musulmanes in our conversation.

KARINA In my parents' house, we were ten, then my mother and father. Ten brothers and sisters. We got along well. Very beautiful. Well, I got along best with my brother Mohamed, may he be in glory. I got along very well. He was a guy that suffered a lot. Because my father was a man that liked women a lot, he liked drinking a lot. He was the kind of man that what he earned was only for him. He used it to go on the streets and have fun.

My mother has struggled, and she suffered a lot for us. My mother worked for us, and has struggled a lot for us, and it is very difficult . . .

I was working on the streets by the time I was twelve. She had to take me out of school and put me to work. And we moved the household forward. Because I am the oldest.

Then I had a brother that also started working when he was young, thirteen or fourteen years old. Then he got into drugs.

GABRIEL Was he into drugs as a user or seller?

KARINA He started consuming. He started selling with a woman, and, apparently, he then got hooked. He died when he was twenty-nine. He left two children, and it has been very hard.

On another occasion, I offhandedly asked Karina to tell me about the most mischievous thing she did as a child.

I spent two days hiding after my father hit my mother, and I went to the police . . . [I spent] two days hiding under my grandmother's bed! [laughter] Two days hiding under my grandmother's bed because my father was going to give it to me. And I saw my mother lying on the floor bleeding, and I walked barefooted from my house to the police several blocks away, and I told the police, "Policeman, policeman, policeman, my father killed my mother!" So I got in their car, and they brought me back here. I will never forget that.

Eventually, Karina did get a beating from her father. The emotional scars that she carries from her childhood have influenced her perspective on what is most troubling in life. Yet her stories also reveal the growth of a young woman whose life did not conform to the Muslim ideals, and that got her in trouble.

I left this place [Ceuta] with a policeman who knew my father. He was from Algeciras. And he would come here on duty, but on the weekends he would go back. So I left my house when I was sixteen or seventeen. It all happened because I liked a young man [not the policeman], and when he came to ask for my hand, my father said no. So the young man asked me to either choose my parents or him. I was stupid, I was stupid. So, I chose him and left my parents.

So I went to live with him. After four or five months, the problems began. So I went to the police headquarters and told this man [the policeman]. I told him "I no longer have a life in Ceuta." All my family lived here, and I was in no condition to live here, and this land was too small. So he told me that if I went with him to his house, I could work there, and I would not need anything.

One day I met him at the port, and he passed me through . . . He talked to the civil guard—that was much different from what it is today. And yes, he took me out and I worked in his house. I was working very well in his house.

After some time had passed, one day he told me that my father had told him that if he saw me to tell me that a letter had arrived to get Spanish citizenship. I did not believe him because I thought that he was going to trick me and bring me home, and then my father would beat me. And I was scared. He told his wife, and she told me that she would go with me to fix the papers and then we would come back with her husband. We did just that and came back. I arranged my papers, bought the stamps, and went to the courthouse . . .

I went back with these people, and he [the policeman] picked up my identification card and brought it to me. And with this married couple they had me as . . . well, she could not have children, so I did not consider myself as a worker, I thought I was another member of the family. She could not have children. I was her passion. They even changed my name. I was everything to her. If she had an argument with her partner, she would come to my room and tell me everything, and if I had problems, I would tell her.

But then there came time when her friends started telling her that it was impossible that her husband loved me as one would love a daughter. That it was too much love. Because when this man got paid, he would take us both out. The truth is that they had a beautiful marriage. Then one day her sister told her that it was impossible, that there had to be something else going on. Then she got jealous. They would fight all the time and she would tell me to go to my room and not come out. This man was used to me being like his daughter. I cooked, cleaned, ironed, and fixed his bags. But then, his wife would no longer let me iron shirts and wanted to do it herself. So I got tired, and I noticed that they did not treat me in the same way they did in the beginning. And I left that house.

There are two contradictory elements in Karina's narrative that I want to highlight. On one hand, she had to leave the confinements of Ceuta because she could neither bear to live with her partner nor with the shame of leaving her house without her father's approval to live "illegitimately" with her partner. Karina's behavior was shameful to her family and her immediate community. On the other hand, Karina then took a job as a domestic servant in the house of cristianos. Initially, she describes her relationship with the policeman and his wife as family-like. However, her situation degenerated to the point where she was merely a domestic servant and made the object of suspected sexual indiscretions by the wife and the wife's sister.

Because Karina was a domestic servant and a suspected object of desire, she embodied a "musulmana" through her class and perceived sexuality, even though one of the main reasons that she left Ceuta was because she was not a "good musulmana." Karina's predicament mirrors broader relationships between musulmanes and cristianos within the domestic realm of cristianos. Rosander (1991)[43] argues that musulmanas have been generally restricted and socially unavailable to cristianos in Ceuta. However, this is partially untrue because even Rosander notes that many musulmanas worked in cristiano households. Today, many musulmanas from Ceuta continue to take care of elderly cristianos and do domestic work. In addition, hundreds of Moroccan women cross the border every day to do similar work. Within cristianos' domestic realm, musulmanas have become accessible in a context of labor domination.

On one occasion, Francisco, a cristiano in his mid-thirties who works for the government, was talking to me about mixed relationships in Ceuta. He first told me that families of musulmanas are more likely to object if someone from their family goes out with a cristiano/a. I asked him if it was more difficult for a cristiano to date a musulmana since her parents would be more protective over her. He said that it was more difficult, but that it happened occasionally. In fact, he had dated a musulmana when he was younger, and he warned me, "Don't be fooled. They are very tricky, they are no saints." He then added that there was truth to his grandparents' generation belief about Moor women being sorcerers that put cristianos under a spell. I met three other men like Francisco who had relationships with musulmanas but did not marry them or have children with them. The way these men related these stories to me conveyed their enjoyment of a sexual adventure that was limited by the willingness of musulmanes as a community to open up to cristianos casually dating musulmanas. Many cristianos also objected to the marriage of a cristiano and a musulmana, but that was not something that Francisco and the other men emphasized during our conversations. Of course, there are a few marriages between musulmanes and cristianos, but they are rare.

I found the most explicit racialization of musulmanas' bodies in the stories of cristianos in bars, usually late at night and after heavy consumption of alcohol. In Melilla, Driessen (1992:182–188)[44] documents the extreme situation in which Moroccan prostitutes and Legionnaires depended on each other for economic sustenance and sexual gratification, respectively. In Ceuta, similar relationships have existed between military men and prostitutes that are either musulmanas from Ceuta or Moroccan. However, during my fieldwork, the most visible prostitutes in the city were all Moroccan women who walked the streets of El Centro. After asking around, it appeared that most customers are older cristiano males, although most of the former clients that I met are cristianos in their thirties. One late night, three ex-military men in their late twenties crudely told me how Moorish women could cast a spell. These men had slept with some musulmanas that were prostitutes and others that were not. They told me that Moor women moved differently in bed. As men, they could enjoy and handle their bodies in a more passionate and forceful manner.

I do not want to overemphasize the domination of cristiano males of musulmanas at the expense of overall gender inequality. My point is that cristiano males' sexual desires of musulmanas exists in Ceuta in a manner that assigns a mystical and exotic (if not prohibited) quality to musulmanas (Cf. Thompson 2006).[45] Had it not been for Karina's stories, I would have had a difficult time contextualizing other life story in this chapter. Her stories at the margins of what most ceutíes would identify as an ideal "musulmán" brought needed ethnographic clarity to social realities of domination and racialization.

Karina was neither a prostitute nor a typical servant in a ceutí household. However, her stories pointed towards the intersections where cristianos routinely exercised power over musulmanas. When I again asked Karina one of the usual questions regarding the current political situation in the city, she again bypassed my framing of politics relative to musulmanes and cristianos. She responded, "There is not enough help for women." She described how the lack of opportunities for musulmanas sometimes led them to the ugly world of drugs.

I know them [women who transport drugs] as if they were my sisters. One . . . well you know that when a woman is on the streets and dedicates herself to the life, then she gets married, and then, the defect that we musulmanes have is that every time there is a fight or an argument, he brings it out and tells you that "I have done this and that for you."[46] They tell you that they picked you up and gave you a home and gave you everything. There comes a time when she said, "no more." She was not going to take the beatings or a man that insulted her, so she separated.

And here in Ceuta it is very difficult to find work, and it is difficult to get any help. To have any sort of help, you need many friends. As they say, "if you do not have a godparent, then you cannot get baptized."

So this woman started going with other people, and they offered her the job of transporting drugs. It has gone very well. She has a house, she has a car, she has her kids, and it has gone very well. But one day, not long ago, they [police] caught her.

Most women transport drugs within their bodies because few manage to own a vehicle in which they can hide their merchandise. The woman in Karina's story lost her freedom and her ability to provide for her children. Karina's concern for women in such situations demonstrates the extreme social and economic isolation that some musulmanas face in Ceuta. Almost all of the prostitutes in Ceuta are musulmanas or Moroccan, and the drug trade overwhelmingly affects musulmanas. These facts again point toward the effects of a social and racial hierarchy.

Over the course of hours and days in which I talked to Karina, I found that a pattern emerged within her stories. Her and other women's experiences outside the realms of the ideal musulmana religious identity were usually closely followed by encounters with cristianos framed by male/female and cristiano/musulmana domination. For example, one can appreciate this pattern in one of Karina's most recent experiences as a city employee cleaning streets and public lands.

KARINA I spent seven months last years working in El Principe.

GABRIEL Working on what?

KARINA On the Plan de Empleo.[47] I would leave my house at six in the morning and wait for my colleagues in El Centro so I could go because I was afraid. And I was working there, and they [musulmanes from El Principe] came out with knives to insult us, throw rocks at us. We always had to be with the police around us.

GABRIEL Why did they do that?

KARINA Well, I do not know. Because women should be at home and men should be working.

GABRIEL And all the people that worked were women?

KARINA Yes, we were thirty, and all thirty were women.

GABRIEL And it was seven months?

KARINA Seven months in there. Seven months.

GABRIEL And those incidents with knives and rocks, were those at the beginning or throughout?

KARINA No, that was at the beginning. At the beginning they [musulmanes from El Principe] behaved very badly. They threw water at us, threw rocks. We would go knock at a door to ask for water, and they would tell us, "Why don't you go to the municipal building to ask for water? Are you not working for them?" They behaved badly. But that was not everywhere, only certain neighborhoods. For example, we had to do Principe Felipe [below Principe Alfonso], and people there made tea for us, gave us pastries, and breakfast at ten in the morning. They brought us breakfast, water bottles, juice, everything. But the upper part [Principe Alfonso], I do not wish that on anyone. Principe Alfonso, that was horrible.

GABRIEL And were the majority of women musulmanas?

KARINA All of them. All of us were musulmanas. And there were women who had been raised in El Principe and still have families in El Principe.

GABRIEL Did that receive any public attention, or did that stay between all of you?

KARINA That whole thing stayed between us. The bosses said that they were going to go to the press to question why people did such things. But it never got anywhere. It remained that way. It stopped. One time, photographers came and took photos and everything, because one time had it not been for the fire truck, things were going to get really bad. Because someone pulled out a knife on one of my colleagues, and she went crazy because, as it turned out, she was on drugs, and she was doing methamphetamine. And she started to fight, and some people could not believe what had happened. It was a big mess. They stopped all work and said they were going to fix it. But what the heck, they did not do anything. At first, they put two police patrols next to us. But the police were afraid. At ten in the morning they would leave and say, "Everything here is calm." Then they would leave and not come back. Those were horrible times, especially in the upper part [Principe Alfonso].

We protested and asked to be switched [from El Principe]. They said "yes, yes, yes," but then came an order that said "no." They said that neighborhood was assigned to us, and we had to stay there until we finished.

MOHAMED MUSTAFA Did they send all the workers that were musulmanes to El Principe, or were all workers musulmanes?

KARINA It was only musulmanas . . . and we protested, because there were Spanish women, and they did not send one with us . . . And we asked why the Spanish women had been sent to El Centro. They were all in El Centro doing gardening or in San Amaro [Park]. There were no Spanish women at the border or in the country with us.

GABRIEL And who made that decision?

KARINA I do not remember their names, but they were both Spaniards. And they told you that it was not in your best interest to complain because we can easily fire you. One time I had a huge argument because they sent us to a ditch, so we went down and worked hard because it was July. And you know that when the sun is hot, and in a ditch full of weeds, if there is some animal, it comes out. So a girl that was with us, who must have been two or three months pregnant, and a snake passed by her feet that made a loud hissing noise. The girl stayed put, and all of us were screaming. And the boss came and took her to the hospital, and she almost lost her baby.

So, we refused to go down [to the ditch], and the Spaniard boss came and said that we had to go down there, that we were workers and that is what we were supposed to do. So I told him that since he is the boss, he should go. My colleagues can go, but I am not going. He wanted to go down, so I told him you can go down if you want, I will give you my clothes if you want, but I am not going. He then asked me for my identification card. I asked him what for, and he said so that I can fill some papers and you can go home if you want.

GABRIEL So what happened?

KARINA Well, we protested but it was of no use. We protested for three days, but they said that they would not pay us our monthly wages, so we had to swallow it and go down.

In this story, both musulmanes and cristianos fail Karina. Yet, there is a familiar pattern in her stories where some musulmanes reject her or other musulmanes, and then cristianos in positions of power oppress her and other musulmanas. Karina, her coworker who uses drugs, and the woman who was caught smuggling drugs all have engaged in behavior outside the boundaries of accepted musulmana identity in Ceuta.[48] Nonetheless, their treatment as subordinate and racialized musulmanas creates a racial continuity within the musulmán community that goes beyond religious identity and is imposed by cristianos from without.

Fatima Mernissi, a Moroccan sociologist and feminist, wrote extensively about the dangers and wonders "crossing of borders" between men and women, native and foreigner. At the very end of *Dreams of Trespass* (1994),[49] Mernissi wrote of a conversation that she had when she was little with Mina, an elderly slave in the Harem where she grew up. After Mernissi tells Mina how her nine-year-old boyfriend would no longer be allowed to be in the women's communal baths, Mina tells her that life would be more difficult because she would be "ruled by difference." Furthermore, that difference would always divide the powerful from the powerless. Mernissi concludes her book saying,

"I asked Mina how would I know on which side I stood. Her answer was quick, short, and very clear: 'If you can't get out, you are on the powerless side'" (1994:242).[50] Similarly, it is clear to me that Karina has lived on the powerless side of racial and sexual hierarchies. She admits to having made mistakes in her life, but her transgressions of boundaries in Ceuta have only resulted in her meeting the rigidity of class, gender, racial, and sexual borders. Still, I cannot help but think of Karina's lifestyle as resilience and a struggle to flourish.

Although Karina's stories did not directly relate her experiences to what Joane Nagel (2003) refers to as the crossing of "ethnosexual frontiers," her stories helped me make sense of the experiences of other ceuties that have crossed those frontiers. Nagel explains that people who cross those frontiers do so with different intentions; they are settlers, sojourners, adventurers, and invaders (2003:14–36).[51] In Ceuta, the children of musulmanes and cristianos are called mestizos, the mixture of Spanish blood. More frequently, cristiano males fanaticize about the adventures of crossing and returning from those boundaries. Women like Karina and some of her friends represent a physical racial crossing point for those cristianos. In turn, those sexual transgressions reinforce and are reinforced by other forms of domination in nonsexual social spheres. Of course, musulmanes, male and female, also participate in their own racialization through the religious valorization or commodification of their bodies (Cf. Goldstein 1999).[52] Karina's insistence on the problem "being with our own race" points to the many occasions in which musulmanes have rejected her for crossing boundaries that cristianos otherwise maintain to oppress musulmanes.

My intention in presenting Karina's life stories has not been to reduce all forms of cristianos' racialization of musulmanes to sexual transgressions, although I do hold that sexuality has an important role in the formation of racial categories. Instead, her narratives disrupted, in my fieldwork and this chapter, the stability with which many cristianos and musulmanes take for granted their collective identities. Although her stories do not appear as historical in the sense that they do not conform to the other ceutíes' communal notions of the past, they do bring clarity to the complexities of the racial niche. I realized in the "here and now" of our interviews how Karina transgressed boundaries in her life stories. One moment she denounced musulmanes for throwing rocks at her and her coworkers, and minutes later she was talking about the discrimination perpetrated by the cristianos in charge of her working crew. One might interpret Karina's life as unstable, but I beleive her life represents the instability and ambiguity that has shaped musulmanes' sense of community throughout the twentieth century, which are different efforts to flourish that Ceuta's racial niche has constricted.

I have explored how the histories of musulmanes in Ceuta have yielded as a sense of community tied to Ceuta as a border-land that is neither here nor there relative to the Spanish and Moroccan states. Nevertheless, the physical, bureaucratic, and hierarchical nature of the borderland that encompasses Spain, Morocco, Ceuta, and the Mediterranean Sea has affected how musulmanes imagine themselves as part of broader communities outside of Ceuta. While cristianos address the incongruity between Ceuta and peninsular Spain through narratives of Ceuta's Spanishness, musulmanes have struggled to expand their communal ties to any broader community outside of Ceuta. For cristianos, Ceuta is Spanish because they are Spanish, and musulmanes are Spanish because they are ceutíes. As Karina's story shows, the sense of community that musulmanes have relative to Ceuta is far from homogenous. It is often best understood from the social margins and the many transgressions that musulmanes experience during their lifetimes. These different senses of community are crucial when interpreting Muslim political ideologies in Ceuta's Local Assembly.

THE ILLIBERAL STATE
AS A RACIAL NICHE

The life histories of musulmanes highlight a phenomenon that historically has been parceled into histories of nation-states and peculiarities of liberal democratic history. Across states, elite representations of nations and governmental ideologies have subverted the illiberal history of liberalism, perhaps even the illiberal nature of liberalism. In this final section, I waver over the nature of liberalism intentionally. I am convinced that for my interlocutors in all three ethnographic sites covered in this book, their respective community histories demonstrate illiberal beginnings; however, claiming the illiberal nature of liberalism is outside the comparative scope of this book. Still, I believe there is a more abstract argument to be made suggesting that it is safer to assume historical illiberalism than not.

To make an anthropological claim about liberalism, it is necessary to conceptually bridge political philosophy and social facts. That is, we cannot assume a neat separation between our social reality and our political, philosophical ideals. The latter are intricately contextualized by the former. However, we also cannot renounce the possibility of formulating new political, philosophical ideals from everyday or social scientific understandings of our social realities. Anthropology, therefore, is part of what John Dewey describes as "the commitment of liberalism to experimental procedure."[53] Dewey utilizes the then-nascent anthropological concept of culture to argue against an absolutist individual in classic liberal philosophy.

> Liberalism knows that an individual is nothing fixed, given ready-made. It is something achieved, and achieved not in isolation, but the aid and support of conditions, cultural and physical, including in "cultural" economic, legal, and political institutions as well as science and art. Liberalism knows that social conditions may restrict, distort, and almost prevent the development of individuality.[54]

Dewey argues that because the growth of individuals necessitates social institutions, the classical liberal opposition of individual freedoms and government intrusion is unsustainable. However, because social conditions change over time, Dewey's experimental method is meant to be a trial-and-error approach to democracy. This approach depends on our analysis of social conditions and, given our analysis, adequate governmental interventions to promote individual growth vis-à-vis individuality and liberty. It is important to remember that individuality in Dewey and others' formulation was closely related to some form of social equality. If one's social condition (race or religion, for example) prevented the full pursuit of liberty, then one's unequal social condition curved the liberty that ideally belongs to the individual.

Anthropology, of course, can offer a reading of social conditions at various scales. In the two hundred to three hundred thousand years of humanity, state-level societies are novel. Bands of hunters and gatherers were the norm up to roughly ten thousand years ago, followed by tribal societies and the independent emergence of states across the globe. States are characterized by hierarchies and division of labor, so by the time we get to the liberal ideologies of the Euro-American revolutions, much of the social realities of inequality that liberalism governed were already set for thousands of years. A more micro-historical overview of the social groups within states between the seventeenth and nineteenth centuries reveals that race and class explain the hierarchies that are the subject of this book. Between-state hierarchies also followed a racial order. Gender hierarchies are universal for social groups within the state, but hierarchies within gender groups also follow the same racial orders.

These evolutionary and micro-historical scales are undoubtedly foundational for my conceptualization of the racial niche. The micro-historical scale is also key in contemporary formulations of systemic racism, which holds that histories of racism have generated contemporary racist ideas (conscious and unconscious) and racist behaviors.[55] However, systemic racism's conceptual condemnation of liberalism is redundant in the sense that racial hierarchies precede liberalism, and racism does not need liberalism to operate. Instead, the illiberal nature of liberalism lies in the political, philosophical void of how government might promote the individual growth of citizens who were denied liberty before and after the installation of liberal democratic governments. More specifically, and to follow Dewey, the processes by which experimentation could take place to improve the pursuit of liberty for racialized peoples were not only institutionalized but also fiercely prevented from being institutionalized.

In Ceuta, we can concretely observe the illiberal mechanisms in place with the ratification of the 1978 constitution following decades of fascism. The colonization, racial subjugation, and economic exploitation of musulmanes shaped their sense of community and sociopolitical marginalization in Ceuta. This racial duality is proper to Ceuta's racial niche, and it explains how musulmanes' struggles for citizenship did not improve their social marginalization and are the foundation for so-called parties of Muslim persuasion. The struggles to be recognized as equal citizens in the 1980s are not even the sort of liberal experimentalism that Dewey had in mind because his experimentalism assumes that all social groups have citizenship. However, once citizenship was forced upon the liberal order, experimentalism with regard to the social equality of musulmanes was either absorbed by traditional Left-Right parties or musulmán parties engaged in clientelism. The first musulmán parties are now known to have been a failed ideological experiment for remedying musulmanes' inequality (the PDSC mentioned at the beginning of this chapter is one of them). However, the UDCE, the so-called party of Muslim persuasion, fashioned a political style to win seats in Ceuta's Local Assembly and experiment with liberal political ideologies that drew on musulmanes' local sense of community. Their success has been limited, but their political ideals are an extension of the transgressions that people like Karina undertook as they formed new subjectivities in Ceuta's borderland.

The US and Puerto Rico have similar intersecting histories of illiberal liberalism. Full citizenship for racialized minorities has come decades and centuries after the constitutional birth of the US. In the case of Puerto Rico, not even full constitutional autonomy has been reached due to colonialism, an important macro-niche context for the colonial nature of racialization of Puerto Ricans and Afro-Puerto Ricans (see Chapter 4). The era of civil rights struggles in the US, like those in Ceuta, are not a proper form of liberal experimentalism; they are the context for equality from which liberal experimentation takes place. Also, like in Ceuta, in the US, the governmental, political, ideological void to remedy social inequality was absorbed by the Left,[56] and struggles for racial equality are mostly made outside governmental politics through social movements and social celebrations of multiculturalism. In Puerto Rico, blackness is not even a broadly recognized body with political subjectivity. What all three ethnographic contexts do have in common is that the same cultural processes of differentiation for racialized peoples are at work in the illiberal nature of liberalism and the racialized bodies from which styles for flourishing emanate. We have seen that these styles have limited political governmental influence. Chapter 6 examines how these styles confront their illiberal beginnings within the parliamentary halls of governance.

6

LIBERAL ANTIRACISM AND THE
ENDS OF FLOURISHING

The emergence of the *Unión Demócrata Ceutí* (the Ceutí Democratic Union or UDCE) in the early 2000s necessitated formal language to talk about parties composed of and voted for exclusively by musulmanes. In response to this need, ceutíes came up with the name *partidos de corte musulmán* (parties of Muslim persuasion). This grammatical construction expresses the influence of musulmanes on the nature of the party.[1] This label is more subtle than it might appear. The UDCE did not incorporate religion into its political agenda, unlike many other Muslim parties in Morocco and the Middle East. In addition, UDCE party leaders went out of their way to say that they are open to all people, regardless of their culture or religious credence.

Exactly what is a "party of Muslim persuasion" if it has no religious affiliations to Islam and is open to all ceutíes? That a party of Muslim persuasion is composed of musulmanes might seem like an obvious answer. That, however, is not a satisfactory response when faced with the fact that none of the local parties formed by cristianos since the 1980s has received the appellation "parties of Christian persuasion" in a city where its people commonly refer to each other as cristianos and musulmanes.

The difference is that what ceutíes would call "parties of Christian persuasion" falls within the accepted range of liberal democratic political groups and ideologies in Ceuta and Spain; therefore, they do not need to be identified by the ethnic or religious party composition. Parties of Muslim persuasion, on the other hand, straddle a political fence in which they have attended to the needs of musulmanes as a marginalized community and carried on with "politics as usual"; that is, attending to the needs of all citizens through the formulation of public policies for the common good. Therefore, the name "party of Muslim persuasion" retains its ambiguity in its English translation.

In my years of fieldwork with musulmanes involved in local politics, it became clear that musulmanes' histories as colonial subjects, stateless noncitizens, and unwanted troublesome citizens shaped members of the UDCE's political ideologies. Elsewhere, I referred to this relationship between political and economic history and political ideology as "knowing the political,"[2] where seemingly the same political and ideological alignments can have varied cultural logics. How one comes to know the political economy through social experience constitutes how knowledge of the political is reasoned, expressed, and felt within liberal democratic governmental order. A so-called party of Muslim persuasion in the case of the UDCE is, in fact, a party that is like social democratic parties in Ceuta, Spain, and Western Europe. But for UDCE members, their social democratic ideologies are rooted in a sense of belonging to Ceuta. The life stories presented in Chapter 5 serve as a cultural foundation for understanding how musulmanes, a racialized minority, have transgressed governmental, political boundaries by forming parties of so-called Muslim persuasion, a political style for flourishing that emerged from Ceuta's racial niche.

In addition to examining the political ideology and actions of musulmanes from the UDCE in the Local Assembly, this chapter engages in a comparative analysis between the styles for flourishing in and outside government politics. My objective is to demonstrate that liberal democratic governance and political ideologies can place serious obstacles in anti-racist social projects. That is, styles for flourishing in the racial niche can quickly find the limits, the ends if you will, in the belly of democratic liberalism. Although I am not presenting these ends as a necessary outcome of anti-racist efforts in governance, I argue that styles for flourishing elsewhere in the racial niche can also inspire strategies for anti-racist politics and governance.

A RACIST BUDGET AND INTERRACIAL CONFLICT

In the May 2019 local elections, the national right-wing populist party, Vox, won six out of twenty-five seats in the Local Assembly, enough to force the ruling center-right *Partido Popular* (Popular Party or PP) to enter into a coalition with some other party to rule. Vox was only bested by two long-established national parties, the *Partido Socialista Obrero Español* (Spanish Socialist Workers Party or PSOE) on the Left and the PP on the Right, which obtained seven and nine seats, respectively. However, in the November 2019 national elections, Vox obtained more votes than any other political party in Ceuta and was able to fill Ceuta's single seat in the National Assembly.

During the second week of January 2020, Ceuta's news media began circulating leaked text messages from Vox Party leadership in Ceuta's Local Assembly. In the leaked texts, Vox representatives lamented Spaniards who accept *moros* (Moors, which is considered a slur by Ceuta's musulmanes and other Muslims throughout Spain) being shoved down their throat, predicting that a Third World War would one day commence against Islam, and envisioning military resistance against moros if political means fail.

A few weeks before the leaked texts, in December 2019, Vox negotiated with the center-right PP to make a pact on Ceuta's annual budget. The Vox-PP pact replaced the tenuous coalition that the PP had made with the PSOE months before—a necessary but unusual Left-Right pact made to prevent Vox from having political influence. However, before the final round of debates to approve the annual budget, scheduled for January 28, 2020, the leaked text messages put the PP in a difficult political position: break with Vox and negotiate a new budget or approve the proposed budgets with the support of a party seen as extremist and racist by other political organizations and parties.

When the parliamentary debate to approve the budget began on January 28, Mohamed Alí, the lone representative from the Caballas Party and former leader of the opposition in previous legislatures, began his first intervention with the following declaration:

> Today, we must begin the budgetary debate—and I will shortly explain why—with another murdered woman. In Cataluña, today, the seventh one [of the year], a woman has been murdered.
>
> And you might ask, "this is a budgetary debate, and what does this have to do with it?" Well, it has a lot to do with this budgetary debate. This is a debate, and this a budget in which the PP, the traditional ruling party of the City of Ceuta, has found support in Vox. And this is not a minor issue. Your finding support in Vox to pass the budget converts this budget into a fascist budget. And I am going to explain it to you. . . .

This budget is converted into a fascist budget, and it converts it into the government's instrument to govern in Ceuta. An instrument that is supported by the ideas and votes from Vox.

Vox, as everybody knows, denies gender violence. You have shared that perspective and have equated gender violence with "intra-family violence." And this is one example of the movement directing the trajectory of this city, the principles of this city, and the city's ruling. You have a responsibility, and your responsibility is to put up a true wall that keeps out fascism. Fascism. That is your responsibility. Because if you don't do it, Mr. Rontoma [PP's spokesperson] and Mr. Vivas [Ceuta's parliamentary president], I will direct myself to you because I have known you for a long time—if you don't do it, then you no longer represent me. Because I am going to sincerely tell you, I am outraged with the government of my city. With the government of my city!

Alí went on to discuss some of the ambiguities surrounding the release of the text messages, focusing on the fact that Vox leaders had not explicitly denounced the content of the messages and that one Vox party member in the assembly had left the party, citing the Islamophobia of party leaders.

If you want to argue that this is a budget of cultural diversity, a budget of the Four Cultures, you cannot have the support of Vox. It is that simple. It is that simple. You cannot have Vox's support to pass your budget because if you do, then you share their ideals. You become complicit. It is that simple.

In his response to Alí, the representative for the ruling PP party, Carlos Rontomé Romero, argued that Alí's party was unwilling to contribute to the debate since they were rejecting the whole budgetary plan; Alí was not presenting amendments to specific parts of the budget. Regarding the PP being complicit with Vox, Rontomé explained that there was a difference between complicity and making political compromises to govern effectively. Besides, Alí had already insinuated that the PP had fascist tendencies, so now he had found a new target in Vox.

Furthermore, and most directly engaging Ali's argument, Rontomé criticized Alí for denying freedom of speech to Vox's representatives who had not been convicted of any crimes. Whatever hateful discourse Vox might have expressed, Rontomé accused Alí of recirculating hate speech. The correct thing to do, explained Rontomé, would have been to make sure that citizens stayed calm and formally accuse Vox in the courts. Visibly upset, Alí often interrupted Rontomé. In one instance, Mohamed Mustafa, a Caballas party member and the colleague who helped me collect the life stories in Chapter 5, began shouting from the public seating area and denounced Vox as "racist" and "fascist," which resulted in President Vivas expulsing him from the Assembly Hall.

That tense atmosphere carried over to the following morning of January 29, 2020, for the Assembly's monthly session. The first proposal was made by Mohamed Alí's party. The proposal urged Ceuta's government to make a formal appeal to Spain's national government to negotiate a treaty with Morocco that would regulate customs at the Spanish-Moroccan border along Ceuta's southern boundaries (the rest of Ceuta's boundaries are water, with the Atlantic Ocean to the northwest and Mediterranean Sea to the north, east, and south), especially since Moroccan border officials had disrupted the flow of commercial goods in previous weeks. The PP refused to back the proposal because they had a different ideological vision for dealing with the border crisis that involved a more independent, economic development of Ceuta. However, Vox explicitly refused to engage the content of the proposal, citing Morocco's history of violating all previous treaties with Spain. Furthermore, Vox took the opportunity to sarcastically claim that Alí's party knew a lot about treaties since they had allegedly recently been in contact with two assembly representatives who had left the Vox party after the leaked voice files.

Immediately after Alí took to the microphone for a second round of debate, the conversation quickly turned into a shouting match that had nothing to do with the proposal on the table and everything to do with the racist conversations. Vox representatives called Alí shameful, and Alí called them the same in return and continued, "and in addition to being shameful, you are cowards. Go out into the streets and tell [Muslim] people you want to kill them . . . and tell them that you want to kick them out [of Spain] . . . have balls, don't write it in chats."

The President stopped the assembly session and called for a break, at which point the two arguing parties kept shouting at each other as they rose from their seats. Alí marched across the assembly hall towards the Vox representatives, stood face to face, and invited them to go outside and tell people [musulmanes] that they wanted to kill them. There were eventually separated by other representatives.

IF NOT OF MUSLIM PERSUASION, THEN WHAT?

In private conversations, my musulmán politician interlocutors were quick to argue that they are not, in fact, "of Muslim persuasion," and their Leftist politics corresponded to their upbringing in Ceuta. Their political ideology was, therefore, shaped by a shared intercultural lifespan with other ceutíes, not just Muslims. It was that fashioning of Leftist politics through lifetimes of racialized experiences that I later sought in the fashioning of boxing styles in a US boxing gym. Leftist politics and boxing are, presumptively, nonracialized practices that are stylized based on racial experiences. Similarly, Muslims and Black/ Latin youth utilize these styles as strategies for flourishing in their respective racial niches.

The behaviors and ideologies of political leaders, like Mohamed Ali, are best understood when considered relative to lifetimes of the racial experiences presented in the previous chapter. Ali's family and community experienced being out of place in Spanish and Moroccan polities that placed borders and exclusive citizenships on the people who became Ceuta's musulmanes. That exclusion, combined with a conflictive integration into Ceuta's civic spaces, explains how traditional, liberal democratic, Leftist ideologies did not properly capture the political ideological minds of many of Ceuta's racialized citizens. Of course, the diversity of musulmanes' life experiences also explains the presence of musulmanes in all political parties, but one must take note of the musulmán electorate embraced Ali and his political party. The political styles of Mohamed Ali and so-called parties of Muslim persuasion are seemingly out of place in liberal because of how these political styles can and cannot translate liberal democratic forms of government. Although not always successful, Ali was able to use his parliamentary forum to question why his politics were popularly labeled "Muslim persuasion" while supposedly nonracial political ideologies were not labeled "Christians" or "fascist," which would register elsewhere in Spain, Western Europe, and the US as "white."

More importantly, Mohamed Ali, the UDCE, and the Caballas Coalition engaged in attempts to flourish through governmental, political actions. These sorts of actions are precisely what most people in Spain, the US, and Puerto Rico think of when asked, "How does one go about solving a social problem?" However, liberal democratic governance has been in historical and philosophical tension with racialized styles of politics for hundreds of years,[3] especially in the three racial niches discussed in this book.

Historically, the ancestors of Black and Mexican Americans in the US, Afro-Puerto Ricans, and Muslims in Ceuta were socially excluded from the autonomy, equality, and freedom promised by the ideal liberal democratic citizen. Mills argues, "Race and liberalism have been intertwined for hundreds of years, for the same developments of modernity that brought liberalism into existence as a supposedly general set of political norms also brought race into existence as a set of restrictions and entitlements governing the application of those norms. This interrogation is relevant to political philosophies and political ideologies of those in power."[4] He argues that liberalism is historical fiction and suggests "racial liberalism" to think about the precise processes through which liberal democratic governance excludes collective racial experiences from democratic deliberation.[5] The history of musulmanes and parties of Muslim persuasion lay bare the inner workings of racial liberalism by exposing what a liberal ideology that emerges from racialized bodies looks like. Anti-racism from within liberal democratic governance has the sensitivity to perceive a budgetary instrument as part of the racial niche. Put differently, the budget that Ali questioned as racist is made racist by its complicity in a racial niche that Ali and his community have experienced for generations; therefore, the liberal democratic assemblage is disassembled and reassembled as racial liberalism.

Although I take Charles Mill's reconceptualization of liberalism as racial liberalism to be a fundamental starting point for any social scientific analysis, it is perplexing how scholars, not to mention public figures in popular culture and politics, often omit the historical foundation of inequality within liberal democratic orders. People continue to speak of liberal democracies in historical contexts as if liberal democracies are not illiberal or undemocratic. However, the historical foundation of inequality within liberal democratic orders is the most serious because it obfuscates the philosophical tension between liberal democracies and racialized styles of politics. The US, Puerto Rican elite, and Spain were all engaged in colonial and oppressive processes during the times that racialized populations became part of body politic, so how can one possibly place racial inequality outside the core of political concerns for any political party striving for the common good? The notion that interethnic conflict occurs in places outside the liberal West is the ultimate, popular philosophical veil of how liberal democracies were built, not just on interethnic conflict but on interethnic (I would say racial) subjugation. The arguments between Mohamed Ali and the ruling party over a racist budget represent a rupture in this veil's seams.

During the parliamentary debate, when Ali explained that the ruling party's support from Vox converted the "budget into a fascist budget," he was criticizing ideals of liberal democratic foundations. How can government budgets be fascist or racist? In parliamentary debate, Ali provides a simple and complex answer. The simple answer is about coalitional politics: if Vox supports the budgetary proposal, then the PP is ideologically in bed with fascist ideologies. Carlos Rontomé's response is restricted to this simple argument: coalitional politics work in complex ways. Since Vox committed no crimes, there is nothing unusual about building alliances with parties holding different ideologies.

Ali's more complex answer equates governance with racial equity. "If you want to argue that this is a budget of cultural diversity, a budget of the Four Cultures, you cannot have the support of Vox." Here, Ali invokes the ideal of convivencia that characterizes Ceuta's multiculturalism between four cultures. Of course, in Ceuta, cristianos and musulmanes account for more than ninety-five percent of the population, so coexistence beyond popular multicultural rhetoric most often refers to the stability of cristiano-musulmán relations. Vox's explicit racism, which led to aggressive shouting and a physical confrontation in the Local Assembly, is a polluting force in a seemingly apolitical government instrument: a budget. The budget, in the ruling party's ideology, is an instrument of liberal democratic governance because it is for all citizens, regardless of whether one is on the Left or the Right. In fact, the Left-Right ideological splits has historically centered on how budgets are used to achieve liberal democratic ideals. However, Ali's argument denies the possibility of a budget functioning for liberal democratic purposes if explicit racists are associated in any way to the budget. Liberalism as illiberalism is racism that taints body politics, even if through a bureaucratic instrument like a budget.

The complexity of Ali's argument can be traced to how the UDCE and the Caballas Coalition came into existence. Ali's UDCE, which I have been researching since 2004 (they were first elected in 2003), called the liberal democratic bluff of citizenship by organizing a party with known friends and associates. Their original motivation for creating the party was that they felt left out of socialist parties, particularly in their belief that Ceuta's musulmanes had experienced decades of racism, and corrective policies were necessary beyond socialist redistribution. Ali and members of the UDCE also felt that the existing parties of Muslim persuasion flirted with Islamic and ethnic favoritism in an undemocratic way, too far from liberal ideals. Therefore, the UDCE drafted a party platform that aligned with social democratic policies, but there were a lot of specific policies that aimed to redirect resources to marginalized Muslim neighbors (based on greater need) and with cultural policies, like Arabic language and Islamic holiday recognition, that were on par with existing cultural policies shaped by cristianos and Catholicism in Ceuta. The UDCE was essentially attempting to realign Ceuta's civic-political assemblage to be inclusive of musulmán community histories.

Furthermore, the UDCE made an open call to all ceutíes to join their party. However, only a handful of cristianos responded to the call. I explained elsewhere that early on in the UDCE's existence, leftist politicians were suspicious of them, not based on public policy but because the UDCE's core group was all musulmanes, which raised suspicions that parties composed of cristianos did not equally raise.[6] Once elected as the main opposition party in 2003, the UDCE's main controversy came in their first term when they challenged the ruling party's budgetary support of Ceuta's carnival, particularly carnival activities that featured participants singing racist lyrics about musulmanes. Therefore, from its inception, the UDCE has been exposing how communal experiences—racial experiences that musulmanes in Ceuta actually talk about as "racial"—shape liberal democratic citizenship.

If their party platform was social democratic in resource distribution and included multicultural policies of identity recognition, then a fair number of leftist cristianos should have joined their cause. Many of those leftist cristianos who initially doubted the UDCE's composition did join forces, which is how the Caballas Coalition formed. However, over the years and in many conversations with UDCE members and affiliates, I have repeatedly heard how the threat of a party of Muslim persuasion is a cultural indication of what occurs when racialized people attempt to take governmental reigns. "That's why I can't stand that denomination!" Farid, who takes on different consulting roles with the party, explained how the concept of parties of Muslim persuasion was tricky in Ceuta. From a voter's perspective, Farid understood that once the UDCE joined forces with a leftist party composed of cristianos, they would lose support from some members of the musulmán community (which they did the first time they presented themselves as the Caballas Coalition). Musulmanes, as it turns out, were suspicious of all cristiano politicians after living on Ceuta's social, economic, and cultural margins for generations. However, Farid also knew that previous parties of Muslim persuasion did, in fact, engage in some forms of Muslim clientelism, and in 2003, the UDCE built a serious and inclusive (of all ceutíes) party platform. Therefore, although Muslim voters might have been voting for reasons of "Muslim persuasion," Farid and other party members were certain that their politics were purely liberal democratic.

UDCE's commitment to liberal democratic principles as foundational to ideological and governance practices demonstrates that racial experiences can result in political subjectivities that attend to the universal citizen *and* the reality of racial inequality, but the latter should be a precondition to the former. This is why the UDCE started a party from a core of musulmanes whose life experiences in the racial niche led to a style of governance prefaced by racial inequality. In an ideal world, Farid said to me as we walked up a still hill along Ceuta's northern coast in 2009, "[truly] being of Muslim persuasion would signal a commitment to resolve the historical injustices that we suffered as second-class citizens, but we govern in the interest of everyone. If we want to fix racism absolutely, then we need a different society. We would need a revolution."

For Farid, the numerical core of Muslims in a party should not be an obstacle for coalitional politics, and class-based Leftist politics should not stumble over debates of whether public policy should be about class or race. As for the Right and righting the wrongs of historical racism, the most that Ali could stomach concerning the budgetary debate was the decency of the center-right party to not add fuel to the fire of racism that had been burning since his ancestors' social existence was reduced to identity cards and the ambiguous statelessness of the Moroccan-Spanish borderland. Indeed, the origins of liberalism are illiberal, and attending to the political subjectivities of racialized people can be a path to more just liberal democratic practices. However, the ruling party's proposed budget was easily approved. The limited success of Ali and his political parties in the budgetary battle, like many other of their political battles, might signal that the ends of racialized styles for flourishing might be in the halls of liberal democratic governance.

The racial niche assemblage is malleable in many of its components, but democratic constitutions are a particularly difficult component to reassemble beyond anthropological theory and political ideologies. David Carroll Cochran argues, "Much of what ails universal citizenship when it comes to racial or ethnic minorities goes well beyond the formal realm of citizenship, so in many cases revising liberal theories of citizenship will do little if anything to overcome these shortcomings. Instead, what is required in such cases is that liberalism makes civil society itself the focus of efforts to rethink its conception of cultural pluralism and to find more flexible and pragmatic responses."[7]

By centering styles for flourishing in the racial niche, this book is an effort to focus on civil society to find more flexible and pragmatic responses to the problem of racial liberalism. I do not want to minimize what Ali and his allies tried to accomplish in Ceuta, but their efforts were one of many possible expressions of styles for flourishing within Ceuta, not to mention within the landscape of liberal democratic politics. Styles for flourishing need systematic input into governmental politics of ideologies. These systemic inputs need to be constant and evolving to keep up with the moving assemblage, especially since established liberal democratic parties tend to co-opt and freeze in time anti-racist politics as part of broader strategies for winning elections regardless of how effective those anti-racist politics are in the long-run.[8] Liberal democratic governance might be the end of flourishing, but the racial niche has generated communities of racialized people that are ready to continue reimagining themselves in order to make a meaningful place for racialized existence. Flourishing is an end in itself.

CONCLUSION

Ceuta's Assembly ratified the 2020 budget. Like many political battles that Alí, the UDCE, and the Caballas Coalition undertook from 2003 until 2022, their ability to institutionalize anti-racism as the business of liberals was limited. One could argue that they failed at musulmanes' racial uplift. First, Vox, like many other populist right-wing parties in Western liberal democracies, presented a significant challenge to politicians associated with anti-racist causes.[1] Second, in forming an alliance with a traditional leftist liberal democratic party, their appeal to musulmanes voters decreased. Third, voters in traditional leftist liberal democratic parties failed to see the purpose of changing their vote for a so-called party of Muslim persuasion. In short, the sociocultural conditions in Ceuta seem to be inadequate for change through the anti-racist leftist politics of Mohamed Alí. This should give pause to people in other liberal democracies who put too much emphasis on the diversity of elected officials as a way to resolve social problems concerning racial diversity because, in Ceuta, not only were there musulmanes in the Local Assembly, but they also had a distinctive ideological prism for translating racial experience into public policy.[2]

Similar right-wing political conditions concerning racialized minorities exist in the US and Puerto Rico. However, efforts to change the lives of at-risk Latinx and Black youth in boxing gyms seem entirely transformational when compared with the failure of Alí to oppose a racist budget. Similarly, in Puerto Rico, weekly bomba classes and social media postings about mangrove conservation reach hundreds of people who support the efforts of an anti-racist community organization. Of course, the scale of potential impact is vastly different in all three places (hundreds in the boxing gym, a few thousand in Piñones, and roughly fifty thousand musulmanes in Ceuta). But, to borrow an old boxing ranking scale meant to compare boxers across different weight classes, "pound for pound," the gym and the community organization appear to have been most transformational for people's lives. The gym concerns itself with whoever comes in, a small number of youths who, if not weeded out in the initial training process, can stick around for years of difficult training. Once in the system, some sort of significant change is almost guaranteed. In Piñones, the community organization touches, modestly but tangibly, the lives of many community members through various anti-poverty relief efforts and expressive culture that fill the community with pride. The community center also creates economic opportunities through ecological tourism micro-businesses and external grants for arts and conservation that employ community members.

A productive way to compare these anti-racist stylistic efforts is to consider them anti-racist liberal experiments (Dewey's liberal experimentalism).[3] With the metaphor of experimentation, the standard for evaluation is relative to the scientific method. A good experiment is good not because it is large but because of its scientific validity. Anti-racist scholarship focused on systemic racism calls for structural changes, which, in turn, is a call for governmental action. However, from the racial niche perspective, with multiple organismal levels and being a moving assemblage, intervention at just one level can be futile. This is especially true if we focus on the governmental level.

In all three cases in this book, governance is liberal and fueled by traditionally liberal Left-Right political ideologies, which I argued have been historically illiberal. Thus, anti-racism as a form of liberal democratic governance is precisely one of the most challenging levels for anti-racist interventions. However, I do not believe we need to renounce anti-racism through governmental politics. The UDCE in Ceuta was perhaps a failed liberal experiment, but that does not mean they or other racialized people elsewhere should stop trying. Indeed, as I completed this book, Mohamed Mustafa, my ethnographic partner in Chapter 5, formed a new political party, *Ceuta Ya* (Ceuta Now), which essentially starts from the coalitional endpoint of Caballas, a coalition between traditionally Leftist parties and so-called parties of Muslim persuasion.

I want to conclude with a reflection on coalitions as a style for flourishing in liberal democracies. Understanding liberal democracy as illiberal forces us to see citizenship contingent on a social group's racial experience within their racial niche. What we have traditionally considered race-based policies (e.g., affirmative action or multicultural holidays) must be reenvisioned, not as allowances for racialized and minoritized populations but as political ideals that always concern all peoples in democratic deliberation. Instead of ambiguous formations of voting coalitions brought together under traditional Left-Right policies, we should take cues from histories of survival elsewhere in the racial niche and place experimental forms of coalitional politics at the center of democracy as a way of life, that is, in a "more fluid and informal realm of civil society. After all, cultural pluralism itself exists in civil society as more fluid, contested, and informal phenomenon, and so sometimes it is better that liberal theory engage it on its own terms rather than trying to reproduce it in the formal realm of citizenship."[4]

Therefore, experimental, coalitional politics can and should reflect racial experiences and styles of flourishing at the individual and community levels, like boxers in a gym. As we saw in Chapter 3, the paradox of racial reification in the Mexican style helps us reimagine how anti-racist social policy need not always attempt to reeducate the public about racial stereotypes. Those stereotypes, like the Mexican warrior, are often attached to other forms of embodiment that can help young people thrive. In such cases, political coalitions can work to redirect government funding to and political advocacy on behalf of community organizations that are not traditionally considered to be effective in transforming individual and community lives. In Chapter 4, the case of Afro-Puerto Ricans presents an opportunity to reconsider the nature and place of grassroots, anti-racist activism, not as an example of democratic pluralism but as a political redefinition of the nation and state as primarily racialized forms of social organization. Grassroots anti-racism is not a corrective to an exclusive society but an assertion of experimental coalitions as foundational for democratic deliberation and governance.

In his eloquent political philosophy for coalitional politics in the US as way to achieve a "blacktopia," Derrick Darby recognizes the historical significance of Charles Mills's racial liberalism but takes exception to political solutions that amount to "small-tent" or "race-first" remedies.[5] These small-tent politics are either too narrowly symbolic or not substantive enough to have the buy-in of other racialized minorities and, more importantly, a significant proportion of white people for whom a color-blind and post-racial America is a desirable future.

Instead, "a realistic blacktopia is the just and equitable world we can pursue free from racial subordination and domination by engaging with other marginalized groups in a collective struggle against all forms of social injustice, subordination, and domination."[6] Invoking the previously presented philosophical principles of democratic pragmatism and continuing the pragmatist approach to race and democracy presented by Cornell West, Darby argues that political solutions like job training, workers' rights, criminal justice reform, educational reform, and a more progressive geographic distribution of low-income housing could be the sort of "big-tent" politics that coalitions can support and can withstand constitutional challenges.[7]

Darby's outlook provides a robust point of departure for thinking about the political philosophical consequences of the ethnographic cases and theory of flourishing in this book. Styles for flourishing in the racial niche, especially when read against Mills's racial liberalism, can certainly come across as the sort of organized community expression that yields the small-tent politics that Darby criticizes. That might be the case, however, the small- and big-tent metaphors are incomplete in helping us more precisely delineate how we get from democratic interests that range from the individual, to community, to racial group, to class, and all the way up to the big-tent coalition (which will vary, of course, depending on how voter representation is differently allocated to elected officials). We cannot assume that coalitional projects are, as they currently exist in various liberal democratic polities, coalitional in ways that are empirically reflective of community-based politics. The boxing gym and Puerto Rico demonstrate that it is quite possible for community solutions to social problems to have no clear political life outside those communities. And the case of musulmanes in Ceuta's government shows that racialized political voices have serious limitations in parliamentary coalitions and maintaining or growing constituent support. The problem with the metaphorical big tent is ensuring equal space for democratic deliberation and representation of varieties of life experiences purportedly gathered under the tent. This process of effective tent-gathering for those in the lower (and perhaps middle) classes is a problem endemic to liberal democracies.

Darby's big tent is a top-down ideological approach to social inequality. The coalition under the big tent gathers similar social groups that seek to redress their lower place in a hierarchical social order. The liberal promise of liberty, freedom, and equality is then pursued through coalitional policies that are pragmatically possible and desirable despite the diverse interests of social groups under the big tent. I do not disagree with this political philosophy and believe it is worth pursuing. In fact, reflecting on all the field sites covered in this book, I have observed a cross-cultural similarity in how people can look outside their communities and recognize similar desires and needs for social uplift elsewhere. That is, there are versions of the bigtent that are cross-culturally translatable.

But what concerns me about this top-down approach is that liberalism is already prepared to accommodate big-tent coalitional policies. I conceptualize this preparedness from a political economic perspective on liberalism's historical intertwinement with capitalism and inequality. Accordingly, big-tent coalitional politics, stripped of ethno-racial concerns and focused on class, is not significantly different from the proletariat that has been of concern to liberal elites, and ideologies of liberalism have always kept an eye (often a fearful eye given the possibilities of revolution) on the lower classes. In his intellectual, historical, and contemporary examination of Keynesianism, Geoff Mann argues that liberalism's concern with "the rabble" of the French

Revolution was ultimately refined by Keynesianism. "Contemporary liberalism in the capitalist global North is constituted, more than anything else, by an effort to ensure that capital does not alienate large enough proportions of the people to destabilize the social order."[8] Keynesianism, with its economic focus on unemployment and techno-bureaucratic solutions to economic problems is, consciously or not, an acceptable alternative to the fading concerns (for both bourgeoisie and proletariat) and actual impossibilities of proletariat revolutions.

The binding fibers between social groups in big-tent coalitions work because they adhere to the cultural logics of representative democracies. Individuals within social groups are like individuals in other social groups because they similarly pursue freedom through autonomous, property-based, electoral-governmental procedures. Anything outside this cultural logic of representative democracy is deemed extreme despite its contemporary recognition of Mills's racial liberalism. Mann, referring to the cultural logic of representative democracy as the logic of "procedural formalism" argues, "It is also the logic behind modern liberal democracies' institutionalized neglect of injustice in favor of endless fretting over the legitimacy of how it might be redressed. Yes, liberals acknowledge, horrible crimes have stained and sustained the past—slavery, colonialism, gendered violence, and oppression—but how can we 'undo' history? Sorry, but what's done is done. Like it or not, we're all in this together."[9] Being in this together is the cultural logic that accommodates big-tent politics within a long history of the liberal welfare state maintaining market stability, accommodating capitalist inequality, and preventing the "rabble" from engaging in revolutions or revolutionary thought.

Again, I do not disagree with Darby's political philosophic best solution to Mills's racial liberalism. I have raised my concern with how the big-tent solution already fits within liberalism's logic, especially Keynesianism, to highlight that we are not necessarily treading new grounds in either advocating for coalitional policies for effecting social change or engaging a governmental order ready to accommodate such demands. Perhaps Mann would agree with Darby, given his reflection on the prevalence of Keynesianism in modern times.

> The importance of acknowledging the ideological power of Keynesianism lies in the fact that it is one of the toughest obstacles any project of more-than-trivial social transformation will face. Currently, I would venture to suggest, it hegemonically defines the horizon of the peacefully possible for both those who understand themselves as in fundamental political opposition to much of the current liberal capitalist order and those whose dogmatic and unwavering faith in austerity is always tacitly backstopped by a Keynesianism-of-last-resort.[10]

If liberal welfare state technocrats are the pragmatic best option for social uplift, then, absent revolutions, the critiques of neoliberalism's withering of the welfare state and increasing governmental influence of private capital are more than justified in modern times.

The neoliberal critique is a triage for revolutionary politics looking to upend social hierarchies. Those revolutions might never come, but they are the most logical antithesis to the forms of structural inequality that characterize the racial niche and any human niche in liberal democracies. Similarly, the reduction of the welfare state in the name of returning power to communities for economic development should raise suspicions of how the liberal order relieves taxation of the wealthy and corporations in the name of something akin to free-market community problem-solving without radical or progressive potential. "The neoliberal trammeling of community development should make us skeptical of any 'new', historically emptied and cleaned up visions of community or society. It should not lead us to reject economic or market considerations, but it should make us wary of any uncritical acceptance of panaceas, dogmas or analyses that offer singular causes or solutions for poverty and injustice."[11] Similar suspicions have been raised in returns of power in the name of multiculturalism.[12] What then of styles for flourishing as ways of survival in the racial niche if modern liberalism triages revolutions and neoliberal policies can "empower" communities at the expense of the welfare state?

Styles for flourishing are a necessity of this revolutionary triage reality. Because styles for flourishing predate the current neoliberal era and liberalism, flourishing in the racial niche is not a singular and modernist response to liberal governance. Moreover, national coalitional politics are not a summative result of styles for flourishing and community efforts. Darby's criticism of Mills does not give enough weight to the empirical historical outcomes of big-tent efforts. Socialist ideals and policies, broadly conceived as class-based coalitional efforts, have consistently failed racialized peoples.[13] The history of Ceuta's musulmanes' exclusion from liberal orders and leftist politics is one example that applies to racialized people in the US Midwest and Afro-Puerto Rican communities. The more significant point that Mills's racial liberalism should help us realize is that the birth of liberalism in an unequal and racialized world hangs over many of the coalitional policies that the liberal state has already been willing to accept to save itself. The problem is that these policies need not equally work for all marginalized, lower-class groups. These policies need to work for just enough racially normalized social groups (e.g., white, mestizo, or Christian) or a middle class that has enough capital worth protecting. The capital is worth protecting because the seemingly necessary revolution that is necessary to upend racial liberalism could put lower- and middle-class capital at risk (whether the risk is real or perceived).

Styles for flourishing as revolutionary triage are necessary, not because they represent a neoliberal capitulation but because they have been a creative source of piecemeal changes to the racial niche assemblage (and the structural inequalities that characterize such niches). Styles for flourishing are a way to create dynamic and civically engaged ideas for the small tent, from which big-tent coalitions can then flourish. Both tents are necessary, but they must be attentive to how the racial niche is a complex and historically moving assemblage. Big tents should source their coalitional models from communities engaged in experimental democracy. Such coalitional experimentation needs to be open to various ideals of citizenship and belonging that include individual drive to uplift through economic and social freedoms and communal freedom through self-governance for marginalized social groups. Strict insistence on theoretical models of liberalism or republicanism does not conform with the realities of generations of exclusion of racialized people in purportedly egalitarian democracies where all individuals have an equal chance to pursue the liberal ideal.[14]

Moreover, the racial niche citizen makes dynamic life adjustments that require shifts in how the self, community, and racial group survive through self-worth, community action, and political participation, but these life adjustments are always in tension with the promise of inclusion and reality of the exclusion of liberal democracies. Racial experience yields liberal senses of individual pursuits of freedom and republican senses of collective preservation and self-government. What coalitional politics need is the institutionalization of dynamic models that allow for community-level styles for flourishing to have an equal ideological space with big tents of party politics. By dynamic I mean something much more profound than pollsters' data on political issues and social values. Instead, I argue for a purposeful destabilization of the Left and Right vis-à-vis community politics and experimental democracy.

This coalitional approach from styles for flourishing in the racial niche reimagines the old concept of racial uplift. Racial uplift might strike us as antiquated because there is an ambiguous assumption of racial inferiority that can be corrected by achieving the same level of civilization as white folks. Uplift implies reaching higher levels of civilization through social policies concerned with education, economic development, and the buttressing of civil society.[15] Figure C.1 illustrates this approach to uplift for a hypothetical "racialized group A" relative to a socially "dominant group B," which I call "liberal uplift."

Under liberal uplift, the social policies for uplift emanate from the liberal state and political ideologies that have been illiberal from historical constitutional beginnings. The welfare

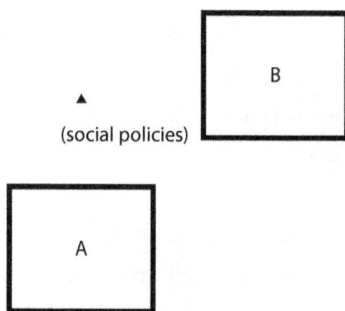

FIGURE C.1 Liberal uplift as achieved through liberal welfare state social policies.

state in liberal democracies is the axis around which questions of social inequality have been politically ideologized, and the social policies of social uplift have primarily relied on these liberal mechanisms. The checkered relationship between racial minorities and the Left demonstrates that, although social scientists might approach race as a class problem, the political ideologies for change tend to follow different and sometimes incompatible cultural logics.[16] Regardless, big-tent coalitions bypass cross-cultural differences when imagining social uplift, so the hypothetical uplift of group A in Figure C.1 can also be hypothesized as a coalition whose parameters for change are delimited by the liberal state.

As an alternative to liberal uplift, I want to propose liberal flourishing as a more democratic and promising model for ameliorating racial inequality. Liberal flourishing first proposes that coalitions be built in a dynamic relationship with Left-Right parties fueled by purposeful experimentation with styles of flourishing in communities. The question of class and the welfare state is not irrelevant here, but the strategies for survival in the racial niche do not occupy a secondary ideological space (as they were not for Mohamed Ali and the UDCE in Ceuta). The business of racial uplift becomes everyone's social problem instead of racial groups being the social problem. Racial uplift becomes societal uplift, echoing what Mohamed Alí expressed in private conversations and in public forums. "What is good for musulmanes is good for all ceutíes." Figure C.2 illustrates this coalitional shift.

Coalitional experimentation then becomes the focus of democratic deliberation, and such experiments should take place at various levels of the racial niche. I would even concede that Keynesianism technocrats have a role to play in outlining the potential translatability of such experiments as they pertain to

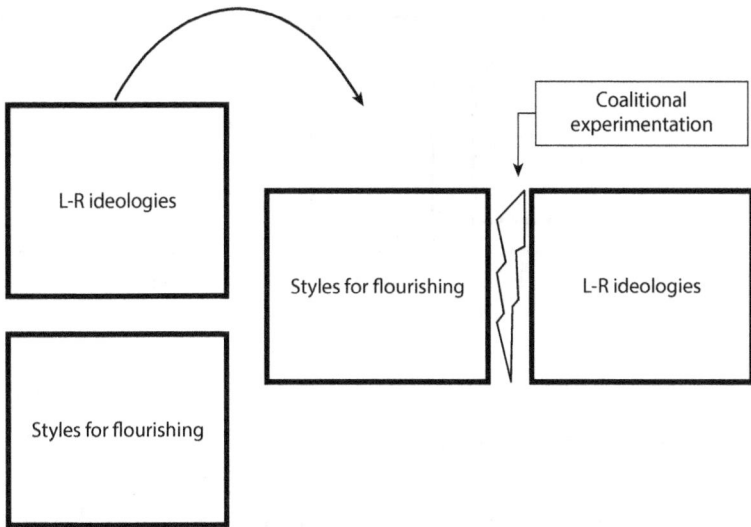

FIGURE C.2 Coalitional politics that place styles for flourishing on an equal footing with Left-Right ideologies.

economic development. However, under this model, the futuristic vision of what counts as racial equality after uplift occurs cannot remain ambiguous. There are economic limits to how much the welfare state can achieve equality for individual citizens. Left-Right political ideologies are primed to compromise (or fight over) wealth redistribution. Therefore, on the question of racial equality relative to economic class, I propose to leave that fight (i.e., revolution) for another day and, instead, aim for a more realistic measure of equality along existing economic classes. Figure C.3 illustrates what I consider to be the inevitable inequality within racial equality. Thus, our hypothetical racial groups, A and B, are equal but class inequality is also accepted or preserved.

I want to ensure that this last point about the inevitable inequality of racial equality does not come across as philosophical

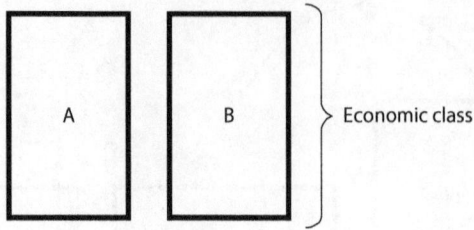

FIGURE C.3 Inequality within racial equality as a realistic goal for liberal flourishing.

pessimism. Instead, one of the lessons that I have learned in over twenty years of fieldwork in various racial niches is that styles for flourishing must flourish within existing political and economic frameworks. Boxing gyms filled with Latinx and Black youth often have police organizations as allies and work with courts that have been historic sites for the reproduction of systemic racism. Afro-Puerto Ricans look to the US for federal grants and Afro-diasporic allies outside of Puerto Rico as ways to protect their ancestral forest and fight anti-blackness within Puerto Rico, respectively. The UDCE took it upon themselves to represent all ceutíes through legislative actions even though cristianos, some explicitly racist, doubted the ability of musulmanes to represent the liberal interests of all citizens. Critical approaches to systemic racism are important to work from within spaces of the racial niche. However, short of revolutionary action, coalitional experimentation—emerging from racial experience and styles for flourishing—is the most authentically democratic way to do right by the history of survival in the racial niche.

NOTES

INTRODUCTION

1. Gabriel A. Torres Colón, "Fighting for Family and Glory: Hope, Racialization, and Exploitation in a U.S. Boxing Gym," *Journal of Sport and Social Issues* 46, no. 2 (April 1, 2022): 156–75, https://doi.org/10.1177/01937235211062626.

2. Thomas M. Alexander, *The Human Eros Eco-Ontology and the Aesthetics of Existence* (New York: Fordham University Press, 2013), 139.

3. Sarah S. Willen and Don Seeman, "Introduction: Experience and Inquiétude," *Ethos* 40, no. 1 (2012): 1–23, https://doi.org/10.1111/j.1548-1352.2011.01228.x.

4. Daniel H. Lende and Greg Downey, *The Encultured Brain: An Introduction to Neuroanthropology* (Cambridge, MA: MIT Press, 2012).

5. Alan H Goodman and Thomas L Leatherman, eds., *Building a New Biocultural Synthesis: Political-Economic Perspectives on Human Biology* (Ann Arbor: University of Michigan Press, 1998).

6. Susan Guise Sheridan and Lesley A. Gregoricka, eds., *Purposeful Pain: The Bioarchaeology of Intentional Suffering* (Switzerland: Springer, 2020).

7. "AAA Statement on Race," American Anthropological Association, accessed February 15, 2023, https://www.americananthro.org/ConnectWithAAA/Content.aspx?ItemNumber=2583; "AABA Statement on Race & Racism," American Association of Biological Anthropologists, accessed August 1, 2022, https://bioanth.org/about/position-statements/aapa-statement-race-and-racism-2019/.

8. Clarence C. Gravlee, "How Race Becomes Biology: Embodiment of Social Inequality," *American Journal of Physical Anthropology* 139, no. 1 (2009): 47–57, https://doi-org.proxy.library.vanderbilt.edu/10.1002/ajpa.20983.

9. Leith Mullings and Alaka Wali, *Stress and Resilience: The Social Context of Reproduction in Central Harlem* (New York: Kluwer Academic/Plenum Publishers, 2001).

10. Marcus Anthony Hunter et al., "Black Placemaking: Celebration, Play, and Poetry," *Theory, Culture & Society* 33, no. 7–8 (2016): 31–56, https://doi.org/10.1177/0263276416635259; Demetrius Miles Murphy, "Aquilomb amento, Entrepreneurial Black Placemaking in an Anti-Black City," *Sociology of Race and Ethnicity* 8, no. 2 (February 18, 2022): 235–49, https://doi.org/10.1177/23326492221077945.

11. e.g., Andrea Elizabeth Shaw, *The Embodiment of Disobedience: Fat Black Women's Unruly Political Bodies* (Lexington Books, 2006); Harvey Young, *Embodying Black Experience: Stillness, Critical Memory, and the Black Body* (Ann Arbor: University of Michigan Press, 2010), https://doi.org/10.3998/mpub.235634.

12. e.g., David J. Leonard, "It's Gotta Be the Body: Race, Commodity, and Surveillance of Contemporary Black Athletes," *Studies in Symbolic Interaction* 33 (October 30, 2009): 165–90, https://doi.org/10.1108/S0163-2396(2009)0000033013; Damani J. Partridge, *Hypersexuality and Headscarves: Race, Sex, and Citizenship in the New Germany* (Bloomington: Indiana University Press, 2012).

13. Pamela A. Popielarz and Zachary P. Neal, "The Niche as a Theoretical Tool," *Annual Review of Sociology* 33 (2007): 65–84, https://doi.org/10.1146/annurev.soc.32.061604.123118.

14. Agustín Fuentes, "Integrative Anthropology and the Human Niche: Toward a Contemporary Approach to Human Evolution," *American Anthropologist* 117, no. 2 (June 2015): 305, https://doi.org/10.1111/aman.12248.

15. Jada Benn Torres and Gabriel A. Torres Colón, "Racial Experience as an Alternative Operationalization of Race," *Human Biology* 87, no. 4 (October 17, 2016): 306–12, https://doi.org/10.13110/humanbiology.87.4.0306; Gabriel A. Torres Colón, "Racial Experience as Bioculturally Embodied Difference and Political Possibilities for Resisting Racism," *The Pluralist* 13, no. 1 (2018): 131–42, https://doi-org.proxy.library.vanderbilt.edu/10.5406/pluralist.13.1.0131.

16. Klaus-Peter Köpping, *Adolf Bastian and the Psychic Unity of Mankind: The Foundations of Anthropology in Nineteenth Century Germany* (Brisbane, Australia: University of Queensland Press, 1983).

17. Henrietta L. Moore, *The Subject of Anthropology: Gender, Symbolism and Psychoanalysis* (Polity, 2007).

18. Cf. Kazuko Suzuki, "A Critical Assessment of Comparative Sociology of Race and Ethnicity," *Sociology of Race and Ethnicity* 3, no. 3 (2017): 287–300, https://doi.org/10.1177/2332649217708580.

19. Moore, *The Subject of Anthropology*; Benedict Anderson, *Imagined Communities: Reflections on the Origin and Spread of Nationalism*, (London, England: Verso, 2006); John Dunham Kelly, *Represented Communities: Fiji and World Decolonization* (Chicago: University of Chicago Press, 2001); Nasar Meer and Tariq Modood, "Refutations of Racism in the 'Muslim Question,'" *Patterns of Prejudice* 43, no. 3-4 (July 2009): 335–54, https://doi.org/10.1080/00313220903109250; Daniel Olmos, "Racialized Im/Migration and Autonomy of Migration Perspectives: New Directions and Opportunities," *Sociology Compass* 13, no. 9 (2019): e12729, https://doi.org/10.1111/soc4.12729.

20. Hilda Lloréns and Bárbara Abadía-Rexach, "In Defense of Black Life: A Brief Cultural History of Anti-Racist Efforts in Puerto Rico," in *Routledge Handbook of Afro-Latin American Studies*, ed. Bernd Reiter and John Antón Sánchez (New York: Routledge, 2022), 448-456.

21. Isar Godreau, *Scripts of Blackness: Race, Cultural Nationalism, and U.S. Colonialism in Puerto Rico* (Urbana: University of Illinois Press, 2015).

1. THE RACIAL NICHE: ORIGIN STORIES OF RACE AND THEORETICAL RESOLUTIONS

1. Cf. Eric R. Wolf, "Contested Concepts," chap. 2 in *Envisioning Power: Ideologies of Dominance and Crisis* (Berkeley: University of California Press, 1999).

2. W.E.B. Du Bois, "Evolution of the Race Problem," in *Proceedings of the National Negro Conference* (New York, NY: s.n., 1909), 142.

3. Cf. Charles R. Hale, "Activist Research v. Cultural Critique: Indigenous Land Rights and the Contradictions of Politically Engaged Anthropology," *Cultural Anthropology* 21, no. 1 (February 1, 2006): 96–120, https://doi.org/10.1525/can.2006.21.1.96.

4. James C. Scott, *Weapons of the Weak: Everyday Forms of Peasant Resistance* (New Haven, CT: Yale University Press, 1985).

5. Eric R. Wolf, *Europe and the People Without History* (Berkeley: University of California Press, 1982).

6. June Nash, "Indigenous Development Alternatives," *Urban Anthropology and Studies of Cultural Systems and World Economic Development* 32, no. 1 (2003): 57–98.

7. Lee D. Baker, *Anthropology and the Racial Politics of Culture* (Durham, NC: Duke University Press, 2010), 9–10.

8. Baker, *Anthropology and the Racial Politics of Culture*, 24.

9. Gabriel A. Torres Colón and Charles A. Hobbs, "Toward a Pragmatist Anthropology of Race," *The Pluralist* 11, no. 1 (2016): 126–35, https://doi.org/10.5406/pluralist.11.1.0126.

10. Norman E. Whitten, "The Longue Durée of Racial Fixity and the Transformative Conjunctures of Racial Blending," *The Journal of Latin American and Caribbean Anthropology* 12, no. 2 (2007): 356–83, https://doi.org/10.1525/jlat.2007.12.2.356; Jada Benn Torres and Gabriel A. Torres Colón, "Racial Experience as an Alternative Operationalization of Race," *Human Biology* 87, no. 4 (October 17, 2016): 306–12.

11. e.g., Reiland Rabaka, *Africana Critical Theory: Reconstructing the Black Radical Tradition, from W. E. B. Du Bois and C. L. R. James to Frantz Fanon and Amilcar Cabral* (Lanham, MD: Lexington Books, 2010).

12. Nash, "Indigenous Development Alternatives," 90–91, emphasis added.

13. Baker, *Anthropology and the Racial Politics of Culture*, 4.

14. Du Bois, "Evolution of the Race Problem," 142.

15. Lawrence Hirschfeld, "The Conceptual Politics of Race: Lessons from Our Children," *Ethos* 25, no. 1 (March, 1997): 63–92, https://doi.org/10.1525/eth.1997.25.1.63.

16. Lawrence Hirschfeld, "Reply," *Ethos* 25, no. 1 (March, 1997): 127, https://doi.org/10.1525/eth.1997.25.1.126.

17. Much of which is presented in a book he published the year before the Ethos debate, see Lawrence Hirschfeld, *Race in the Making: Cognition, Culture, and the Child's Construction of Human Kinds*, (Cambridge, Massachusetts: MIT Press, 1996).

18. Virginia R Dominguez, "The Racialist Politics of Concepts, or Is It the Racialist Concepts of Politics?," *Ethos* 25, no. 1 (March, 1997): 93–100, https://doi.org/10.1525/eth.1997.25.1.93; Ann Laura Stoler, "On Political

and Psychological Essentialisms," *Ethos* 25, no. 1 (March, 1997): 101–6, https://doi.org/10.1525/eth.1997.25.1.101.

19. Stoler, "On Political," 104.
20. Stoler, "On Political," 104–5.
21. Stoler, "On Political," 105.
22. Dominguez, "Racialist Politics," 97.
23. Dominguez, "Racialist Politics," 98.
24. Hirschfeld, "Reply," 131–32.
25. Hirschfeld, "Conceptual Politics," 87.
26. Hirschfeld, "Reply," 132.
27. Dominguez, "Racialist Politics," 94.
28. Hirschfeld, "Conceptual Politics," 63.
29. Dominguez, "Racialist Politics," 94.
30. e.g., Andrew Webb, "Negotiating Optimum Distinctiveness: Cognitive Tendencies toward Primordialism among Mapuche Youth," *Ethnic and Racial Studies* 36, no. 12 (2013): 2055–74, https://doi.org/10.1080/0141987 0.2012.676202; Kazuko Suzuki, "A Critical Assessment of Comparative Sociology of Race and Ethnicity," *Sociology of Race and Ethnicity* 3, no. 3 (017): 287–300, https://doi.org/10.1177/2332649217708580.
31. Lars Rodseth, "Reality Remodeled: Practical Fictions for a More-than-Empirical World," *HAU: Journal of Ethnographic Theory* 12, no. 1 (2022): 217–34, https://doi.org/10.1086/719660.
32. Cf. Daniel Hausman, "Are There Causal Relations among Dependent Variables?," *Philosophy of Science* 50, no. 1 (1983): 58–81.
33. e.g., Leith Mullings, "Interrogating Racism: Toward an Antiracist Anthropology," *Annual Review of Anthropology* 34, no. 1 (October 21, 2005): 667–93, https://doi.org/10.1146/annurev.anthro.32.061002.093435; Paul Silverstein, "Immigrant Racialization and the New Savage Slot: Race, Migration, and Immigration in the New Europe," *Annual Review of Anthropology* 34 (2005): 363–84; Deborah Thomas and M. Clarke, "Globalization and Race: Structures of Inequality, New Sovereignties, and Citizenship in a Neoliberal Era," *Annual Review of Anthropology* 42, no. 1 (2013): 305–25.
34. Hirschfeld, "Conceptual Politics," 69.
35. This book represents such an effort, but also see Abigail Bakan and Enakshi Dua, *Theorizing Anti-Racism: Linkages in Marxism and Critical Race Theories* (University of Toronto Press, 2014) and Charles R. Hale,

Más Que Un Indio = *More Than an Indian: Racial Ambivalence and Neo-liberal Multiculturalism in Guatemala* (Santa Fe, CA: School of American Research Press, 2006).

36. Lawrence Hirschfeld, "Seven Myths of Race and the Young Child," *Du Bois Review* 9, no. 1 (2012): 17–39, https://doi.org/10.1017/S1742058 X12000033.

37. W.E.B. Du Bois, "Strivings of the Negro People," *Atlantic Monthly*, 1897; see also Moustafa Bayoumi, *How Does It Feel to Be a Problem? Being Young and Arab in America* (New York: Penguin Press, 2008) for a contemporary reinterpretation regarding young Muslims.

38. Hirschfeld, "Conceptual Politics," 63.

39. Baker, *Anthropology and the Racial Politics of Culture*; Gabriel A. Torres Colón and Charles A. Hobbs, "The Intertwining of Culture and Nature: Franz Boas, John Dewey, and Deweyan Strands of American Anthropology," *Journal of the History of Ideas* 76, no. 1 (January 2015): 139–62; Torres Colón and Hobbs, "Toward a Pragmatist Anthropology of Race"; Jada Benn Torres and Gabriel A. Torres Colón, "Anténor Firmin and Biological Anthropology as Anti-Racism" chap. 5 in *Genetic Ancestry: Our Stories, Our Pasts*, (New York: Routledge, 2021).

40. e.g., Mullings, "Interrogating Racism"; Clarence C. Gravlee, "How Race Becomes Biology: Embodiment of Social Inequality," *American Journal of Physical Anthropology* 139, no. 1 (2009): 47–57; Thomas and Clarke, "Globalization and Race"; Mary Bucholtz, *White Kids: Language, Race, and Styles of Youth Identity* (Cambridge University Press, 2010), https://doi.org/10.1017/CBO9780511975776.

41. Webb, "Negotiating Optimum Distinctiveness," 2058.

42. Ali Rattansi, "Race's Recurrence," *Theory, Culture & Society* 28, no. 1 (January 31, 2011): 117, https://doi.org/10.1177/0263276410387623.

43. Maria Kromidas, "The 'Savage' Child and the Nature of Race: Posthuman Interventions from New York City," *Anthropological Theory* 14, no. 4 (November 19, 2014): 424, https://doi.org/10.1177/1463499614552739.

44. Hirschfeld, "Conceptual Politics," 81.

45. e.g., Rachel Caspari, "Race, Then and Now: 1918 Revisited," *American Journal of Physical Anthropology* 165, no. 4 (March 25, 2018): 934–35, https://doi.org/10.1002/ajpa.23417; Susan A. Gelman, *The Essential Child: Origins of Essentialism in Everyday Thought* (New York: Oxford University Press, 2003), https://doi.org/10.1093/acprof:oso/9780195154061.001.0001.

46. Francisco J. Gil-White, "Are Ethnic Groups Biological 'Species' to the Human Brain?: Essentialism in Our Cognition of Some Social Categories," *Current Anthropology* 42, no. 4 (2001): 515–53, https://doi.org/10.1086/321802.

47. Hirschfeld, "Conceptual Politics," 87.

48. Dominguez, "Racialist Politics," 94.

49. Hirschfeld, "Seven Myths of Race and the Young Child."

50. Baker, *Anthropology and the Racial Politics of Culture*, 4.

51. Benn Torres and Torres Colón, "Racial Experience as an Alternative."

52. Torres Colón and Hobbs, "The Intertwining of Culture and Nature"; Torres Colón and Hobbs, "Toward a Pragmatist Anthropology of Race"; Benn Torres and Torres Colón, *Genetic Ancestry*, chap. 5.

53. John Dewey, *The Middle Works of John Dewey, 1899–1924: Human Nature and Conduct*, vol. 14: 1922, ed. Jo Ann Boydston (Carbondale: Southern Illinois University Press, 2008).

54. Jo Ann Boydston, ed., *The Later Works of John Dewey, Volume 1, 1925–1953: 1925, Experience and Nature* (Carbondale: Southern Illinois University Press, 2008); Dewey, *Art as Experience* (New York: Penguin, 2005); Thomas M. Alexander, *The Human Eros: Eco-Ontology and the Aesthetics of Existence* (New York: Fordham University Press, 2013), 59.

55. Boydston, *Later Works of John*, 55.

56. John Dewey, *Unmodern Philosophy and Modern Philosophy*, ed. Phillip Deen (Carbondale: Southern Illinois University Press, 2012).

57. Alexander, *The Human Eros*, chaps. 3–4.

58. Alexander, *The Human Eros*, 57.

59. Henrietta L. Moore, "Global Anxieties: Concept-Metaphors and Pre-Theoretical Commitments in Anthropology," *Anthropological Theory* 4, no. 1 (March, 2004): 73, https://doi.org/10.1177/1463499604040848.

60. Moore, "Global Anxieties," 74.

61. Sarah S. Willen and Don Seeman, "Introduction: Experience and Inquiétude," *Ethos* 40, no. 1 (2012): 2, https://doi.org/10.1111/j.1548-1352.2011.01228.x.

62. e.g., Pierre Bourdieu, *Outline of a Theory of Practice* (England: Cambridge University Press, 1977).

63. Douglas Hollan, "On the Varieties and Particularities of Cultural Experience," *Ethos* 40, no. 1 (2012): 43, https://doi.org/10.1111/j.1548-1352.2011.01230.x.

64. Hollan, "Varieties," 45.

65. Alexander, *The Human Eros*, 139.

66. Patricia Hill Collins, *Black Feminist Thought: Knowledge, Consciousness, and the Politics of Empowerment* (New York: Routledge, 2008); Patricia Hill Collins, *Black Sexual Politics: African Americans, Gender, and the New Racism* (New York: Routledge, 2004); Patricia Hill Collins, "Intersectionality's Definitional Dilemmas," *Annual Review of Sociology* 41, no. 1 (2015): 1–20.

67. Gravlee, "How Race Becomes Biology"; Zaneta M. Thayer and Christopher W. Kuzawa, "Biological Memories of Past Environments: Epigenetic Pathways to Health Disparities," *Epigenetics* 6, no. 7 (July 1, 2011): 798–803, https://doi.org/10.4161/epi.6.7.16222; William W. Dressler, Kathryn S. Oths, and Clarence C. Gravlee, "Race and Ethnicity in Public Health Research: Models to Explain Health Disparities," *Annual Review of Anthropology* 34, no. 1 (2005): 231–52, https://doi.org/10.1146/annurev.anthro.34.081804.120505; Jo C. Phelan and Bruce G. Link, "Is Racism a Fundamental Cause of Inequalities in Health?," *Annual Review of Sociology* 41, no. 1 (2015): 311–30, https://doi.org/10.1146/annurev-soc-073014-112305; Lynne D. Richardson and Marlaina Norris, "Access to Health and Health Care: How Race and Ethnicity Matter," *Mount Sinai Journal of Medicine* 77, no. 2 (2010): 166–77.

68. e.g., Gwen Latendresse, "The Interaction Between Chronic Stress and Pregnancy: Preterm Birth from A Biobehavioral Perspective," *Journal of Midwifery & Women's Health* 54, no. 1 (January 1, 2009): 8–17, https://doi.org/10.1016/j.jmwh.2008.08.001; Jasmine D. Johnson and Judette M. Louis, "Does Race or Ethnicity Play a Role in the Origin, Pathophysiology, and Outcomes of Preeclampsia? An Expert Review of the Literature," *American Journal of Obstetrics and Gynecology*, Preeclampsia and Eclampsia, 226, no. 2, Supplement (February 1, 2022): S876–85, https://doi.org/10.1016/j.ajog.2020.07.038.

69. Kia C. Fuller et al., "ACE Gene Haplotypes and Social Networks: Using a Biocultural Framework to Investigate Blood Pressure Variation in African Americans," *PloS One* 13, no. 9 (2018): e0204127, https://doi.org/10.1371/journal.pone.0204127.

70. Fuller et al., "ACE Gene Haplotypes," 12.

71. R. J. Taylor et al., "Developments in Research on Black Families: A Decade Review," *Journal of Marriage and Family* 52, no. 4 (November, 1990): 993–1014, https://doi.org/10.2307/353315; William Dressler, Susan

Haworth Hoeppner, and Barbara J. Pitts, "Household Structure in a Southern Black Community," *American Anthropologist* 87, no. 4 (December, 1985): 853–62, https://doi.org/10.1525/aa.1985.87.4.02a00070.

72. Carol B Stack, *All Our Kin: Strategies for Survival in a Black Community* (New York: Harper & Row, 1974); Andrew Billingsley, *Black Families in White America* (Englewood Cliffs, NJ: Prentice-Hall, 1968).

73. Cecily R. Hardaway and Vonnie C. McLoyd, "Escaping Poverty and Securing Middle Class Status: How Race and Socioeconomic Status Shape Mobility Prospects for African Americans During the Transition to Adulthood," *Journal of Youth and Adolescence* 38, no. 2 (2009): 242–56, https://doi.org/10.1007/s10964-008-9354-z.

74. Angela Rose Black and Nadine Peacock, "Pleasing the Masses: Messages for Daily Life Management in African American Women's Popular Media Sources," *American Journal of Public Health* 101, no. 1 (September 20, 2011): 144–50, https://doi.org/10.2105/AJPH.2009.167817; Cheryl L. Woods-Giscombé et al., "Whose Stress Is Making Me Sick? Network-Stress and Emotional Distress in African-American Women," *Issues in Mental Health Nursing* 36, no. 9 (October 6, 2015): 710–17, https://doi.org/10.3109/01612840.2015.1011759.

75. Leith Mullings and Alaka Wali, *Stress and Resilience: The Social Context of Reproduction in Central Harlem* (New York: Kluwer Academic /Plenum Publishers, 2001).

76. Agustín Fuentes, "The Extended Evolutionary Synthesis, Ethnography, and the Human Niche: Toward an Integrated Anthropology," *Current Anthropology* 57, no. S13 (April 4, 2016): S13–26.

77. Fuentes, "Extended Evolutionary Synthesis," S18.

78. Roy A. Rappaport, *Pigs for the Ancestors: Ritual in the Ecology of a New Guinea People* (New Haven, CT: Yale University Press, 1984).

79. Fuentes, "Extended Evolutionary Synthesis," S18.

80. Fuentes, "Extended Evolutionary Synthesis," S18.

81. e.g., Benn Torres and Torres Colón, *Genetic Ancestry*, chap. 5; Nicole Madrilejo, Holden Lombard, and Jada Benn Torres, "Origins of Marronage: Mitochondrial Lineages of Jamaica's Accompong Town Maroons," *American Journal of Human Biology* 27, no. 3 (May 6, 2015): 432–37 https://doi-org.proxy.library.vanderbilt.edu/10.1002/ajhb.22656; Jada Benn Torres, Anne C. Stone, and Rick Kittles, "An Anthropological Genetic Perspective on Creolization in the Anglophone Caribbean," *American Journal of*

Physical Anthropology 151, no. 1 (May 1, 2013): 135–43. https://doi-org.proxy .library.vanderbilt.edu/10.1002/ajpa.22261

82. Agustín Fuentes, "Integrative Anthropology and the Human Niche: Toward a Contemporary Approach to Human Evolution," *American Anthropologist* 117, no. 2 (2015): 305, https://doi.org/10.1111/aman.12248.

83. Fuentes, "Extended Evolutionary Synthesis," S19.

84. Greg Downey, "Being Human in Cities: Phenotypic Bias from Urban Niche Construction," *Current Anthropology* 57, no. S13 (2016): S54, https:// doi.org/10.1086/685710.

85. Fuentes, "Extended Evolutionary Synthesis," S19.

86. Michael Omi and Howard Winant, *Racial Formation in the United States: From the 1960s to the 1990s*, 2nd ed. (New York: Routledge, 1994); Daniel HoSang, Oneka LaBennett, and Laura Pulido, eds., *Racial Formation in the Twenty-First Century* (Berkeley: University of California Press, 2012), https://doi.org/10.1525/9780520953765; Alexander G. Weheliye, *Habeas Viscus: Racializing Assemblages, Biopolitics, and Black Feminist Theories of the Human* (Durham, NC: Duke University Press, 2014).

2. STYLES FOR FLOURISHING: RECONFIGURING SELVES THROUGH THE RACIAL NICHE

1. Lawrence Hirschfeld, "Reply," *Ethos* 25, no. 1 (March, 1997): 127, https:// doi.org/10.1525/eth.1997.25.1.126.

2. Leith Mullings and Alaka Wali, *Stress and Resilience: The Social Context of Reproduction in Central Harlem* (New York: Springer, 2001).

3. Naomi Priest et al., "A Systematic Review of Studies Examining the Relationship between Reported Racism and Health and Wellbeing for Children and Young People," *Social Science & Medicine* 95, (October, 2013): 115–27, https://doi.org/10.1016/j.socscimed.2012.11.031.

4. Priest et al., "Systematic Review."

5. Gwen Latendresse, "The Interaction Between Chronic Stress and Pregnancy: Preterm Birth from A Biobehavioral Perspective," *Journal of Midwifery & Women's Health* 54, no. 1 (January 1, 2009): 8–17, https:// doi.org/10.1016/j.jmwh.2008.08.001; Priest et al., "Systematic Review"; Margaret T. Hicken et al., "Racial/Ethnic Disparities in Hypertension Prevalence: Reconsidering the Role of Chronic Stress," *American*

Journal of Public Health 104, no. 1 (January 2014): 117–23, https://doi.org/10.2105/AJPH.2013.301395.

6. Adam J. Hoffman et al., "Peer Support Development Among Black American and Latinx Adolescents: The Role of Ethnic-Racial Centrality," *Developmental Psychology* 55, no. 12 (2019): 9, https://doi.org/10.1037/dev0000829.

7. Deborah Rivas-Drake et al., "Feeling Good, Happy, and Proud: A Meta-Analysis of Positive Ethnic-Racial Affect and Adjustment," *Child Development* 85, no. 1 (February 3, 2014): 95, https://doi.org/10.1111/cdev.12175.

8. e.g., Faye V. Harrison, "The Persistent Power of 'Race' in the Cultural and Political Economy of Racism," *Annual Review of Anthropology* 24, no. 1 (1995): 47–74; Clarence C. Gravlee, "How Race Becomes Biology: Embodiment of Social Inequality," *American Journal of Physical Anthropology* 139, no. 1 (2009): 47–57, https://doi.org/10.1002/ajpa.20983; Jo C. Phelan and Bruce G. Link, "Is Racism a Fundamental Cause of Inequalities in Health?," *Annual Review of Sociology* 41, no. 1 (2015): 311–30, https://doi.org/10.1146/annurev-soc-073014-112305; Tanya Golash-Boza, "A Critical and Comprehensive Sociological Theory of Race and Racism," *Sociology of Race and Ethnicity* 2, no. 2 (February 23, 2016): 129–41, https://doi.org/10.1177/2332649216632242.

9. S. M. Quintana, "Racial and Ethnic Identity; Developmental Perspectives and Research," *Journal of Counseling Psychology* 54, no. 3 (2007): 259–70, https://doi.org/10.1037/0022-0167.54.3.259.

10. Quintana, "Racial and Ethnic Identity," 262.

11. Quintana, "Racial and Ethnic Identity," 267.

12. Adriana J. Umaña-Taylor, Melinda A. Gonzales-Backen, and Amy B. Guimond, "Latino Adolescents Ethnic Identity: Is There a Developmental Progression and Does Growth in Ethnic Identity Predict Growth in Self-Esteem?," *Child Development* 80, no. 2 (April 29, 2009): 391–405, https://doi.org/10.1111/j.1467-8624.2009.01267.x; Ciara Smalls, "African American Adolescent Engagement in the Classroom and Beyond: The Roles of Mother's Racial Socialization and Democratic-Involved Parenting," *Journal of Youth and Adolescence* 38, no. 2 (2009): 204–13, https://doi.org/10.1007/s10964-008-9316-5; Adriana J. Umaña-Taylor et al., "Mexican-Origin Early Adolescents' Ethnic Socialization, Ethnic Identity, and Psychosocial Functioning," *The Counseling Psychologist* 42, no. 2 (2014): 170–200, https://doi.org/10.1177/0011000013477903.

13. Jelani Mandara et al., "The Effects of Changes in Racial Identity and Self-Esteem on Changes in African American Adolescents Mental Health," *Child Development* 80, no. 6 (November 12, 2009): 1671, https://doi.org/10.1111/j.1467-8624.2009.01360.x.

14. Aerika S. Brittian, "Understanding African American Adolescents' Identity Development: A Relational Developmental Systems Perspective," *Journal of Black Psychology* 38, no. 2 (July 22, 2011): 178, https://doi.org/10.1177/0095798411414570.

15. Joanna L. Williams et al., "The Protective Role of Ethnic Identity for Urban Adolescent Males Facing Multiple Stressors," *Journal of Youth and Adolescence* 43, no. 10 (2013): 1739, https://doi.org/10.1007/s10964-013-0071-x.

16. Aihwa Ong and Stephen J. Collier, eds., *Global Assemblages: Technology, Politics, and Ethics as Anthropological Problems* (Malden, MA: Blackwell Publishing, 2005), 12.

17. Stephen Campbell, "Rendering Assemblage Dialectical," *Anthropological Theory* 21, no. 2 (2021): 243, https://doi.org/10.1177/1463499619875904.

18. Tania Murray Li, "Practices of Assemblage and Community Forest Management," *Economy and Society* 36, no. 2 (March 26, 2007): 263–93, https://doi.org/10.1080/03085140701254308.

19. Pierre Bourdieu, *The Logic of Practice*, trans. Richard Nice. (Stanford, CA: Stanford University Press, 1990), 53.

20. Ulla D. Berg and Ana Y. Ramos-Zayas, "Racializing Affect: A Theoretical Proposition," *Current Anthropology* 56, no. 5 (2015): 654, https://doi.org/10.1086/683053.

21. Ulla D. Berg and Ana Y. Ramos-Zayas, "Racializing Affect:," 664.

22. Ulla D. Berg and Ana Y. Ramos-Zayas, "Racializing Affect:," 664.

23. Judith T. Irvine, "'Style' as Distinctiveness: The Culture and Ideology of Linguistic Differentiation," in *Style and Sociolinguistic Variation*, ed. Penelope Eckert and John R. Rickford (Cambridge, United Kingdom: Cambridge University Press, 2002), 21–43, https://doi.org/10.1017/CBO9780511613258.002.

24. Irvine, "'Style' as Distinctiveness," 31.

25. Irvine, "'Style' as Distinctiveness," 22.

26. Irvine, "'Style' as Distinctiveness," 22.

27. Pierre Bourdieu, *Distinction: A Social Critique of the Judgement of Taste* (Cambridge, Mass: Harvard University Press, 1984), 223.

28. Bourdieu, *Distinction: A Social Critique*, 376.

29. e.g., Dick Hebdige, *Subculture, the Meaning of Style*, New Accents (London: Methuen, 1979); Keith Gildart et al., eds., *Hebdige and Subculture in the Twenty-First Century: Through the Subcultural Lens* (Palgrave Macmillan, 2020), https://doi.org/10.1007/978-3-030-28475-6.

30. Aimee Meredith Cox, *Shapeshifters: Black Girls and the Choreography of Citizenship* (Durham, NC: Duke University Press, 2015), 28–29, https://doi.org/10.1515/9780822375371.

31. Henrietta L. Moore, *The Subject of Anthropology: Gender, Symbolism and Psychoanalysis* (Polity, 2007).

32. Moore, *The Subject of Anthropology*, 8.

33. Jussi A. Saarinen, "What Can the Concept of Affective Scaffolding Do for Us?," *Philosophical Psychology* 33, no. 6 (2020): 820, https://doi.org/10.1080/09515089.2020.1761542.

34. Pierre Bourdieu, *Outline of a Theory of Practice* (England: Cambridge University Press, 1977).

35. Laura Candiotto and Roberta Dreon, "Affective Scaffoldings as Habits: A Pragmatist Approach," *Frontiers in Psychology* 12 (2021): 2, https://doi.org/10.3389/fpsyg.2021.629046.

36. Candiotto and Dreon, "Affective Scaffoldings as Habits," 11–12.

37. Karla Slocum, *Black Towns, Black Futures: The Enduring Allure of a Black Place in the American West* (Chapel Hill: The University of North Carolina Press, 2019), 133.

38. Matei Candea, *Comparison in Anthropology: The Impossible Method*, (New York: Cambridge University Press, 2019), 349–50.

3. GOING TO THE BODY AS MEXICAN BOXERS DO: FASHIONING STYLES FROM RACIAL EXPERIENCES

1. Cf. David Epstein, *The Sports Gene: Inside the Science of Extraordinary Athletic Performance* (New York: Penguin, 2014).

2. Susan A. Gelman and Cristine H. Legare, "Concepts and Folk Theories," *Annual Review of Anthropology* 40, no. 1 (October, 2011): 379–98, https://doi.org/10.1146/annurev-anthro-081309-145822.

3. Steven High, *Industrial Sunset: The Making of North America's Rust Belt, 1969–1984* (University of Toronto Press, 2015); Justin B. Hollander, *Sunburnt Cities: The Great Recession, Depopulation and Urban Planning in the American Sunbelt* (London: Routledge, 2011); David Wilson,

Cities and Race: America's New Black Ghetto (London: Routledge, 2006); Christabel Devadoss, "Examining Rust Belt Narratives: Race, Rural Representation, and Everyday Experiences," *Journal of Rural Studies* 100, (May, 2023): 103010, https://doi.org/10.1016/j.jrurstud.2023.103010; Jason Hackworth, *Manufacturing Decline: How Racism and the Conservative Movement Crush the American Rust Belt* (New York: Columbia University Press, 2019), https://doi.org/10.7312/hack19372.

4. Toua Antoine Coulibaly et al., "Inter Personal Violence-Related Facial Injuries: A 10-Year Survey," *Journal of Oral Medicine and Oral Surgery* 24, no. 1 (January 1, 2018): 2–5, https://doi.org/10.1051/mbcb/2017038.

5. Megan Brickley and Martin Smith, "Culturally Determined Patterns of Violence: Biological Anthropological Investigations at a Historic Urban Cemetery," *American Anthropologist* 108, no. 1 (March 1, 2006): 163–77, https://doi.org/10.1525/aa.2006.108.1.163.

6. In boxing, a "Mexican boxer" can refer to a fighter from Mexico or someone with Mexican heritage in the United States.

7. Allen, Stephen D. 2017. *A History of Boxing in Mexico: Masculinity, Modernity, and Nationalism.* Albuquerque, New Mexico: University of New Mexico Press.

8. As a result of demographic and historical immigration patterns, a gym in Miami or New York would yield a more complex social grouping of Latin American US identifications

9. Ruth Gomberg-Muñoz, *Labor and Legality: An Ethnography of a Mexican Immigrant Network* (Oxford University Press, 2011); Rusty Barrett, "Language Ideology and Racial Inequality: Competing Functions of Spanish in an Anglo-Owned Mexican Restaurant," *Language in Society* 35, no. 02 (April 2006): 163–204, https://doi.org/10.1017/S0047404506060088.

10. Faye V. Harrison, "The Persistent Power of 'Race' in the Cultural and Political Economy of Racism," *Annual Review of Anthropology* 24, no. 1 (1995): 47–74; Deborah Thomas and M. Clarke, "Globalization and Race: Structures of Inequality, New Sovereignties, and Citizenship in a Neoliberal Era," *Annual Review of Anthropology* 42, no. 1 (2013): 305–25.

11. Umaña-Taylor et al., "Ethnic and Racial Identity During Adolescence and Into Young Adulthood: An Integrated Conceptualization," *Child Development* 85, no. 1 (2014): 22.

12. Lawrence D. Bobo, "Racialization, Assimilation, and the Mexican American Experience: Racialization in Ascendance," *Du Bois Review* 8, no. 2 (October 24, 2011): 497–502, https://doi.org/10.1017/S1742058X11000452; Victor M. Rodriguez Dominguez, "The Racialization of Mexican Americans and Puerto Ricans: 1890's-1930's," *Centro Journal* 17, no. 1 (2005): 70–105; Edward Fergus, "Because I'm Light Skin . . . They Think I'm Italian: Mexican Students' Experiences of Racialization in Predominantly White Schools," *Urban Education* 52, no. 4 (2017): 460–90, https://doi.org/10.1177/0042085916666931; Alex E. Chávez, *Sounds of Crossing: Music, Migration, and the Aural Poetics of Huapango Arribeño* (Durham, NC: Duke University Press, 2017); Daniel Olmos, "Racialized Im/migration and Autonomy of Migration Perspectives: New Directions and Opportunities," *Sociology Compass* 13, no. 9 (August, 2019): e12729, https://doi.org/10.1111/soc4.12729.

13. Alan Tomlinson and Christopher Young, *National Identity and Global Sports Events: Culture, Politics, and Spectacle in the Olympics and the Football World Cup* (State University of New York Press, 2006).

14. Torres Colón, Gabriel A. 2022. "Fighting for Family and Glory: Hope, Racialization, and Exploitation in a U.S. Boxing Gym." *Journal of Sport and Social Issues* 46 (2): 156–75. https://doi.org/10.1177/01937235211062627.

15. Asking youth a direct question about whether a white boy would beat them seemed inappropriate to me for two reasons. First, we often had a few white boxers in the gym, and having non-white youth entertain the inferiority of white boxers who were also their teammates was not something I was willing to do. Second, I had a responsibility as a coach to correct a young person who thought that they could beat someone because they were white. In fact, I did correct young boxers a couple of times, but I did not want to set them up to be corrected and potentially embarrass themselves after prompting them for a wrong answer.

16. Howard Sackler, *The Great White Hope: A Play* (New York: Dial Press, 1968), http://archive.org/details/greatwhitehfeploosack; Ben Carrington, *Race, Sport and Politics: The Sporting Black Diaspora* (SAGE Publications, 2010), 88–97.

17. Stephen D. Allen, *A History of Boxing in Mexico: Masculinity, Modernity, and Nationalism* (Albuquerque: University of New Mexico Press, 2017);

David Brown and George Jennings, "In Search of a Martial Habitus: Identifying Core Dispositions in Wing Chun and Taijiquan," in *Fighting Scholars: Habitus and Ethnographies of Martial Arts and Combat Sports*, ed. Raul Sanchez Garcia and Dale C. Spencer (New York: Anthem Press, 2013), 33–48; Constancio R. Arnaldo Jr., "'Undisputed' Racialised Masculinities: Boxing Fandom, Identity, and the Cultural Politics of Masculinity," *Identities* 27, no. 6 (June 3, 2019): 655–74, https://doi.org/10.1080/1070289X.2019.1624068; Louis Moore, *I Fight for a Living: Boxing and the Battle for Black Manhood, 1880–1915* (University of Illinois Press, 2017).

18. Justin D. García, "Boxing, Masculinity, and *Latinidad*: Oscar De La Hoya, Fernando Vargas, and Raza Representations," *The Journal of American Culture* 36, no. 4 (December 1, 2013): 323–41, https://doi.org/10.1111/jacc.12053; Isabel Molina Guzman and Angharad N. Valdivia, "Brain, Brow, and Booty: Latina Iconicity in U.S. Popular Culture," *The Communication Review* 7, no. 2 (April 1, 2004): 205–21, https://doi.org 10.1080/10714420490448723.

19. Lee D. Baker, *Anthropology and the Racial Politics of Culture* (Durham, NC: Duke University Press, 2010), 4.

20. e.g., Marcus Anthony Hunter et al., "Black Placemaking: Celebration, Play, and Poetry," *Theory, Culture & Society* 33, no. 7–8 (December 1, 2016): 31–56, https://doi.org/10.1177/0263276416635259; Demetrius Miles Murphy, "*Aquilombamento*, Entrepreneurial Black Placemaking in an Anti-Black City," *Sociology of Race and Ethnicity* 8, no. 2 (2022): 235–49, https://doi.org/10.1177/23326492221077945.

21. Patricia Hill Collins, "Intersectionality's Definitional Dilemmas," *Annual Review of Sociology* 41, no. 1 (2015): 1–20, https://doi.org/10.1146 /annurev-soc-073014-112142.

22. Moore, Henrietta L. 2007. *The Subject of Anthropology: Gender, Symbolism and Psychoanalysis*. Polity.

23. Henrietta L. Moore, *The Subject of Anthropology: Gender, Symbolism and Psychoanalysis* (Polity, 2007), 8.

24. Henrietta L. Moore, The Subject of Anthropology: Gender, Symbolism and Psychoanalysis (Polity, 2007), 123-124.

25. e.g., Thomas and Clarke, "Globalization and Race"; Olmos, "Racialized Im/migration and Autonomy of Migration Perspectives."

26. Umaña-Taylor et al., "Ethnic and Racial Identity During Adolescence and Into Young Adulthood."

27. Tanya Golash-Boza, "A Critical and Comprehensive Sociological Theory of Race and Racism," *Sociology of Race and Ethnicity* 2, no. 2 (2016): 129–41, https://doi.org/10.1177/2332649216632242.

4. BOMBA STYLES: SURVIVING ANTI-BLACKNESS IN THE RACIAL NICHE OF EMPIRES

1. Isar Godreau, *Scripts of Blackness: Race, Cultural Nationalism, and U.S. Colonialism in Puerto Rico* (Urbana: University of Illinois Press, 2015).

2. Jada Benn Torres and Gabriel A. Torres Colón, *Genetic Ancestry: Our Stories, Our Pasts*, New Biological Anthropology (New York: Routledge, 2021), chap. 2.

3. Benn Torres and Torres Colón, *Genetic Ancestry*.

4. Geoff Mann, *In the Long Run We Are All Dead: Keynesianism, Political Economy, and Revolution* (Verso Books, 2017).

5. Orlando J. Sotomayor, "Poverty and Income Inequality in Puerto Rico, 1969–89: Trends and Sources," *Review of Income and Wealth* 42, no. 1 (1996): 49–61, https://doi.org/10.1111/j.1475-4991.1996.tb00145.x.

6. José Caraballo Cueto, "Notas Del Centro De Información Censal (CIC)" (Centro De Información Censal, Universidad de Puerto Rico en Cayey, 2018).

7. e.g., Clarence C. Gravlee, "Ethnic Classification in Southeastern Puerto Rico: The Cultural Model of 'Color,'" *Social Forces* 83, no. 3 (2005): 949–70, https://doi.org/10.1353/sof.2005.0033; Hilda Lloréns, "Beyond Blanqueamiento: Black Affirmation in Contemporary Puerto Rico," *Latin American and Caribbean Ethnic Studies* 13, no. 2 (May 4, 2018): 157–78, https://doi.org/10.1080/17442222.2018.1466646; Hilda Lloréns, *Making Livable Worlds: Afro-Puerto Rican Women Building Environmental Justice* (Seattle: University of Washington Press, 2021).

8. Gerd Baumann and André Gingrich, *Grammars of Identity/Alterity: A Structural Approach* (New York: Berghahn Books, 2005).

9. Cf. Isar Godreau and Yarimar Bonilla, "Nonsovereign Racecraft: How Colonialism, Debt, and Disaster Are Transforming Puerto Rican Racial Subjectivities," *American Anthropologist* 123, no. 3 (2021): 509–25, https://doi.org/10.1111/aman.13601.

10. J. C. Martinez-Cruzado et al., "Mitochondrial DNA Analysis Reveals Substantial Native American Ancestry in Puerto Rico," *Human Biology* 73, no. 4 (August 1, 2001): 491–511, https://doi.org/10.1353/hub.2001.0056.

11. Benn Torres and Torres Colón, *Genetic Ancestry*, chap. 6.

12. Michelle Thompson, "Land, Law and Community Among the Accompong Maroons in Post-Emancipation Jamaica" (PhD diss., New York University, 2012), http://search.proquest.com.proxy.library .nd.edu/docview/965607417/abstract/13E61B580DC43040F07/3?accou ntid=12874; Jean Besson, "Folk Law and Legal Pluralism in Jamaica: A View from the Plantation-Peasant Interface," *The Journal of Legal Pluralism and Unofficial Law* 31, no. 43 (1999): 31–56; Jacqueline Cogdell DjeDje, "Remembering Kojo: History, Music, and Gender in the January Sixth Celebration of the Jamaican Accompong Maroons," *Black Music Research Journal* 18, no. 1/2 (April 1, 1998): 67–120, https:// doi.org/10.2307/779395; Nicole Madrilejo, Holden Lombard, and Jada Benn Torres, "Origins of Maroonage: Mitochondrial Lineages of Jamaica's Accompong Town Maroons," *American Journal of Human Biology* 27, no. 3 (May 6, 2015): 432–37, https://doi.org/10.1002/ajhb.22656.

13. Benn Torres and Torres Colón, *Genetic Ancestry*, chap. 6.

14. Rebecca J. Scott, "Exploring the Meaning of Freedom: Postemancipation Societies in Comparative Perspective," *The Hispanic American Historical Review* 68, no. 3 (1988): 407–8, https://doi.org/10.1215/00182168-68.3.407.

15. Scott, "Exploring the Meaning of Freedom," 408.

16. Scott, "Exploring the Meaning of Freedom," 409.

17. Aline Helg, *Our Rightful Share: The Afro-Cuban Struggle for Equality, 1886–1912* (Chapel Hill: University of North Carolina Press, 1995); Danielle S. Allen, *Our Declaration: A Reading of the Declaration of Independence in Defense of Equality* (New York: Liveright Publishing, 2014).

18. Godreau, *Scripts of Blackness*.

19. Godreau, *Scripts of Blackness*, 230.

20. Godreau, *Scripts of Blackness*, 238.

21. Fernando Picó, "Esclavos, Cimarrones, Libertos Y Negros Libres En Rio Piedras, 1774–1873," *Anuario de Estudios Americanos; Sevilla* 43 (January 1,

1986): 28; Sidney W. Mintz, *Caribbean Transformations* (Chicago: Aldine Publishing Company, 1974), 86–91.

22. Susan A. Gelman and Cristine H. Legare, "Concepts and Folk Theories," *Annual Review of Anthropology* 40, no. 1 (2011): 379–98, https://doi.org/10.1146/annurev-anthro-081309-145822.

23. Juan A. Giusti Cordero, "Trabajo y Vida En El Mangle: 'Madera Negra' y Carbón En Piñones (Loíza), Puerto Rico (1880–1950)," *Caribbean Studies* 43, no. 1 (2015): 3–71, https://doi.org/10.1353/crb.2015.0001.

24. Luis Antonio Figueroa, *Sugar, Slavery, and Freedom in Nineteenth-Century Puerto Rico* (University of North Carolina Press, 2005).

25. Benn Torres and Torres Colón, *Genetic Ancestry*, chap. 6.

26. e.g., Godreau, *Scripts of Blackness*; Lloréns, *Making Livable Worlds*.

27. Lloréns, *Making Livable Worlds*, chap. 3.

28. Gavin Webb, "Bomba, Puerto Rico," in *Music Around the World: A Global Encyclopedia*, ed. Andrew R. Martin and Matthew Mihalka (Santa Barbara, CA: ABC-CLIO, 2020), 110.

29. Godreau, *Scripts of Blackness*, 55–56.

30. Halbert Barton, "The Challenges of Puerto Rican Bomba," in *Caribbean Dance from Abakuá to Zouk: How Movement Shapes Identity*, ed. Susanna Sloat (Gainsville: University Press of Florida, 2002), 183–96, http://hdl.handle.net/2027/heb.05772; I. Abadía-Rexach, *Musicalizando la Raza: La racialización en Puerto Rico a través de la música* (San Juan, Puerto Rico: Ediciones Puerto, 2012); Bárbara I. Abadía-Rexach, "¡Saludando al tambor!: el nuevo movimiento de la Bomba puertorriqueña" (Austin: University of Texas, 2015).

31. Abadía-Rexach, *Musicalizando la Raza*.

32. e.g., Katherine Everhart, "Cultura-Identidad: The Use of Art in the University of Puerto Rico Student Movement, 2010," *Humanity & Society* 36, no. 3 (2012): 213–14, https://doi.org/10.1177/0160597612451243; Paulina Guerrero, "A Story Told through Plena: Claiming Identity and Cultural Autonomy in the Street Festivals of San Juan, Puerto Rico," *Island Studies Journal* 8, no. 1 (2013): 165–78, https://doi.org/10.24043/isj.282.

33. Olavo Alén, "Rhythm as Duration of Sounds in Tumba Francesa," *Ethnomusicology* 39, no. 1 (1995): 55–71, https://doi.org/10.2307/852200.

34. Giusti Cordero, "Trabajo y Vida En El Mangle."

35. Giusti Cordero, "Trabajo y Vida En El Mangle," 39–40.

36. Lloréns, *Making Livable Worlds*.

37. See Bárbara I. Abadía-Rexach, "Adolfina Villanueva Osorio, Presente," *NACLA Report on the Americas* 53, no. 2 (April 3, 2021): 174–80, https://doi.org/10.1080/10714839.2021.1923222.

38. Lloréns, "Beyond Blanqueamiento."

39. Lloréns, *Making Livable Worlds*.

5. THE ORIGINS OF RACIALIZED CITIZENS IN THE ILLIBERAL STATE: LIFE STORIES IN THE SPANISH-MOROCCAN BORDERLAND

1. Charles W. Mills, "Racial Liberalism," *PMLA* 123, no. 5 (2008): 1380–97, https://doi.org/10.1632/pmla.2008.123.5.1380.

2. I use the terms "cristianos" (m. cristiano, f. cristiana) and "musulmanes" (m. musulmán, f. musulmana) to identify these two self-identified communities in Ceuta. I use the English words "Christians" and "Muslims" to refer generally to the practitioners of those religions. The reader should keep in mind that the use of cristianos and musulmanes in plural form are gender neutral; so unless I specify that I am talking just about males, then these terms are inclusive of males and females in those groups.

3. Since the 1990s, Chinese immigrants have also set up several restaurants, general stores, and wholesale businesses; however, they are not yet represented as part of the city's heritage. There is also a constant stream of hundreds of migrants from Northern and sub-Saharan Africa, the Middle East, and East Asia. They sneak into Ceuta with hopes of continuing to various destinations in Western Europe. However, most of these immigrants end up as detainees in a low-security facility outside Ceuta's urban center, awaiting response to their asylum petitions, and do not settle in Ceuta.

4. Feld, Steven, and Keith H. Basso, eds. 1996 Senses of Place. Santa Fe: School of American Research Press.

5. Bruner, Edward M., ed. 1984 Text, Play, and Story: The Construction and Reconstruction of Self and Society. Washington, D.C.: American Ethnological Society.

6. James L. Peacock and Dorothy C. Holland, "The Narrated Self: Life Stories in Process," *Ethos* 21, no. 4 (1993): 367–83, https://doi.org/10.1525/eth.1993.21.4.02a00010.

7. Dorothy Holland Herring and Jean Lave, eds., History in Person: Enduring Struggles, Contentious Practice, Intimate Identities (Santa Fe, N.M: School of American Research Press, 2001); Elinor Ochs, Living Narrative: Creating Lives in Everyday Storytelling (Cambridge, Mass: Harvard University Press, 2001); Elinor Ochs and Lisa Capps, "Narrating the Self," Annual Review of Anthropology 25, no. 1 (1996): 19–43, https://doi.org/10.1146/annurev.anthro.25.1.19; George C. Rosenwald and Richard L. Ochberg, eds., Storied Lives: The Cultural Politics of Self-Understanding (New Haven: Yale University Press, 1992).

8. Lamb, Sarah 2001 Being a Widow and Other Life Stories: The Interplay between Lives and Words. Anthropology & Humanism 26(1):16–34.

9. Rosander, Eva Evers 1991 Women in a Borderland: Managing Muslim Identity where Morocco Meets Spain. Stockholm: Department of Social Anthropology Stockholm University.

10. Driessen, Henk 1992 On the Spanish-Moroccan Frontier: A Study in Ritual, Power, and Ethnicity. New York: Berg.

11. Driessen, Henk 1992 On the Spanish-Moroccan Frontier: A Study in Ritual, Power, and Ethnicity. New York: Berg.

12. Driessen, Henk 1992 On the Spanish-Moroccan Frontier: A Study in Ritual, Power, and Ethnicity. New York: Berg.

13. Rosander, Eva Evers 1991 Women in a Borderland: Managing Muslim Identity where Morocco Meets Spain. Stockholm: Department of Social Anthropology Stockholm University.

14. Balfour, Sebastian 303 2002 Deadly Embrace: Morocco and the Road to the Spanish Civil War. Oxford: Oxford University Press.

15. Pennell, C. R. 2000 Morocco since 1830: A History. London: Hurst & Company.

16. Rosander, Eva Evers 1991 Women in a Borderland: Managing Muslim Identity where Morocco Meets Spain. Stockholm: Department of Social Anthropology Stockholm University.

17. These violent confrontations included civil wars and conflicts between Berbers and Arabs.

18. A multibillion-dollar port near Tangiers is one example of economic investments by the Moroccan government.

19. By "active," I mean voting, participating in neighborhood association, volunteering for a party, or simply being aware of governmental politics.

Karim has been, since the mid-1980s, an unelected member of a party of Muslim persuasion.

20. Tetuan's urban center naturally extends up the Mediterranean coast until Ceuta.

21. e.g., Philip Corrigan and Derek Sayer, *The Great Arch: English State Formation as Cultural Revolution* (Hoboken, NJ: Blackwell, 1991).

22. Laroui, Abdallah 1997 Orígenes sociales y culturales del nacionalismo marroquí 1830-1912. Madrid: Mapfre.

23. Rosander, Eva Evers 1991 Women in a Borderland: Managing Muslim Identity where Morocco Meets Spain. Stockholm: Department of Social Anthropology Stockholm University.

24. Driessen, Henk 1992 On the Spanish-Moroccan Frontier: A Study in Ritual, Power, and Ethnicity. New York: Berg. Stallaert, Christiane (1998). Etnogénesis y etnicidad. Barcelona: Proyecto A ediciones.

25. The Legion is a special tactical force of the Spanish army.

26. By "civil phase," Karim is referring to the gradual decrease of musulmanes that took place after Moroccan independence. This is different from the civil society that emerged in Ceuta at the end of the nineteenth century.

27. Mohamed Lahchiri, Cuentos Ceutíes (Casablanca: Dar Al Karaouine, 2004), 59–60.

28. Gold, Peter 1994 A stone in Spain's Shoe: The Search for a Solution to the Problem of Gibraltar. Liverpool: Liverpool University Press.

29. Rosander, Eva Evers 1991 Women in a Borderland: Managing Muslim Identity where Morocco Meets Spain. Stockholm: Department of Social Anthropology Stockholm University.

30. Rosander, Eva Evers 1991 Women in a Borderland: Managing Muslim Identity where Morocco Meets Spain. Stockholm: Department of Social Anthropology Stockholm University.

31. Arango, Joaquín 2000 Becoming a Country of Immigration at the End of the Twentieth Century: The Case of Spain. In Eldorado or fortress? : Migration in Southern Europe. R. King, G. Lazaridis, and C.G. Tsardanidis, eds. Pp. 253-276. New York: St. Martin's Press.

32. Officially, the 1985 Immigration Law was called Ley Orgánica sobre los derechos y libertades de los extranjeros or Ley de Extranjería.

33. i.e., Spanish citizenship

34. A faquí is a scholar or intellectual of Islamic law.

35. Haraam is anything prohibited by Islamic faith.

36. Brochmann, Grete, and Tomas Hammar, eds. 1999 Mechanisms of Immigration Control: A Comparative Analysis of European Regulation Policies. New York: Berg. King, Russell, Gabriella Lazaridis, and Charalampos G. Tsardanidis, eds. 2000 Eldorado or Fortress? Migration in Southern Europe. New York: St. Martin's Press.

37. Mernissi, Fatima 1994 Dreams of Trespass: Tales of a Harem Girlhood. Reading: Addison-Wesley. Mernissi, Fatima 2001 Scheherazade Goes West: Different Cultures, Different Harems. New York: Washington Square Press.

38. Rosander, Eva Evers 1991 Women in a Borderland: Managing Muslim Identity where Morocco Meets Spain. Stockholm: Department of Social Anthropology Stockholm University.

39. Rosander, Eva Evers 1991 Women in a Borderland: Managing Muslim Identity where Morocco Meets Spain. Stockholm: Department of Social Anthropology Stockholm University.

40. Berber language

41. The PSOE controlled Ceuta's local government and the national government at the time.

42. Rosander, Eva Evers 1991 Women in a Borderland: Managing Muslim Identity where Morocco Meets Spain. Stockholm: Department of Social Anthropology Stockholm University.

43. Driessen, Henk 1992 On the Spanish-Moroccan Frontier: A Study in Ritual, Power, and Ethnicity. New York: Berg.

44. Thompson, Carlyle Van 2006 Eating the Black Body: Miscegenation as Sexual Consumption in African American Literature and Culture. New York: Peter Lang.

45. Karina used the word "payo" to refer to cristianos, although in peninsular Spain it usually refers to a non-Gypsy.

46. A woman who "is on the streets and dedicates herself to the life" is a prostitute.

47. Literally, "Employment Plan." It is a program funded by the local government with the purpose of training (through temporary employment) people in difficult financial situations.

48. Mernissi, Fatima 1994 Dreams of Trespass: Tales of a Harem Girlhood. Reading: Addison-Wesley.

49. Mernissi, Fatima 1994 Dreams of Trespass: Tales of a Harem Girlhood. Reading: Addison-Wesley.

50. Nagel, Joane 2003 Race, Ethnicity, and Sexuality: Intimate Intersections, Forbidden Frontiers. New York: Oxford University Press.

51. Goldstein, Donna 1999 "Interracial" Sex and Racial Democracy in Brazil: Twin Concepts? American Anthropologist 101(3):563–578.

52. Many musulmanes told me that, over the last twenty years or so, religion has become more important in their community, and that the current generation might be more conservative than previous ones (especially with regards to the behavior of women).

53. John Dewey, "The Future of Liberalism," *The Journal of Philosophy* 32, no. 9 (April, 1935): 227–28, https://doi.org/10.2307/2015856.

54. Dewey, "The Future of Liberalism," 227.

55. Eduardo Bonilla-Silva, "What Makes Systemic Racism Systemic?," *Sociological Inquiry* 91, no. 3 (2021): 513–33, https://doi.org/10.1111/soin.12420.

56. Robert C. Smith, *We Have No Leaders: African Americans in the Post-Civil Rights Era* (Albany: State University of New York Press, 1996). Charles W. Mills

6. LIBERAL ANTIRACISM AND THE ENDS OF FLOURISHING

1. In the Spanish language, many expressions use the formula *X de corte Y* (X of Y persuasion) to describe the influence of Y over X.

2. Gabriel A. Torres Colón, "Racial Experience and Knowing the Political in Liberal Democracies," *Identities* 30, no. 5 (September 3, 2023): 644–63, https://doi.org/10.1080/1070289X.2023.2213939.

3. Uday Singh Mehta, *Liberalism and Empire: A Study in Nineteenth-Century British Liberal Thought* (University of Chicago Press, 1999); Charles W. Mills, "Racial Liberalism," *PMLA* 123, no. 5 (2008): 1380–97, https://doi.org/10.1632/pmla.2008.123.5.1380.

4. Mills, "Racial Liberalism," 1394.

5. Mills, "Racial Liberalism," 1381–86.

6. Gabriel A. Torres Colón, "Parties of Muslim Persuasion and the Left in Ceuta, Spain," in *Migration and Activism in Europe since 1945*, ed. Wendy Pojmann (New York: Palgrave Macmillan, 2008), 111–28.

7. David Carroll Cochran, "Liberal Political Theory's Multicultural Blind Spot and Race in the United States," in *Racial Liberalism and the Politics of*

Urban America, ed. Curtis Stokes and Theresa Meléndez (East Lansing: Michigan State University Press, 2003), 72.

8. Robert C. Smith, *We Have No Leaders: African Americans in the Post-Civil Rights Era* (Albany: State University of New York Press, 1996); Anthony J. Badger, *Why White Liberals Fail: Race and Southern Politics from FDR to Trump* (Cambridge, MA: Harvard University Press, 2022), https://doi.org/10.4159/9780674276116.

CONCLUSION

1. Aurélien Mondon and Aaron Winter, *Reactionary Democracy: How Racism and the Populist Far Right Became Mainstream* (London: Verso, 2020).

2. Cf. John D. Griffin, "When and Why Minority Legislators Matter," *Annual Review of Political Science* 17, no. 1 (2014): 327–36, https://doi.org/10.1146/annurev-polisci-033011-205028.

3. John Dewey, "The Future of Liberalism," *The Journal of Philosophy* 32, no. 9 (1935): 225–30, https://doi.org/10.2307/2015856.

4. David Carroll Cochran, "Liberal Political Theory's Multicultural Blind Spot and Race in the United States," in *Racial Liberalism and the Politics of Urban America*, ed. Curtis Stokes and Theresa Meléndez (East Lansing: Michigan State University Press, 2003), 72.

5. Derrick Darby, *A Realistic Blacktopia: Why We Must Unite to Fight*, Philosophy of Race Series (New York: Oxford University Press, 2023).

6. Darby, *Realistic Blacktopia*, 11.

7. *Race Matters*, Twenty-fifth anniversary edition. (Boston: Beacon Press, 2017), 6–8; *Democracy Matters: Winning the Fight against Imperialism / Cornel West.* (New York: Penguin Press, 2004).

8. Geoff Mann, *In the Long Run We Are All Dead: Keynesianism, Political Economy, and Revolution* (Verso Books, 2017), 22.

9. Mann, *In the Long Run*, 188.

10. Mann, *In the Long Run*, 389.

11. Ingrid Burkett, "Organizing in the New Marketplace: Contradictions and Opportunities for Community Development Organizations in the Ashes of Neoliberalism," *Community Development Journal* 46, no. suppl_2 (April 1, 2011): iii13, https://doi.org/10.1093/cdj/bsr002.

12. Charles R. Hale, "Neoliberal Multiculturalism," *PoLAR: Political and Legal Anthropology Review* 28, no. 1 (2005): 10–19, https://doi.org/10.1525/pol.2005.28.1.10; Nancy Grey Postero, *Now We Are Citizens: Indigenous Politics in Postmulticultural Bolivia* (CA: Stanford University Press, 2007); Will Kymlicka, "Solidarity in Diverse Societies: Beyond Neoliberal Multiculturalism and Welfare Chauvinism," *Comparative Migration Studies* 3, no. 1 (2015), https://doi.org/10.1186/s40878-015-0017-4.

13. e.g., Charles R Hale, *Más Que Un Indio = More Than an Indian: Racial Ambivalence and Neoliberal Multiculturalism in Guatemala* (Santa Fe, CA: School of American Research Press, 2006); Abigail Bakan and Enakshi Dua, *Theorizing Anti-Racism: Linkages in Marxism and Critical Race Theories* (University of Toronto Press, 2014).

14. Rogers M. Smith, "Grasping the 'Invisible Hands': Race and Political Theory Today," in *Racial Liberalism and the Politics of Urban America* (East Lansing: Michigan State University Press, 2003), 77–78.

15. Gabriel A. Torres Colón and Charles A. Hobbs, "Toward a Pragmatist Anthropology of Race," *The Pluralist* 11, no. 1 (2016): 129–31, https://doi.org/10.5406/pluralist.11.1.0126.

16. Abigail Bakan and Enakshi Dua, *Theorizing Anti-Racism: Linkages in Marxism and Critical Race Theories* (University of Toronto Press, 2014); Gabriel A. Torres Colón, "Parties of Muslim Persuasion and the Left in Ceuta, Spain," in *Migration and Activism in Europe since 1945*, ed. Wendy Pojmann (New York: Palgrave Macmillan, 2008), 111–28; Gabriel A. Torres Colón, "Racial Experience and Knowing the Political in Liberal Democracies," *Identities* 30, no. 5 (September 3, 2023): 644–63, https://doi.org/10.1080/1070289X.2023.2213939.

INDEX

GPSR Authorized Representative: Easy Access System Europe, Mustamäe tee
50, 10621 Tallinn, Estonia, gpsr.requests@easproject.com

www.ingramcontent.com/pod-product-compliance
Lightning Source LLC
Chambersburg PA
CBHW021852020426
42334CB00013B/296